THE TORY'S WIFE

The Revolutionary Age

FRANCIS D. COGLIANO AND
PATRICK GRIFFIN, EDITORS

The Tory's Wife

*A Woman and Her Family in
Revolutionary America*

Cynthia A. Kierner

UNIVERSITY OF VIRGINIA PRESS
Charlottesville and London

University of Virginia Press
© 2023 by Cynthia A. Kierner
Printed in the United States of America on acid-free paper

First published 2023

1 3 5 7 9 8 6 4 2

Library of Congress Cataloging-in-Publication Data

Names: Kierner, Cynthia A., author.
Title: The Tory's wife : a woman and her family in Revolutionary America / Cynthia A. Kierner.
Description: Charlottesville : University of Virginia Press, 2023. | Series: The revolutionary age | Includes bibliographical references and index.
Identifiers: LCCN 2023003673 (print) | LCCN 2023003674 (ebook) |
ISBN 9780813949918 (hardcover) | ISBN 9780813949932 (ebook)
Subjects: LCSH: Spurgin, Jane Welborn, 1736–1803. | Abandoned wives—North Carolina—
Biography. | North Carolina—History—Revolution, 1775–1783 | United States—History—
Revolution, 1775–1783—Women. | Spurgin, William, 1734–1806. | American Loyalists—North
Carolina—Biography. | Runaway husbands—North Carolina—Biography. | North Carolina—
Biography.
Classification: LCC F257.S68 K54 2023 (print) | LCC F257.S68 (ebook) | DDC 975.602092
[B]—dc23/eng/20230127
LC record available at https://lccn.loc.gov/2023003673
LC ebook record available at https://lccn.loc.gov/2023003674

Cover art: Detail from *The Petticoat Duellists,* published by W. & J. Stratfords, 1792.
(Wellcome Collection, 568670i)

In memory of my parents

CONTENTS

ILLUSTRATIONS

Figures

Maps

PREFACE

I first encountered Jane Spurgin in the State Archives of North Carolina in Raleigh in the mid-1990s. At the time, I was writing a book on southern women during the colonial and revolutionary eras. I turned to legislative petitions in the hope of recovering women's voices, to better understand their political culture and what the American Revolution meant to them and their families. The holy grail I hoped to find was a cache of documents in which women petitioners, in their own words, employed revolutionary rhetoric and presented themselves as rights-bearing citizens of an independent republic.

As it turned out, the petitioners were savvier than I was. Aware that the men who would evaluate their requests likely preferred women who were dependent and self-effacing, nearly all of the petitioners adopted that conventionally feminine demeanor. Among North Carolinians, the one standout exception was Jane Welborn Spurgin of Rowan County, the mother of twelve living offspring and wife of a prosperous backcountry farmer. The essential details of her story were that she was a Whig supporter of the Revolution, and her husband, William, was a committed Tory who opposed it. When the war was over, the family had lost their property, Jane and William were estranged, and she approached the legislature to ask that the state accord her the "Common rights of other Citizens."

Although I worked on other research topics over the years, I never really stopped thinking about Jane and her boldly worded petitions. Fast-forward to 2020 and telling Jane's story became my perfect pandemic project. Stuck at home, I researched and wrote the bulk of this book in my Washington, DC, study while my husband taught physics in the next room over. The digitization of public records and other primary sources, as well as online access to scholarly books and articles, made my work possible. Online genealogies, used judiciously, also led me to all sorts of information that was unknown to me—despite my due diligence—when I first attempted to fill in the details of Jane's life, however briefly, in the 1990s. That being said, this project was also an object lesson in the limits of online research. Some essential sources were accessible only in libraries or archives. More important still, it was through that initial deep dive into the archives in Raleigh that I discovered Jane.

Although I had written about comparatively underdocumented people in the past, I worried that it would be difficult to write an entire book about Jane based on her three petitions and not much else. Encouraging responses to two preliminary attempts to tell her story helped to convince me otherwise. The first was a public talk for Women's History Month, which I gave at Mount Vernon's Fred W. Smith National Library for the Study of George Washington. I thank Doug Bradburn and Stephen McLeod for inviting me (and for letting me speak about someone so obscure) and also Charlene Boyer Lewis, that evening's fabulous moderator. The second was a more scholarly presentation at the last prepandemic meeting of the Southern Historical Association, where my paper on Jane, Charlene's work on Margaret Shippen Arnold, and Lorri Glover's on Eliza Lucas Pinckney together made for one of the best women's history panels ever (or at least I thought so). Thanks especially to Ami Pflugrad-Jackisch for her insightful comments. Best of all, however, was the fact that our panel led to a discussion with Nadine Zimmerli, then the newly installed editor at the University of Virginia Press. "I think it could be a book," Nadine said emphatically, adding, "a little book." After that conversation, I never looked back.

This project benefited from the support of several institutions. A prepandemic Archie K. Davis Fellowship from the North Caroliniana Society funded essential research in Chapel Hill and Raleigh. As the recipient of the Amelie W. Cagle Fellowship from the Fred W. Smith National Library for the Study of George Washington in January 2021, I enjoyed full access to a very quiet and mostly deserted library, where I wrote my first chapter. The (safe) reopening of the Library of Virginia, long before most other libraries, allowed me to do some much-needed remedial research at a crucial point in the project. Funding from the Department of History and Art History at my home institution, George Mason University, paid for a trip to North Carolina to find Jane's gravestone, as well as for some of the book's illustrations. Three other public institutions—the Library of Congress, the State Archives of North Carolina, and the Wilson Special Collections Library at the University of North Carolina at Chapel Hill—provided images and permission to use them free of charge.

Librarians and archivists made research viable during the pandemic by responding promptly to my queries and providing digital reproductions of documents via email. I am especially grateful for the assistance of Finley Turner at the Z. Smith Reynolds Library Special Collections & Archives at Wake Forest University, Yvette Toledo at the New Hampshire State Archives, Gayle Martinson at the Wisconsin Historical Society, and Terese Austin at the William L. Clements Library at the University of Michigan. Michael Stephenson of Ontario Genealogy got me a copy of William Spurgin's will at a time when my traveling to Canada would have been impossible. At the State Archives of North Carolina, William H. Brown and Joseph Beatty expedited approval of my use of images from their collections, as did Matt Turi at the Wilson Special Collections Library at the University of North Carolina at Chapel Hill.

My research also profited immensely from the efforts of local people who have preserved the history of Rowan County and its environs and made their work accessible to others. I never met either Jo White Linn or James W. Klutz, who gathered, transcribed, and published essential county records, but my debt to them is amply acknowledged in my notes. In the nineteenth century, the Reverend Eli Washington Caruthers collected oral histories—he would have probably called them "reminiscences"—from elderly people in Rowan County who lived through the Revolution, some of whom recounted their impressions of William Spurgin and shared one remarkable story about Jane.

This book also benefited from colleagues' insights and other sorts of help. Jon Kukla alerted me to the availability of online revolutionary military pension records, which turned out to be incredibly valuable. Martha J. King sent me articles about the differences between petitions and memorials, which nonetheless remain at best imprecise to me (and apparently to many other people, too). Jim Ambuske helped with some military history. Megan Shockley chatted with me about Jane and her world as we drove around the Carolina Piedmont looking for her grave-stone. At George Mason, Stephanie Sheridan in the Department of History and Art History and Alyssa Toby Fahringer at Fenwick Library helped with digital images. Anders Bright, Jane Turner Censer, Charlene Boyer Lewis, and George Oberle kindly read and commented on parts of the manuscript as it neared completion.

Finally, at the University of Virginia Press, my excellent editor, Nadine Zimmerli, carefully read every word, and her probing questions and smart suggestions surely improved the finished product. Nadine also sent the manuscript to two thorough and thoughtful readers, Woody Holton and T. Cole Jones, who offered their enthusiastic support for the project while also providing constructive criticism from their very different perspectives. Ellen Satrom and my terrific copy editor, Susan Murray, ably guided the book through production. It was a pleasure working (again) with both of them.

Given the paucity of sources that document Jane's life and experiences, much of the material in *The Tory's Wife* is necessarily contextual and sometimes speculative. But it is worth remembering that the historical record is never as complete as we would like it to be. The historian's job is to find and interpret what remains. Our work is always speculative to some degree, and we can only understand the people we study if we situate them in their larger historical and cultural contexts. I hope I got Jane's story right. I know that it is a story worth telling both because of its unlikely twists and turns but even more so because it offers an unusually thought-provoking perspective on life in revolutionary America.

INTRODUCTION

Woman on the Verge

IN JANUARY 1791, a fifty-five-year-old North Carolina woman anxiously awaited news from the state capital, where the recently convened legislature would decide a question of immense importance to her and her large and struggling family. A month earlier, Jane Welborn Spurgin had composed and submitted a petition to the general assembly—this one was, in fact, her third—in an attempt to regain title to land that she and her family had lost during the American Revolution. Jane was the mother of twelve surviving offspring, half of whom still lived with her at home. If the assembly denied her petition, she would be homeless and without property and, at best, dependent on her older sons. If the legislators granted her request, Jane would preserve her position as the de facto head of a farming household in eastern Rowan County, a thriving backcountry area that had been inhabited by few white setters when she and her husband, William, arrived there in the mid-1750s.

Jane Spurgin was a Whig, a patriot who had supported the war effort of the Continental Congress and North Carolina's revolutionary state government, most notably by aiding General Nathanael Greene when the American commander brought his army to her Abbotts Creek neighborhood in early 1781. Her husband, William, who had been a prosperous farmer and a justice of the peace, was the only Rowan County magistrate who remained steadfastly loyal to the king after North Carolina and

1

twelve other colonies declared their independence in 1776. William was an officer in the loyalist militia, and he fought for the king—and against most of his fellow North Carolinians—during the Revolution. The state government enacted legislation that formally banished him and other active loyalists in early 1777.

By the time Jane submitted her third petition in 1791, she and William were estranged and, perhaps because the stakes were so high for her and her children, when she addressed the legislature, she emphasized that she had "always behaved herself as a good Citizen," despite the fact that her husband had been a notorious—and now disgraced—"enemy to his country." In making her case to North Carolina's postrevolutionary leaders, Jane boldly claimed what she called "the Common rights" that "other Citizens" enjoyed in a now independent American republic. If the legislators took these words seriously, they might have wondered what "rights" this woman claimed and whether, indeed, she qualified as a "citizen" of their state. Contemporary definitions of citizenship and what it entailed were at best ill-defined; legal and constitutional fuzziness about what it meant to be a "citizen" perhaps emboldened Jane to publicly claim that status and whatever rights and privileges it conferred on those who held it. Whatever her reasoning, the blunt assertiveness of Jane's rhetoric and her use of the language of citizenship made her petition unusual among those submitted by women of the era and unique among female petitioners in postrevolutionary North Carolina. Jane presented herself as a member of a political community, a constituent whose concerns warranted the careful attention of North Carolina's elected governors, though as a woman she herself lacked the right to vote as well as most other political and civil rights.[1]

Women did have the right to petition, however, and the disruption and loss occasioned by the long and costly war led them to do so in unprecedented numbers. Female petitioners sought tax relief, military arrears of pay and pensions owed to deceased soldiers, and payment of other public debts. Wives of loyalists petitioned to recover property seized by the state as a result of their husbands' political offenses. Most of these women petitioners meekly described themselves as frail, faultlessly apolitical, and dependent on the mercy of the benevolent men who weighed the merits of their requests, an approach that must have seemed more likely to succeed because it conformed to conventional ideas about women and their place both in the domestic sphere and in the wider world. By contrast, the strident rhetoric of Jane's petition, along with scattered evidence of her activities during the war, indicates that she truly was a Whig whose political beliefs and actions differed from her spouse's. Legislative petitions collectively offer an illuminating glimpse of women's political culture during this period, but Jane's petition represents a remarkably rare instance in which a woman publicly asserted both a claim to citizenship and a political identity distinct from that of her husband.

Jane Welborn Spurgin participated in the settlement of the western frontier of British colonial America and experienced the subsequent violent replacement of British imperial rule with an independent republican regime. Despite her involvement in such key developments in early American history, it would be impossible to write a conventional biography of Jane because so few surviving sources document her life. In America as elsewhere, public archives were established and curated to bolster the authority of the state by preserving documents pertaining to politics, property, war, and the like, so their collections tend to lack materials that explicitly pertain to women and their experiences. Even most family archives, housed in private historical societies and in other institutions, until relatively recently privileged the collection and preservation of documents produced by and for men, especially if those men were politically influential or economically powerful.

Much of the evidence that historians use to reconstruct the lives of nonelite people—both women and men—comes from their occasional encounters with public officials and institutions when they appeared in court, filed their wills, or (in the case of many men) applied for military pensions. In Jane's case, her postrevolutionary petitions, which are included in the official records of North Carolina's state assembly, are the only surviving documents in which she told her own story, or at least part of it. The carved stone that marks her grave, a few entries in court or land records, a line in the 1790 federal census, and a brief anecdote in a nineteenth-century history written by a Rowan County author are the only other surviving evidence of her life. There are no family portraits, and, though both Jane and William were literate, there are no collected Spurgin family papers.

Despite these challenges, Jane's story can be told, and it is well worth telling both because of its intrinsic drama and because making history more diverse and inclusive—going beyond the familiar narratives that focus on the exploits of presidents, generals, and other great white men—is a more honest approach to the past and also a precondition for attaining a more complete and nuanced understanding of it. Recent scholarship includes countless examples of the transformative power of historians' reconstruction of the stories of people who themselves produced few documents—or at least few that have been preserved—by interrogating the silences in the archives and providing more complete historical contexts to interpret whatever materials they find there. For instance, using documents produced by white men and the institutions they established to enforce their system of race-based chattel slavery, but then correcting for their inherent biases, scholars have learned much about the experiences of enslaved people in the Americas. That new understanding, in turn, has challenged the once pervasive belief that slavery was virtually unchallenged—by either Blacks or whites—in eighteenth-century America, in favor of one that recasts the war for independence as North America's most significant slave uprising—an occasion when thousands of enslaved people, at great risk, flocked to the British to gain their freedom—and also as the impetus for the emergence of a robust antislavery movement in the postrevolutionary era.[2]

By focusing on one woman's experiences in an environment far removed from Boston, Saratoga, Yorktown, or other marquee venues of the imperial crisis and the ensuing war, Jane's story likewise offers a different perspective on the American Revolution, one that in many respects was more representative, given that the overwhelming majority of Americans were rural people who were neither soldiers nor government functionaries. *The Tory's Wife* is a microhistory whose protagonist is at once unique and representative of the experiences of a significant subset of the people of her era and one whose story reveals much about family, community, war, debt, and other fundamental aspects of life in revolutionary America. In the words of one historian, a microhistorical approach is akin to "holding our eye up to a peephole . . . [that] reveals a wide expanse of culture and society." By placing Jane at the center of this wide-ranging vista, her story becomes a compelling window onto life in the late eighteenth-century American backcountry, a place with a revolutionary history that belies the traditional narrative of the imperial crisis that began with the Stamp Act in 1765 and the war between Britain and its thirteen rebellious colonies that commenced a decade later in Massachusetts with the Battles of Lexington and Concord.[3]

While that familiar narrative emphasizes popular unity in the heroic pursuit of liberty and rights, the Revolution in reality divided Americans, whose allegiances were often complicated, conflicted, or fluid. Scholars estimate that as much as 40 percent of the American population was apathetic or simply unwilling to commit to one side or the other and did their best to remain neutral throughout the long and costly war. Known as the "disaffected," these people were often persecuted and sometimes yielded under pressure to recognize the authority of whichever side wielded power over them and thereby threatened their lives and livelihoods. Among those whose ideals or interests did lead them to support one side or the other, not only did families and communities divide into hostile patriot and loyalist (or Whig and Tory) factions, but Whigs became Tories, or Tories became Whigs, to avoid harassment or to protest the offensive and sometimes draconian policies of the ascendant power. In sum, historians of the Revolution increasingly emphasize its pervasive violence, shifting allegiances, and internal divisions, characterizing it not only as a fight for colonial independence but also as a brutal civil war.[4]

Perhaps nowhere were these attributes more stunningly displayed than in the Carolina backcountry, where the years before independence were punctuated by local controversies and violence, culminating at the Battle of Alamance in May 1771. Although distinctions between dissident farmers (known as Regulators) and government officials did not neatly translate into later divisions between Whigs and Tories, this recent history—and the class, religious, and ethnic antagonisms that drove both the Regulators and their enemies—shaped the region's response to the Revolution. Disaffection was widespread. Wartime violence played out not only in confrontations between generals on battlefields but also in scores of obscure skirmishes and attacks that involved soldiers and civilians, blurring the lines between battlefield and home front, especially in the war's later years when the southern states became the focus of its most significant military offensives.[5]

The history of Jane Welborn Spurgin and her family therefore reveals much about the lived experiences of revolutionary Americans and the issues surrounding the meaning of war and independence for many non-famous people in late eighteenth-century America. Most fundamentally, the Spurgins' family story stands in marked contrast to the still-powerful but simplistic notion that virtuous Americans united to wrest liberty and independence from a tyrannical king and his evil minions, an interpretation that is at least as old as George Bancroft's monumental *History of the United States*, the first volume of which was published in 1834. Although this view of the republic's origins persists to this day, especially in popular culture, earlier histories suggest that Bancroft's elderly readers who themselves had lived through the revolutionary era would have found his version of it nearly unrecognizable. David Ramsay, a South Carolina physician who himself experienced the Revolution and wrote one of the first histories of it, candidly reported divisions among the populace, and, though clearly a Whig himself, vilified neither the Tories nor the king to whom they remained loyal. "The revolution had its enemies, as well as its friends, in every period of the war," he wrote, adding, "Country, religion, local policy, as well as private views, operated in disposing the inhabitants to take different sides." More than a half century later, E. W. Caruthers, a Rowan County native who drew heavily on interviews with elderly acquaintances as sources for his two books on North Carolina's revolutionary history, devoted most of both volumes to describing hostilities between Whigs and Tories, especially in the backcountry, where enmities from the colonial era evolved into revolutionary divisions and violent altercations between opposing patriot and loyalist militias.[6]

In both obvious and more insidious ways, the Revolution changed everything for Jane and her family, often moving their lives in directions that she likely neither expected nor welcomed. As a farming family in North Carolina's colonial backcountry, the Spurgins were both prosperous and upwardly mobile until the imperial crisis gradually distinguished Whigs from Tories and stigmatized the latter. The revolutionary movement, which culminated with colonists' renunciation of royal authority and a formal declaration of independence in July 1776, forced William to choose sides. The choice he made—to remain loyal to king and empire—set him in opposition to the most influential men in Rowan County and in North Carolina generally. Indeed, William became one of North Carolina's most notorious Tories, one of a select group whom the colony's last royal governor commissioned to raise troops to fight for the king and whom he later singled out for special praise in a letter to London authorities. North Carolina's Whig leaders also recognized the depths of William's commitment to king and empire, mentioning him by name in several statutes mandating the banishment of those who would not swear allegiance to the Revolution and the confiscation and sale of their property.[7]

William's loyalism, and especially his determination to accept a military commission to bear arms in support of the king, in turn, set in motion a spiraling wave of events and circumstances that had dire consequences for his family. Whatever satisfaction she received from the ultimate American victory, Jane experienced the war years as a series of everyday struggles to preserve her family's property, feed her children, and ward off threats from William's Whig enemies in Rowan County and beyond. She also spent most of the war apart from William, who was either hiding from his Whig enemies or off fighting as an officer in the Tory militia. Political differences and William's extended absences either caused or aggravated tensions between him and Jane.

Jane's family story is also a backcountry story, both in terms of the particular context in which the Revolution unfolded and also in the continuing centrality of migration as a route to prosperity and upward mobility. Like many denizens of North Carolina's revolutionary backcountry, Jane and William were born in Maryland and moved first to Virginia and then to North Carolina in the hope of improving their own prospects and those of their extended family. War temporarily disrupted the migration of white settlers into less densely populated areas, but people moved at unprecedented rates in the postrevolutionary era. After the war, Black and white loyalist refugees flocked to Britain and its remaining colonies. In the United States, white settlers moved westward, encouraged by government incentives to populate land claimed and occupied by Native Americans and thereby establish US control of those territories.

Although Jane remained in North Carolina, her and William's descendants continued their family's tradition of migration in the postrevolutionary decades.[8]

Finally, and most important, Jane's story is also a woman's story, and one that provides an unusual perspective on women's experiences and identity in revolutionary America. The best-known women from the revolutionary era were those who were married to famous men and supported or shared their political objectives. Martha Washington spent winters with her husband at Valley Forge and other winter army encampments. Abigail Adams, who famously warned her congressman husband, John, against putting "unlimited power into the hands of the Husbands," was, like him, a fervent Whig. Margaret Shippen Arnold was complicit, even instrumental, in her husband Benedict's fateful decision to turn traitor in 1780.[9] These women and some others like them have well-documented and widely known personal stories. By contrast, Jane Spurgin was the wife of a middling farmer who espoused political views that differed markedly from those of her husband—and she sometimes acted on those views. Her actions were, on the one hand, patriotic, but, on the other hand, conspicuously and unconventionally antipatriarchal.

The extent to which Jane transgressed the marital conventions of her time and place is worth emphasizing because, notwithstanding the egalitarian rhetoric of male revolutionaries, postrevolutionary America remained profoundly patriarchal. Although contemporary political theory and revolutionary rhetoric drew parallels between the authority of kings and that of fathers and husbands as domestic rulers, the revolutionary transformation of a monarchical political culture into a republican one did little to formally diminish the authority of fathers and husbands in their households. Revolutionary-era legal reforms neither eradicated nor weakened the prevailing interpretation of the English common law of marriage, which characterized wives as dependents and husbands as their protectors, and accordingly endowed husbands, fathers, and masters with near-complete authority over wives, children, and bonded labor (which included people held in servitude either by contract or as a result of having been enslaved). In fact, in the postrevolutionary era, as the law increasingly rendered private households immune from governmental or judicial oversight, men actually acquired more power over their wives and other domestic dependents.[10]

In the 1770s and 1780s, however, the Revolution and war that upended monarchy in America could—however inadvertently—destabilize, undermine, and even destroy customary hierarchies and relationships in families and in society more generally. Jane Spurgin's revolutionary experience reflected that reality. Her postrevolutionary petitions chronicled that experience, while leaving unanswered any questions of whether she looked on the Revolution as a happy development overall or whether the revolutionary experience ultimately was more liberation or loss from her perspective. In revolutionary North Carolina, Jane Spurgin renounced her Tory husband and challenged her Whig governors to redress her grievances and to view her as a rights-bearing "citizen." Although her story and her voice were far from typical, both showed how the Revolution could test personal and political relationships and transform women's political consciousness.

1

Settling the Backcountry

JANE WELBORN AND HER HUSBAND, William Spurgin, were born in Maryland, welcomed their firstborn child in Virginia, and joined the massive southward migration down the Great Wagon Road into North Carolina shortly thereafter. By 1757, when Jane gave birth to their second child, she and William were living in the Abbotts Creek neighborhood of Rowan County in North Carolina's backcountry, the fastest-growing section of the fastest-growing province in British North America. The first white settlers had arrived in western North Carolina in the mid-1740s, and within a few years Governor Gabriel Johnston reported to his superiors in London that "People from all parts are Crowding in Here Daily," necessitating the creation of new county governments to foster order and stability. Established in 1753, Rowan became North Carolina's third backcountry county when it was cut off from Anson County to make court sessions and other county functions more readily accessible to the area's burgeoning population. By the mid-1760s, Rowan County's "taxable" population of 3,059—a category that included only adult white males and Black adults of both sexes, based on the fiction that white women's work had no economic value—was exceeded by only that of nearby Orange County, another backcountry jurisdiction that had been established in 1752.[1]

Although William Spurgin would attain a place among the local elite within a decade of his arrival in North Carolina, in other respects the Spurgins' family story largely typified the experiences of Rowan County's early white settlers. Because North Carolina lacked a deepwater port and because plantation-based agriculture increasingly predominated in its eastern counties, white people who migrated into the colony's western, or backcountry, region came overwhelmingly from the north—chiefly Pennsylvania and the western parts of Maryland and Virginia—rather than directly from Europe, as was more often the case in other British provinces. Most settlers were experienced farmers, having grown grain and raised livestock on family farms they either owned or rented, and they expected to continue to engage in this sort of mixed agriculture after they relocated to North Carolina. "None take up lands . . . but with a view to cultivate and improve them, as fast as they can," observed Governor Arthur Dobbs in 1754, "all the back[country] settlers being very industrious."[2] These people came to North Carolina to pursue upward mobility by securing fertile land on easy terms, acreage they would clear, cultivate, and then pass on to future generations. Like Jane and William, whose surviving parents and brothers accompanied them to North Carolina, many traveled south with family members, neighbors, or fellow church members with whom they would establish new communities.

Jane Welborn Spurgin, who would eventually bear twelve living children in North Carolina, began her life as a second-generation Marylander. Born in 1736, Jane was one of eight children of William Welborn and Ann Crabtree, Maryland natives who married according to the rites of the Church of England at St. George's Parish in northern Baltimore County (present-day Harford County) in 1731. The Welborns also had their children baptized at St. George's. Despite its origins as a haven for persecuted English Catholics, Maryland had been a majority-Protestant province since the 1660s. In the eighteenth century, Maryland's provincial government, like its counterparts in most other colonies, followed the English practice of officially tolerating religious dissent while also giving preferential treatment to a tax-supported ecclesiastical establishment, the Protestant Church of England.[3]

Three of Jane's four grandparents were born in England and came to Maryland as part of the unprecedented flood of immigrants that arrived in the colony after 1715, when its population grew markedly, likely in part due to a rare decades-long cessation of the deadly and disruptive Anglo-French wars in Europe and North America. Although not much is known about Jane's maternal grandparents, by 1722 her paternal grandfather, Edward Welborn, owned a tract of land in Maryland known as "Willburn's Venture." Edward was both a landowner and a blacksmith; Jane's father, William Welborn, followed in his father's footsteps. When Edward died in 1731, he divided his other property equally among his three children, but he left most of his land and all of his "Smiths Tools" to William, who married Ann Crabtree and with her raised their children in Baltimore County. In the early 1750s, however, William sold the land he inherited from his father and purchased at least 150 acres in Frederick County in western Maryland. Jane and her siblings, all apparently still unmarried, accompanied their parents when they moved west.[4]

Perhaps because they had been relatively prosperous in Baltimore County, the Welborns were latecomers to the Maryland backcountry. The remote western extremities of the originally oversized counties of Baltimore and Prince George's were the site of white settlements as early as the 1720s. By 1748, this western area had become sufficiently populated by white colonists—most of whom were Scots-Irish and German farmers from Pennsylvania and New Jersey, or English settlers from eastern Maryland—to warrant its designation as the separate county of Frederick. Among the early residents of Monocacy, the first white settlement in western Maryland, were William and James Spurgin, two brothers who had come to Maryland from England in 1718. Like the Welborns, the Spurgin brothers were English Protestants who had moved to the backcountry from eastern Maryland. Unlike them, their roots in America were comparatively shallow, and they did not emigrate to the colonies voluntarily.[5]

The Spurgin brothers were transported to Maryland aboard a prison ship as convict labor. Although America had long been an occasional dumping ground for England's convicted felons, the use of convicts as forced workers in labor-scarce English colonies became both systematic and widespread after Parliament passed the Transportation Act of 1718. That law aimed both to rid Britain of criminals and to lessen the number of executions in an era when many crimes were capital offenses by offering all but the most heinous offenders the option of avoiding corporal punishment or execution by serving a term of seven to fourteen years as bonded labor in America. After 1718, approximately fifty thousand convicts came to British colonial America as a result of this legislation, including more than two-thirds of all felons convicted and sentenced at the Old Bailey, London's central criminal court. Although the government contracted with merchants to transport convicts to at least eighteen different colonies during the eighteenth century, between 1718 and 1744 nearly all of those transported criminals who left England went to Maryland and Virginia. Taking convict labor to the Chesapeake region was doubly profitable for government contractors, who could easily dispose of their human cargo in these tobacco-producing colonies where labor was in high demand (even as the use of enslaved Africans became increasingly widespread) and then return home with their ships laden with tobacco and other marketable commodities.[6]

On 25 February 1719, the Spurgin brothers were among a group of forty-eight men and women who were tried, found guilty, and then sentenced in the Old Bailey for having committed various property-related offenses. The Spurgins were common thieves. The elder brother, twenty-four-year-old James, was found guilty of "taking . . . a Camblet Coat, 2 pair of Plush Breeches, 23 Coats and Waistcoats, &c." from the home of Mary Fletcher. The younger brother, the teenaged William, had stolen "a Flaxen Sheet, a Holland Smock and other Linnen" from a "Garden," where their owner had hung them to dry, and had then fenced these purloined goods to Mary Stiles (who was herself transported to America after being apprehended and convicted of another crime in 1728). Of the forty-eight convicts whom the court sentenced that day, twelve were to be executed, four received prison terms, and two women who "pleaded their Bellies" escaped punishment, at least temporarily, as a result of being "found with Quick Child." Twenty-nine of the remaining thirty convicted felons—ten women and nineteen men, including James and William Spurgin—opted for transportation to Maryland, where they would serve terms as forced labor in lieu of "whipping or Burning in the hand." Like most of their fellow soon-to-be exiles, the Spurgin brothers were young unmarried men from the lower strata of English society.[7]

On 11 May 1719, the brothers left England on the prison ship *Margaret* as part of a cargo of 109 convicts bound for Maryland. Conditions aboard the ship were likely horrific, with prisoners chained together and kept in stiflingly close quarters below the deck with little air or light. Many of their shipmates would have died during their arduous Atlantic crossing: mortality rates on ships transporting prisoners were more than 10 percent in the early years of the convict trade. On arriving in Maryland in September, those who survived their months-long voyage aboard the *Margaret* were sold to local buyers. Most newly arrived convicts likely served their sentences as field workers on plantations in and around Baltimore. The most careful study of convict labor in the colonies indicates that these people did not commit crimes once they fulfilled the terms of their punishment and attained their freedom. Nevertheless, in part because they lacked capital, skills, and local connections, few transported convicts who survived their sentences later attained prosperity as free inhabitants in America.[8]

In comparison to most of their fellow prisoners, the Spurgin brothers were remarkably successful. Their first lucky break may have come when Richard Snowden purchased the services of both brothers on their arrival in Maryland. Staying together was likely a comfort for the brothers, especially for young William. Equally important was the fact that Snowden, besides being an important landowner and merchant, was the proprietor of an iron mine in Anne Arundel County, and in 1705 he had formed a partnership with four other men "for the Carrying on an Iron Work or Works" on the Patuxent River. Although the Patuxent ironworks does not appear to have materialized in the years following the formation of this partnership, the provincial assembly's passage of a law to encourage iron production in 1719 may have revived Snowden's commitment to the project. As an incentive to prospective ironmasters, the legislature designated up to eighty workers at any ironworks as "levy free," which was a boon to masters who were normally required by law to pay taxes on all the bonded laborers they employed, whether enslaved or free. Although there is no way to know for sure whether the Spurgin brothers became part of Snowden's iron-making workforce, ironmasters in both Maryland and Virginia used convict labor, as well as enslaved people and indentured servants, for both skilled and unskilled tasks. Acquiring any sort of metal-working artisanal skills would have helped the Spurgins to prosper once they completed their terms of servitude and attained their freedom. Such skills would have been especially welcome—and profitable—in newly settled western communities.[9]

At some point after they fulfilled their contractual obligations to Snowden, James and William moved to western Maryland. The names of both men appeared on a list of taxables for the backcountry community of "Monocoise Hundred" in 1733, and the brothers were also among the signers of a petition requesting that a Church of England parish be established there in 1742. By then, both James and William had married, and they had also begun acquiring land in the area. The younger brother, William, owned acreage on both the Maryland and Virginia sides of the Potomac River. He also had three sons—William, John, and Samuel—all of whom were born in the Maryland backcountry between 1732 and 1738.[10]

The death of the elder William Spurgin in 1750 initiated a chain of events that resulted in the removal of his extended family to North Carolina. The death of a family patriarch was always a transitional moment, resulting in the passing of land to one or more of the children of the deceased and often prompting the relocation of those siblings who inherited other forms of property instead of land, or perhaps received nothing at all and were left to fend for themselves. Because backcountry people were unusually mobile, the death of a father or patriarch in a backcountry family was particularly likely to result in the liquidation of the family landholdings in order to move to a more remote location, where farmland was less expensive and more readily available.[11]

The elder William Spurgin had three sons, but he seems to have left land only to his eldest son and namesake, who, after 1750, resided on a tract on the Virginia side of the Potomac River adjacent to the property occupied by his widowed mother. By swapping his Virginia holdings for cheaper land elsewhere, the younger William could secure his own future prosperity while also keeping the family together by making it easier for his younger brothers to attain what contemporaries called a "competency," or a comfortable independence. By 1750, the western parts of both Virginia and Maryland were comparatively densely populated, and Lord Fairfax, the proprietor of much of Virginia's backcountry acreage, insisted on the payment of small annual fees known as quitrents by western farmers. White settlers in Virginia and Maryland also suffered brutal

Indian attacks as a result of both their seizure of Native lands and the ongoing French and Indian wars. For all these reasons, William Spurgin and his family joined the ranks of the mostly middling farmers who were leaving southeastern Pennsylvania, as well as the Maryland and Virginia backcountry, for North Carolina, where they hoped to prosper by investing both capital and labor in acreage on which they would continue to practice their familiar form of grain-based agriculture.[12]

Jane Welborn married William Spurgin in 1751 or 1752, not long after he became the effective head of the Spurgin family by inheriting the bulk of his father's landed estate. Jane likely brought some property to the marriage, as was the custom, in the form of household goods or livestock. In theory at least, marriage was a lifetime commitment for both husband and wife. In British colonial America, divorce was an option only in New England, where descendants of the Puritan founders retained their belief that marriage was a civil contract, not a sacred bond, and therefore could be dissolvable. In other colonies, most of which had the Church of England as their established church, marriage was subject to ecclesiastical law, which did not allow for divorce except by rare private acts of Parliament. As imperial authorities insisted when they quashed Pennsylvanians' effort to enact a general divorce law in the 1770s, colonial governors could "not, upon any pretence whatsoever . . . assent to any Bill or Bills that may have been, or shall hereafter be, passed . . . for the Divorce of Persons joined together in Holy Marriage." None of the provinces in which Jane and William resided—Maryland, Virginia, and North Carolina—granted a single divorce during the colonial era.[13]

In the absence of the possibility of obtaining a legal divorce, some unhappily married couples found other ways to make the best of their bad situations. For couples who either had no property or who separated amicably, the easiest option was what one historian has called a "do-it-yourself divorce," which usually involved a mutually acceptable separation agreement whereby the couple remained legally married but pledged to treat each other legally and in property-related matters as if their union had never occurred. Colonial newspapers and court records provide ample evidence of less cordial permanent or temporary separations. Abandoned wives went to court to secure financial support for themselves and their children. Angry husbands placed newspaper adver-

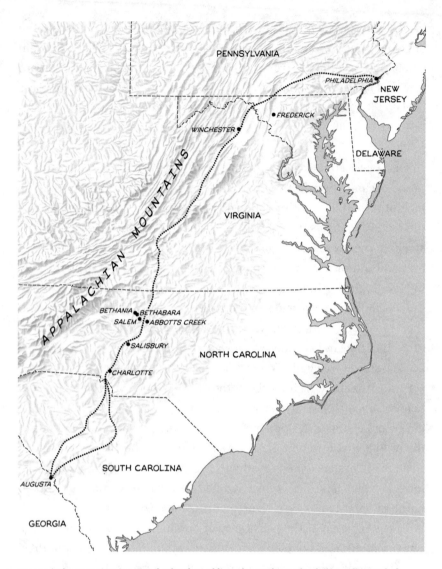

MAP 1 | The Great Wagon Road. The dotted line shows the path of this well-traveled road, which began in Philadelphia. This road was the principal route taken by white settlers migrating to the interior parts of Maryland, Virginia, and the Carolinas, known collectively as the southern backcountry. Note the location of the Abbotts Creek settlement, where the Spurgins and their extended family arrived in the mid-1750s. (Map by Franchesca Mireku)

tisements to inform the public that their wives had behaved scandalously, had run off with another man, and that, as a result, they would no longer be liable for the offending woman's debts.[14]

Marriage was a particularly high-stakes proposition for women because the English common law at least theoretically gave men virtually limitless power within their households. Under the common-law doctrine of coverture, a wife's legal rights and duties—including her control of property and liability for debts and other contractual obligations— were subsumed by those of her husband; by law and custom, fathers also governed their children with near-absolute authority. Because men's powers within marriage derived in part from the belief that women and children were inherently weak and inferior, they were also at least notionally tied to men's corresponding responsibility to protect and provide for their domestic dependents. In reality, however, both law and custom less rigorously enforced men's protective obligations than the authority they wielded over their wives and other subordinates.

Wives' legal disabilities did not, however, preclude companionship and cooperation in marriage, and it seems likely that Jane, whose Welborn kin were was also part of the southward migration out of Maryland and Virginia, supported or possibly instigated William's decision to move to North Carolina. Not long after they married, both of Jane's parents and all of her brothers were in the process of relocating to Rowan County. Jane's mother, Ann, died there in 1756, around the time that Jane, William, and their young son, John, arrived, accompanied by William's brothers and their widowed mother. In May 1758, William and his mother, Mary, sold their landholdings in Virginia and Maryland, and the following February each registered a deed for land in Rowan County on Abbotts Creek, a tributary of the north fork of the Yadkin River (slightly west of the present-day city of High Point). The Spurgins' land was adjacent to a tract farmed by Isaac Welborn, one of Jane's older brothers. William's brothers also acquired land in the area. Samuel spent the rest of his life as a resident of Abbotts Creek, though John subsequently left and resettled in South Carolina.[15]

In part because it had not been cleared and improved, land was, indeed, significantly cheaper in North Carolina. William, who sold 200 acres he owned in Virginia for £100 in local currency, purchased 310 acres in

Rowan County for only £56 in "Virginia money," despite its fine waterside location. William may have planned to erect a gristmill either on Abbotts Creek or on the smaller waterway that became known as Spurgin's (or Spurgeon's) Creek because of its proximity to his property, though there is no evidence that a mill was erected there during his lifetime. Years later, when he was seeking land on which to launch a new farm, William purposefully targeted a tract near a stream that would "Afford Water to Set up a Small Gristt mill" to service farmers in the surrounding settlements whose wheat needed to be ground to become usable as flour. Seemingly knowledgeable about the process of establishing such an enterprise, William expressed confidence in his ability to procure the "mill Stones and Irons, All ye Wheels Runni[n]g-Gears," and to have the whole mill operating within a few weeks of beginning construction.[16]

Grain—corn, rye, oats, barley, and especially wheat—were the most important crops that North Carolina's backcountry farmers cultivated during the colonial era. The area's first grain-producing white settlers, mostly Scots-Irish and German families, had arrived in western North Carolina in the mid-1740s, more than a decade before the Spurgins, establishing their farms on the west side of the Yadkin River. Among those earliest white settlers was Morgan Bryan, an important landowner and justice of the peace in Frederick County, Virginia, who established his large extended family on prime North Carolina fields that had once been occupied by Cherokee Indians. By 1749, when the provincial government designated Anson County as North Carolina's first backcountry jurisdiction, three distinct settlements had coalesced in the Yadkin-Catawba river basin. Land in the forks of the Yadkin, including the Spurgins' neighborhood on Abbotts Creek, was settled later, in part because it was rockier, hillier, and slightly less accessible to key waterways that facilitated the movement of crops to market. Nevertheless, Governor Arthur Dobbs described the land in and around Abbotts Creek as "all a rich dark red, and some inclining to yellow of the richest Loams" and consequently ideal for cultivating wheat and other grains. White settlers who came to the Abbotts Creek area were predominantly English, like the Spurgins and the Welborns, though significant numbers of Germans also established farms in the area.[17]

As the experiences of the Spurgins and the Welborns suggest, settlers

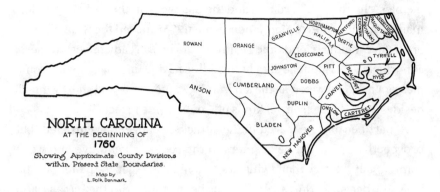

MAP 2 | North Carolina at the beginning of 1760. When the Spurgin and Welborn families arrived in North Carolina in the mid-1750s, the newly formed backcountry counties of Anson (1749) and Rowan (1753), with their unspecified western boundaries, were among the fastest-growing in the province. (Authored by L. Polk Denmark; provided courtesy of the North Carolina Department of Natural and Cultural Resources)

often came to the backcountry in family or community groups, leaving their previous homes together to establish new farming communities. The best-known examples of collective migration and community formation in the North Carolina backcountry were the Moravian settlements, the first of which, Bethabara, was founded in 1753, a year after Bishop Gottlieb Augustus Spangenberg led an expedition to survey the area that became known as the Wachovia Tract. When he toured the area, Spangenberg liked what he saw. The bishop concluded that the land was "reserved by the Lord for the Brethren," some of whom soon left their town of Bethlehem, Pennsylvania, to establish a new Moravian community.[18]

When he visited North Carolina in 1752, Spangenberg found that "many families are moving in from Virginia, Maryland, Pennsylvania, [New] Jersey, and even New England"—and, indeed, that as many as four hundred had arrived in the past year alone—but he still found plenty of fertile acreage for sale by the Earl of Granville, who was eager to populate his vast landholdings in the province. Granville was the proprietor of a sixty-mile-wide swath of land that officially ran from the Atlantic Ocean to the "South Seas" (the Pacific Ocean) in the west. Known as the Granville District, this tract encompassed some 26,000 square miles of land, most of which was not populated by white settlers and was still claimed by Native peoples, chiefly the Cherokees and the Catawbas, in the early 1750s. Herman Husband, a native Marylander who in 1755 toured the Granville Patent before joining friends and relatives who had already relocated there, admiringly described the area he visited as having unusually "wholesome pleasant air, good water, fertile land, and . . . a moderate and short winter," besides being "free from all kinds of troublesome insects."[19]

In part because he feared Indian attacks, Spangenberg insisted that prospective Moravian newcomers to the region should live and work communally. "Every man living alone is in . . . danger in the forest," he believed, because "North Carolina has been at war with the Indians, and they have been defeated and lost their lands . . . [and] all of the Indians are resentful and take every opportunity to show it." Angry Indians, he reported, "have not only killed the cattle of the whites, but have murdered the settlers themselves when they had a chance." Spangenberg also worried that families living in isolation would face other, more quotidian, difficulties, which would not have troubled them as Pennsylvania town-dwellers. He noted the prevalence of vicious beasts, such as wolves and panthers, and was especially concerned about the potential health-related hazards confronting Moravian farm women. "For instance a woman is ill, has high fever," he queried, "where is the nurse, medicine, proper food?" In an era when women suffered high mortality rates in childbirth and relied on each other, rather than male physicians, to navigate various maladies that afflicted themselves and their children, Spangenberg's apprehension was duly warranted. In the North Carolina wilderness, he explained, "The wife of a neighbor lives half a mile, perhaps several miles away, and she has her children, her cattle, her own household to care for, and can give only a couple of hours, or at most one day or one night" to an ailing mother.[20]

On behalf of his brethren, Spangenberg purchased 100,000 acres from the Earl of Granville, on which Moravians built three towns—Bethabara, Bethania, and Salem—by the 1760s. Although most Moravian settlers were farmers, Bethabara and Salem became important commercial hubs in Rowan County, the sites of stores, mills, taverns, and an impressive variety of artisanal activities. As commercial centers, the Moravian towns were rivaled only by the county seat of Salisbury, which benefited from its location on the Great Wagon Road, at the intersection of two Native

American trading routes, and also from its status as the meeting place of the county court, which convened there quarterly. Less than a decade after its founding in 1753, Salisbury's residents included two lawyers, a physician, three hatters, a candlemaker, a potter, a weaver, a tailor, a tanner, a wagonmaker, and merchants and storekeepers, as well as several taverns.[21]

Although there is no surviving record chronicling the settlement of Abbotts Creek that is comparable to Spangenberg's diary or the remarkably detailed daily records Moravian ministers subsequently kept in their respective communities, circumstantial evidence suggests that the Spurgins and the Welborns were part of a somewhat organized exodus that left Frederick County, Maryland and Virginia, in the mid-1750s. Jane Welborn's marriage to William Spurgin linked their two families, both of which moved south and settled in Abbotts Creek at roughly the same time. Back in Virginia, Jane's brother James had married Isabella Mary Teague, and many members of the Teague family, including Isabella's parents and her aunt Charity, also settled in Abbotts Creek around this time. The Teague family left Virginia en masse, just as they had departed from Cecil County, Maryland, decades earlier. Accompanying Charity Teague was her husband, John Swaim, a New York native who had migrated south to Virginia, married into the Teague family, and then accompanied his wife's extended family when they went to North Carolina.[22]

Members of all three of these families—the Spurgins, Welborns, and Teagues—had been baptized in the Church of England, either in Maryland or Virginia, but at Abbotts Creek they would form the nucleus of a new Baptist church community. Clergy were scarce in the Carolina backcountry, and there were no Church of England ministers in the area until 1767. Most backcountry settlers were Scots-Irish Presbyterians, Quakers, Baptists, and members of various German pietist denominations. Many of these newly arrived backcountry settlers had been influenced by the northern religious revivals known as the Great Awakening, and many were openly hostile to the Church of England. Moravian diarists reported that one of their own ministers held services in various Abbotts Creek houses, including the Spurgins', but the neighborhood quickly became a significant Baptist enclave. A Welsh Baptist preacher named James Younger held religious services in the area before the establishment of a permanent church there in 1756 with the Connecticut-born Daniel Marshall as its pastor. Both Younger and Marshall were linked by marriage to the Welborn family.[23]

Moving with family and neighbors enhanced settlers' safety, as Spangenberg noted, while also enabling prospective farmers to share the burden of clearing fields and erecting the structures needed to create new farms and family houses. William Few, who was ten years old when his family left Maryland for Orange County in 1758, recalled that his father sold his land and "such of his goods and chattels as were not moveable" before setting out for North Carolina, where his family arrived with only what they were able to pile into "a wagon drawn by four horses and in a cart drawn by two horses." The lands Few's father purchased "were in their natural state" and "not a tree had been cut," and, as he recalled decades later, the family's "first employment was to cut down the timber and prepare the land for cultivation." The laborious project of clearing the land and establishing a farm there, he noted, "progressed very slowly." Although Few's account of settling the backcountry did not mention any women in his family, middling women like Jane would have worked alongside their husbands and other men in varying capacities during the process of farm formation, even if they were spared the heaviest sorts of physical labor.[24]

Once the land was cleared and the crops were planted, men and women worked together to ensure the success of the family venture. Although contemporary advice manuals, like some modern historians, sometimes envisioned women and men—and their respective activities—as inhabiting distinct, or separate, spheres, the reality was more complex. A leading historian of eighteenth-century rural women and families instead likens the division of labor in early American farm families to the squares on a piece of blue-and-white-checkered gingham cloth. "Think of the white threads as women's activities, the blue as men's," she writes, "then imagine the resulting social web" of interwoven blue and white threads as the activities that "brought men and women together" within and beyond the household. In the farmyard, for instance, women and men jointly cared for livestock and attended to gardens and orchards, though dairying, raising poultry, and tending kitchen gardens were generally considered women's work, whereas men typically attended to the horses, plows, and other tools and farming implements.[25]

Eighteenth-century family farms produced a wide range of commodities, but even backcountry families never envisioned their farms or households as self-sufficient entities. Backcountry families like the Spurgins worked cooperatively, exchanging goods and services within their neighborhoods, but they also expected to sell at least some of their produce. Women produced butter, cheese, and eggs for home consumption, but they sent whatever surplus remained to merchants or stores in Salisbury or Bethabara, where it could be exchanged for imported sugar, spices, nails, tools, cloth, buttons, gunpowder, flints, paper, and patent medicines, as well as items that were made locally, such as textiles and pottery. Farm families—and especially farmers' wives—made much of the cider, beer, and other alcoholic beverages served at local taverns. Rowan County farmers also sold meat from slaughtered livestock to nearby townspeople.[26]

By the time Jane and William arrived in Abbotts Creek, a growing network of roads was also connecting backcountry farmers and their produce to more distant markets. Building and maintaining roads was one of the chief responsibilities of county government, and Rowan County magistrates sanctioned the creation of six roads, including two connecting Salisbury to the coastal ports of Wilmington and Charleston, between 1753 and 1759. The more important of the two proved to be the road to Wilmington, on which merchants from that town established a trading post and mills at Cross Creek (present-day Fayetteville) approximately eighty miles inland on a tributary of the Cape Fear River. Wilmington merchants' agents in Cross Creek purchased and ground western grain, which they sent downriver for sale or export. By the 1760s, Cross Creek was the main entrepôt for backcountry wheat, a vital link for both commerce and communication between the eastern and western sections of North Carolina.[27]

While William oversaw the production and sale of wheat, Jane's work as a farmer's wife was also both productive and essential to their family's welfare. Like William's work in the wheat fields, some of Jane's work was seasonal. Especially when her children were too young to work with

William in the fields, Jane herself likely helped with the grain harvest during the fall; once they established a fruit-bearing orchard, she would have made cider after apple-picking season. In November, men typically butchered hogs, but women preserved the meat in brine and rendered the fat for lard and tallow, which they could then use for making candles and soap. If their farms produced flax for making linen, women spun and carded its fibers for linen-making during the winter, though they may have sent their spun flax to nearby Moravian weavers rather than weaving it into fabric by themselves. In the spring, Jane would have planted her vegetable gardens, milked her cows daily, and made cheese and butter. When the garden yielded vegetables in summertime, she harvested, pickled, and preserved their produce.[28]

Jane worked year-round to keep her family fed and clothed. Cooking necessitated not only labor-intensive food preparation but also the endless building and maintaining of fires. Women also made most of the clothes their family wore and the bed linens and other cloth goods their households used, even if they purchased textiles from local shopkeepers or weavers. Laundry was a particularly onerous task. Keeping clothing and linens in good repair meant that sewing was another constant household chore. A popular advice book (which most backcountry women never read) aptly summarized the conventional wisdom regarding the scope and value of women's most basic domestic work: "After her knowledge of preserving and feeding her Family, [a housewife] must also learn how . . . to cloath them outwardly and inwardly: outwardly for the defence from the cold and comeliness to the person, and inwardly for cleanliness and neatness of skin, whereby it may be kept from the filth of sweat or vermin."[29]

Jane's work at Abbotts Creek would have been the most taxing in the early years, when the life cycles of both her family and the family farm demanded extra labor. In addition to whatever work she contributed to the process of farm formation, Jane arrived in North Carolina with one young son to tend, and she bore four more children—three daughters and one son—between 1757 and 1762, followed by two daughters and three sons between 1766 and 1775. Given the high rates of infant mortality in eighteenth-century America, as well as Jane's record of giving birth every one to two years after settling at Abbotts Creek, it seems probable that she was also pregnant at least once more in the mid-1760s but that she either suffered a miscarriage or her child was stillborn or died in infancy. Childcare and child-rearing were time-consuming responsibilities, and, though daughters eventually could be expected to help with household work, they typically learned domestic skills from their mothers, mostly by watching, between the ages of five and ten, before they became full-fledged members of the family workforce. "No family," as one historian has observed, "gave birth to full-grown workers." Jane's oldest daughters, Rebecca and Margaret, turned ten in 1767 and 1768, respectively.[30]

Nor did Jane have regular access to other forms of assistance, though many housewives of her era brought nieces or other female kin into their homes to work, and some also had access to bonded labor or hired help. At Abbotts Creek, aside from their aged parents, who had their own new farmsteads to establish and tend, the Spurgins' extended family was made up of couples like themselves who had young children and fledgling farms. Tax records indicate that William was the only tithable member of the Spurgin household during this period, which meant that Jane and her family, like most Abbotts Creek residents, had neither white servants nor enslaved Blacks working on their farm or in their house. In 1759, there were only 36 enslaved adults—out of 652 taxable inhabitants—in Rowan County, and the few families who employed indentured servants or en-slaved workers devoted those scarce resources to agricultural labor. In sum, while Jane may have worked cooperatively with neighboring farm women on certain tasks, especially during harvests, she was mostly on her own for at least her first decade in Abbotts Creek in running an in-creasingly crowded household.[31]

Especially during the early years, living conditions in the Abbotts Creek settlements would have been rustic. E. W. Caruthers, an early his-torian of North Carolina who was born and raised in Rowan County and who drew on the recollections of aged county residents when he wrote about life in the colonial backcountry, described each settler family there as living initially in "a small log house, with only one room below, which served for both parlor and bedroom, and one [room] above." Newcomers, he reported, "expected that in such a house they could be comfortable and contented for a few years, and hoped that by the blessing of Prov-idence on their own industry and economy, they would be able, after a while, to get a better [house]." If the Spurgins followed this pattern, they may have expanded their dwelling space after 1761, when William purchased an additional 273 acres in the area, and perhaps used timber from his newly cleared land to construct expanded quarters for his growing family. If so, Jane and William would have spent several years living with four or five small children in the original two-room house that would have required Jane's constant cleaning. "In a house of this description on a farm considerable mud and dust will every hour be deposited on the floor, in spite of all the care than can be taken," Caruthers observed, adding that "if it were swept clean in going to bed," the dirt would return as a result of "the bringing of wood and water in the morning."[32]

Whatever their material circumstances, within a few years of their arrival in North Carolina, the Spurgins were ascending the social ladder in Abbotts Creek and in Rowan County more generally. The most compelling evidence of William's rise was his appointment, in 1764, as one of twenty-two justices of the peace for Rowan County, a position he retained for the rest of the colonial era. Justices of the peace (or JPs) represented the authority of the king and were the main source of law and governance in most rural colonial communities. It is unclear exactly how William secured this coveted appointment. Although ownership of 583 acres made him a substantial farmer, his economic status was significantly below that of those men who owned thousands of acres and, in some cases, also numbered among the county's small slaveholding elite.

It seems reasonable to suppose that William cultivated connections with powerful and prominent men in Rowan County and its environs who, in turn, rewarded him with their patronage, which was an essential prerequisite for obtaining an appointment as a county magistrate. The colony's governor, as the king's representative in America, made all official appointments, but he heavily relied on the advice of his elite contacts across the province, choosing new county justices from lists of recommendations submitted by members of the provincial legislature who were also sitting justices. Acting on such advice, in 1764 Governor Arthur Dobbs commissioned William Spurgin as a justice of the peace for Rowan County. The decision to appoint William to the county bench may have derived in part from the fact that there was no sitting justice from the comparatively remote and recently settled Abbotts Creek area, and the governor's elevation of William to this position marked him as a leader in his community. In October 1764, William appeared at his first court session as a county justice, after having subscribed to the oath by which he avowed his allegiance to the Crown and his commitment to upholding the king's laws.[33]

Although there were no educational requirements for becoming a county magistrate, the justices of the peace and their functions were both ubiquitous and essential in eighteenth-century America. As one North Carolina governor observed, appointment as a county justice was "much desired on account of the many Trusts reposed in them by the Laws of the Country which indeed gives them very great influence in their several Counties."[34]

In North Carolina as in other colonies, the vast and varied powers of the county courts and their justices served both judicial and governmental functions. As a court, the justices convened quarterly to adjudicate civil cases and criminal matters except those in which a guilty verdict could result in the loss of life or limb for a free defendant (in other words, one who was neither enslaved nor indentured). Justices had the power to impose fines, prison terms, and whippings and other types of corporal punishment. They chose the juries for their district's superior court, a higher tribunal that decided the most serious criminal cases, on which they also served as judges. At the same time, the county court was also the main source of local government in rural colonial communities. The justices established local tax rates, oversaw tax collection, and confiscated property for nonpayment of taxes and other debts. They registered land titles and deeds, licensed taverns and mills, and decided where to locate roads and ferries. They enforced the wills of the deceased and committed orphans and poor children to apprenticeships and other forms of bonded labor. They regulated weights and measures and set prices for trips on ferries and drinks in taverns.[35]

Although most of his fellow-justices in Rowan County exceeded William in wealth and personal connections, like him they all were upwardly mobile men who had settled relatively recently in North Carolina. A few of the justices had been born in Great Britain, but all of them had come to North Carolina after settling initially in Pennsylvania, Maryland, or Virginia, and often, like the Spurgins, after residing in more than one of those older colonies. Rowan County's justices were farmers who moved south in the hope of acquiring cheap and fertile land in comparatively larger quantities. Like the Spurgins and the Welborns, most had also migrated in family groups and settled amid clusters of families who intermarried with each other.[36]

Although some of William's new colleagues on the county bench had come to North Carolina in the late 1740s and were among those chosen as the first magistrates of Anson County when it was established in 1749, even those early arrivals who attained the pinnacle of success in colonial officeholding by representing their county in the provincial legislature had risen from relatively humble origins. James Carter had spent some time in debtors' prison in Cecil County, Maryland, before decamping first to the Shenandoah Valley and then to the Carolina backcountry, where he became a justice of the peace and later represented Rowan County in the provincial assembly. John Brandon was a modest "husbandman" in Lancaster County, Pennsylvania, before moving first to Virginia and then on to North Carolina, where he, too, became both a county magistrate and a provincial legislator. So, too, did Alexander Osborne, a New Jersey native, thrive in the North Carolina backcountry, where he was both a county justice—first in Anson and then later in Rowan—and a member of the colonial assembly. All three men owned substantial property in North Carolina, and both Carter and Osborne were also part of the relatively small group of backcountry elites who were also slaveholders. In 1759, Osborne, who claimed ownership of at least three enslaved people, paid taxes on more enslaved workers than any other county resident.[37]

Court day was an important occasion in Rowan County, as in other colonial communities, bringing local people together to conduct business, socialize in taverns, and witness the ceremonial and substantive aspects of the court's proceedings. As he took his place among the justices on the elevated bench in Salisbury's recently completed wooden courthouse, William likely felt a combination of awe at the power of the law to both protect and punish and pride that he was now among the select few who were entrusted with wielding such power. In 1764, he and Jane would have been entirely justified in looking optimistically toward the future, perhaps even seeing William's appointment as a JP as the start of a family dynasty in North Carolina. After all, the colonial legislature was made up almost entirely of sitting justices, and though political positions were not exactly hereditary, it was common for sons to succeed their fathers as officeholders. Indeed, some of William's colleagues on the court had either a father or a son who also served as a county magistrate.[38]

As it turned out, however, William's tenure on the court coincided with the most tumultuous years of North Carolina's early history. In the coming years, the authority of the courts and of even the king himself would face unprecedented challenges, both locally and on a far grander scale, forcing the Spurgins and their neighbors to make difficult and sometimes life-changing choices.

2

An Enemy to His Country

WILLIAM'S YEARS AS a Rowan County justice coincided with the imperial crisis that led to the American Revolution. Britain's decisive defeat of France and its Native American allies in 1763, after decades of intermittent warfare, raised administrative and financial issues that ultimately resulted in the breakup of its vastly enlarged American empire. To promote peace with the Indians, the royal Proclamation of 1763 prohibited colonists from acquiring land west of the Appalachians, a policy that enraged both wealthy speculators and poorer settlers who hoped to become landowners by occupying Native territory. To pay the costs of administering an enlarged and unwieldy empire, which included the permanent posting of troops in North America, Parliament enacted the Sugar Act and the Stamp Act, the first of several laws that aimed to extract revenue from the king's American subjects. Colonists denounced these laws and later imperial measures as unconstitutional, contending that only their own elected representatives legitimately possessed the power to tax them. Although they professed allegiance to King George III, most colonists, including many who would remain loyal to the Crown after 1776, believed that this onslaught of new imperial policies violated their rights as subjects of the king and denizens of the British Empire. For supporting evidence, they cited the Magna Carta, centuries of English common-law precedents, and their own legislatures' past histories as governing bodies in British colonial America.

Although some North Carolinians participated in the increasingly intercolonial debates and protests that punctuated the well-known story of the coming of the Revolution, during much of this period inhabitants of the western part of the province experienced a different political reality. In the late 1760s and early 1770s, backcountry farmers, too, protested unfair government policies and what they saw as ongoing efforts to deprive them of their property and violate their rights. Unlike the Stamp Act rioters in the colony's coastal towns, however, dissidents in Rowan and neighboring counties located the source of their suffering not in Parliament or among London's imperial functionaries but rather within the ranks of the local magistracy to which William Spurgin had so recently ascended. Although William deftly avoided taking a strong stance either for or against the dissident farmers, who were known as Regulators, for him the imperial crisis posed more serious and enduring problems. By late 1775, as colonists defiantly edged their way toward independence, William's refusal to renounce what he believed to be his sworn duty as a magistrate to uphold the authority of the king made him—in the words of the Rowan County Committee of Safety—an "Enemy to his Country." His political choice ended the upward trajectory of Spurgins' fortunes in North Carolina, with dire consequences for Jane and her ever-growing family.

In the fall of 1765, the Moravian diarists reported that there was "great bitterness throughout the land" as a result of Parliament's passage of the Stamp Act, which imposed taxes on newspapers, pamphlets, almanacs, and other printed matter, as well as on legal documents such as leases, land titles, wills, and licenses. Unlike the Sugar Act, which was a duty that merchants paid on imported foreign sugar and then quietly passed on to their customers, the Stamp Act was a direct tax on essential goods and services that nearly everyone would have to pay. Rowan County residents complained about this controversial law when they gathered for the November 1765 meeting of the county court in Salisbury. They sympathized with protesters in Boston and New York and other faraway communities and learned that North Carolinians in Wilmington and in some other eastern towns had also taken to the streets in what their recently arrived royal governor, William Tryon, condemned as "riotous Assembly." In March 1766, in large part because many colonial merchants agreed to stop buying British imports to protest the hated law, Parliament prudently repealed the Stamp Act, but they did so without acceding to colonists' demands that they be taxed only by their own representatives. In fact, the repeal of the Stamp Act was accompanied by the passing of another law called the Declaratory Act, which emphatically affirmed Parliament's authority to legislate for the colonies "in all cases whatsoever."[1]

Although there were no Stamp Act riots in the backcountry, at least initially discontented farmers there drew inspiration from the Stamp Act protesters' demands for lawful and equitable government. By 1766, backcountry farmers had a long list of grievances, most of which involved the unresponsiveness and rampant corruption of North Carolina's local and provincial governments. Particularly vexing was the difficulty securing land titles and the extortionate and illicit fees that land agents and county officials—who were often the same people—charged for surveying tracts and then for securing and registering the documents required to verify landownership. Farmers also resented North Carolina's colony-wide tax system, which favored the wealthy by deriving all revenue from a poll tax levied on each person whose labor was deemed remunerative—white males aged sixteen or older and all Blacks over the age of twelve—which left the vast landholdings and commercial wealth of the most affluent colonists untaxed. Laws requiring that taxes be paid in currency, not commodities, also were burdensome for cash-poor farmers, as was tax collectors' aggressive confiscation of livestock and other property in lieu of unpaid taxes. Among the southern colonies, according to a leading historian of early American taxation, North Carolina's tax system was "the most regressive . . . and the most corrupt." Farmers also complained that wealthy and powerful men who dismissed their concerns or, worse yet, extorted money from them and wantonly profited from their misery, controlled both the county courts and the provincial legislature, with the latter body disproportionately dominated by representatives from the eastern counties, despite the backcountry's rapidly growing population.[2]

Although unrest as a result of these and other backcountry grievances arose from time to time, most historians see the Regulator movement as beginning with the founding of the Sandy Creek Association in August 1766. This group of Orange County farmers, most of whom were Quakers, composed and circulated a manifesto that began by invoking the precedent of "the sons of Liberty [who] withstood the Lords in Parliament in behalf of true Liberty" by protesting the Stamp Act and then went on to condemn the "unjust Oppression in our own Province." The Sandy Creek associators called on "each Neighbourhood throughout the Country" to send one or more men to a meeting to be held in the Orange County town of Hillsborough, where they planned to discuss "whether the free men of this Country labor under any abuses of power or not." Such a candid airing of grievances, they confidently predicted, would "certainly cause the wicked men in power to tremble." As it turned out, they were wrong. Edmund Fanning, a wealthy and well-connected lawyer, who was also a local official in Orange County and a member of the colonial assembly, refused to meet with the associators. A second meeting between aggrieved farmers and local authorities, planned for 1768, also never happened.[3]

More so than in most other places, local officials in the Carolina backcountry were men on the make, relatively recent arrivals from comparatively humble origins who came to the area specifically to have a chance to become wealthy and powerful. Even Edmund Fanning, a New York native whose degrees from Yale and Harvard marked him as one of very few college attendees among the backcountry's residents, was a Long Island innkeeper's son who left New York to rise from his middling beginnings to enter the ranks of North Carolina's provincial elite. Such men, as the Regulator leader Herman Husband noted, were "active to gain all offices and posts of profit." As early as 1765, Fanning's critics were singing a ballad that his condemned his illicit rise to wealth and power:

When Fanning first to Orange came
He looked both pale and wan,
An old patched coat upon his back
An old mare he rode on.

An Enemy to His Country

Both man and mare wa'nt worth five pounds
As I've been often told
But by his civil robberies
He's laced his coat with gold.

After settling in Orange County, Fanning became Hillsborough's town commissioner and recorder of deeds, besides holding several local judicial appointments. He amassed a huge estate, which included more than 10,000 acres, as a result of holding these multiple official posts.[4]

In Rowan County, James Carter was arguably the most corrupt of William Spurgin's colleagues on the county bench. This former inmate in a Maryland debtors' prison became a justice of the peace, a major in the county militia, and a surveyor for Lord Granville, the absentee landlord who owned most of Rowan County and the surrounding area. Like Fanning, Carter accumulated vast wealth by charging exorbitant fees and by not verifying land purchases for farmers who had paid him to perform that service. As early as 1755, Herman Husband accused Carter of filing only about 170 land titles, though he had received payment for the land, along with the fees for surveying and the recording of the deeds, from "not quite a thousand" farmers.[5]

Because of the unchecked rapacity of men like Fanning and Carter, the Regulators attracted widespread support, especially in the counties of Orange, Anson, and Rowan. One measure of the movement's appeal was farmers' increasingly widespread refusal to pay their taxes. Beginning in 1765, as colonists throughout British North America rejected the new Parliamentary levies, residents of North Carolina's backcountry thwarted their county sheriffs' efforts to collect annual local taxes. That year, in Rowan County alone there were 838 tax delinquents, whom local authorities disparaged as "either insolvents or insurgent Mobs." The next year, fewer than one-third of the county's 3,059 households paid their taxes. By 1769 more than 1,200 Rowan County households still had not paid their taxes for 1766, and some of these delinquent families owed additional sums from subsequent years as well. Indeed, in 1770 the Rowan County sheriff reported having secured payment of the levies for 1768 from only 205 households in the entire county. He attributed his difficulties to "a refractory disposition of a set of people calling themselves Regulators," who, by "refusing to pay any taxes or other publick money to a sheriff or any other officer," also encouraged "many well disposed people [to] neglect to discharge their public dues." The end result, in Rowan and in other backcountry counties, was widespread resistance and sometimes violent opposition to the collection of local taxes.[6]

Like colonists who opposed the Stamp Act and other new imperial laws and policies, Regulators used the written word to explain their grievances, seek reform, and justify crowd actions. In particular, they went over the heads of seemingly incorrigible local magistrates by addressing petitions to the provincial legislature in 1768 and 1769, after Governor William Tryon called on the colony's militia to restore order in Orange County, where angry residents attacked the local sheriff for confiscating a farmer's mare as payment for delinquent taxes. In their first petition, signed by twenty-nine men from Orange and Rowan Counties and submitted in October 1768, the Regulators complained of the corruption of "Publick Officers" who "Continually Sqez'd and pressed" them for both taxes and illicit fees, while noting the special problems posed by the lack of currency in the backcountry. Perhaps to make their plight more tangible to the "Gentlemen Rowling in affluence" who considered the merit of their requests, the petitioners lamented that they would have to sell "their Bed and Bedclothes [and] their Wives Petticoats" to pay these taxes and fees. A second petition, which 144 men from Orange County submitted that November, called for the creation of new, smaller backcountry counties to make courts, militia musters, and voting accessible to more people. Because each county sent delegates to the provincial legislature, the addition of new counties in the backcountry also would have made that body more representative of the area's growing population.[7]

Although the legislature granted neither petition outright, these efforts were modestly successful, at least in the short term. In late 1768, the assembly passed a law that allowed payment of some taxes with commodities instead of currency. The following year, when the governor dissolved the assembly and called for new elections, four Regulators—Herman Husband, Christopher Nation, Thomas Person, and John Pryor—were elected and forty-five of the legislature's seventy-seven seats overall were won by newly elected members. When the new assembly convened in October 1769, Husband presented the Regulators' third petition, signed by forty-nine men from Orange and Rowan Counties, who reiterated their desire for a more representative assembly, as well as their denunciation of official corruption and "very grievous and oppressive taxes." Unfortunately for the Regulators, the assembly never truly considered their requests because Governor William Tryon, wary of North Carolina's leaders joining the intercolonial opposition to the Townshend Duties Act (another objectionable Parliamentary tax) summarily dissolved the legislature in early November. Husband returned to Orange County, where he wrote the first of two pamphlets in which he explained the origins of the Regulator movement, justified the farmers' actions, and encouraged the insurgents to continue and even expand their protest efforts. "We lose our liberty by not asserting it properly," he argued, adding, "It serves no purpose to cry out against government and officers if we don't properly bestir ourselves" to action.[8]

The situation in the backcountry grew increasingly dire in the coming months, with a major riot occurring in Hillsborough in September 1770. Governor Tryon issued a proclamation in response to the violence and retroactively invoked the Johnston Riot Act, which the assembly swiftly enacted when Tryon reconvened that body in December. Under the terms of that draconian law, any group of ten or more people who assembled "unlawfully, tumultuously and riotously," and who did not disperse within an hour after receiving an official warning to do so, would be charged with a capital offense. In the same legislative session, the assembly voted to eject Herman Husband, who, along with several other Regulator leaders, was indicted by a Special Court of Oyer and Terminer for his role in the Hillsborough riot. Tryon then called on militia from throughout the province to assemble in Hillsborough to maintain order during the expected trials.[9]

The Regulators would not back down, however, and the two sides clashed in battle at Alamance Creek on 16 May 1771. Within two hours, some twenty farmers were dead, along with nine militia men; a total of 150 men were wounded. The governor's militia soundly defeated the Regulators, one of whom was summarily executed on the battlefield. After the battle was over, many of the Regulators fled North Carolina, fearing retribution. While some moved to South Carolina, a significant number of the movement's Quaker supporters crossed the boundary line into Virginia, where they established the Chestnut Creek community. For those Regulators who remained in North Carolina, Tryon offered pardons to all but the insurgents' leaders, twelve of whom were tried and convicted in Hillsborough and condemned to death. Ultimately, six of those men were publicly executed, by hanging, on 19 June 1771. One of the six who escaped execution was Thomas Welborn, whom those petitioning on his behalf described as "A true and Loyal Tenant to his Majesty, Excepting the Late Insurrection and Rebellion." A farmer from Orange County, Welborn also happened to be Jane Spurgin's older brother.[10]

Although Jane must have strongly supported the efforts of the friends and neighbors who petitioned to spare her brother's life, no surviving evidence sheds light on her opinion of the Regulators or the role that county magistrates and other officials played in their ultimately violent suppression. The Regulators kept no lists of their supporters, and women, whatever their status in the community, neither signed Regulator petitions nor participated in their meetings, though the wives and children of the condemned men were among the crowd that gathered to witness the hangings in Hillsborough in June 1771.[11]

Nor does William Spurgin appear anywhere in the documentary record of what became known as the War of the Regulation, despite his official position as a Rowan County justice. William was not among those backcountry magistrates who reported the Regulators' activities to Governor Tryon and who requested military assistance from the provincial government to suppress the dissident farmers. Nor was he among those local officials whom the Regulators mentioned by name as being particularly arrogant or corrupt.

Although there is no way of knowing whether William profited financially from his appointment as a justice of the peace, it is clear that, unlike some of his colleagues, he did not become wealthy as a result of his tenure as a county justice. William owned 583 acres when he joined the court in October 1764; in 1768, he purchased an additional 396 acres but then sold 273 acres the following year. In 1769, at the height of the Regulation, William therefore possessed 706 acres, which made him a prosperous landowner but not by any means a member of the uppermost tier of the county's landed elite. Although he would eventually acquire at least one enslaved worker, the tax lists indicated that at this point he had not yet entered the small but slowly growing ranks of Rowan County slaveholders.[12]

One reason why William may not have profited from his position was that, as his subsequent conduct would amply demonstrate, he took his official oath seriously. As everyone from the governor to the struggling farmers knew, justices of the peace were unpaid officials whom both law and custom barred from profiting from their service. As Tryon explained in a letter to his superiors in London, "besides the Oaths to the [King's] Government which these Justices in common with all other Officers Civil and Military are obliged to take . . . they also take an Oath of Fidelity among other Things importing they shall accept no Fee or Reward whatever for doing their Duty in that Office." While comfortably affluent men in the eastern plantation counties aspired to become JPs and did their "Duty" in pursuit of prestige and opportunities for further political advancement, backcountry justices were mostly ambitious men who sought to profit financially from local officeholding. The Regulators understood that, and, as a result, they advocated the granting of publicly funded salaries to officeholders as a means of stemming official corruption. Yet in an era when many people regarded oath-keeping not only as a test of personal integrity but also as a measure of one's fidelity to God, swearing to forgo fees and other forms of payment must have deterred at least some JPs from the sort of illicit and oppressive conduct that enriched so many of their colleagues and enraged so many backcountry farmers.[13]

William's attendance record at the court's quarterly sessions indicates that he was well informed about the turmoil in the region and that he took an interest in the Regulators and their relations with local authorities. From his appointment as a justice in October 1764 through December 1767, William attended a total of only five (of a possible thirteen) court sessions. Although some justices appeared at court more consistently than he did, his spotty attendance was not unusual, especially in view of the roughly fifty-mile distance between Abbotts Creek and Salisbury and the fact that the presence of only a small subset of the total number of justices was required to form the quorum needed to conduct court business. From 1768 through 1770, however, William attended six of twelve quarterly court meetings, and he was present at all of the sessions when county sheriffs reported problems they encountered as a result of the farmers' refusal to pay taxes and likely discussed strategies for suppressing the Regulator insurgency. William was also at court on various occasions during these years when Rowan County farmers sought to use grand jury presentments to initiate criminal proceedings against corrupt local officials, and when their repeated failures to secure indictments exacerbated Regulator outrage and led to accusations that the magistrates used their power to stack the juries against them.[14]

Circumstantial evidence suggests that William (and perhaps even more so Jane) sympathized with the Regulators, though his position as a justice prevented him from supporting them openly. The Spurgins remained on good terms with their kin and with their other neighbors in Abbotts Creek, an area widely known as a hotbed of Regulator activism. Jane's brothers, James and William Welborn, both of whom resided in Abbotts Creek, supported the Regulators, though they were not nearly as prominent in the movement as their brother Thomas, who narrowly escaped execution for his activities in Orange County. Members of the Teague family, who had settled in Abbotts Creek around the same time as the Spurgins and who had intermarried with the Welborns, also sided with the Regulators, as did James Younger, a Baptist minister who was associated with the Abbotts Creek congregation. Rowan County Regulators often convened at "the Meeting House near Moses Teague's" where the Baptists held their services, a building commonly known as "Welborn's Meeting House" because of the prominence of Jane's brothers and their extended family in the local Baptist community.[15]

As worshippers at Abbotts Creek Baptist Church, the Spurgins were members of a community that had good reason to be enraged with both corrupt local officials and the colony's current royal governor. Although the Church of England was, overall, weak in North Carolina and virtually nonexistent in the backcountry, Tryon, who assumed the governorship in 1765, made augmenting the power and visibility of the colony's established church one of his top priorities. The new governor did not attempt to suppress non-Anglican Protestant denominations, but he resolutely sought to increase the number of Church of England clergy in the province, an initiative that included sending the first-ever Anglican minister to the backcountry and forcing the region's overwhelmingly non-Anglican inhabitants to elect a vestry charged with overseeing the operation of a newly established tax-supported parish. More important still, Tryon adamantly demanded the enforcement of laws that gave Anglican clergy the exclusive authority to officiate in marriage ceremonies (and to collect the fees for those services), which effectively rendered illegitimate marriages performed by other Protestant clergy. The governor eventually offered some concessions to Presbyterians, who constituted the bulk of backcountry elites, in part to retain them as allies in his efforts to defeat the Regulators, but he made no such concessions to the Baptists, who were overall less affluent and less powerful, and whom he denounced as "Enemies to Society, & [a] Scandal to common Sense."[16]

In addition to their denominational and economic interests, the Baptists' religious beliefs and social ethos led them to criticize the greed and pretension of established secular and ecclesiastical authorities. Even among Protestant evangelicals, the early Baptists were radical in privileging individual conscience over church dogma and especially in their egalitarian disregard for conventional social hierarchies. Baptist ministers were mostly uneducated and often of modest social origins. They lived simply, adhered to Scripture, and preached from the heart. The belief that all people were brothers and sisters, and children of God, led Baptists to welcome poor men, and even women and free and enslaved Blacks, into their congregations as near-equals. This approach to religion subverted the prevailing social hierarchy with its presumptive deference toward the elite white men who held official posts—both ecclesiastical and secular—regardless of their conduct. Accordingly, Governor Tryon blamed the Baptists (and the equally radical Quakers) for the Regulator uprisings. Although the Regulators were more denominationally diverse than Tryon claimed, historians agree that Baptists in Sandy Creek, Abbotts Creek, and elsewhere accounted for a large proportion of the backcountry's dissident farmers.[17]

Regardless of the extent to which Jane and William shared (or perhaps rejected) this radical worldview, three pieces of evidence suggest that they sympathized with their Regulator neighbors and coreligionists. First, perhaps at Jane's urging, William shielded one of her brothers from possible official retaliation after the decisive defeat of the Regulators at Alamance in May 1771. In July, perhaps fearing that he would be arrested and his property confiscated, James Welborn sold 323 acres to the Spurgins for £50; once the crisis had passed, William and Jane sold the same land back to James for an identical £50 price. Other evidence comes from E. W. Caruthers, the nineteenth-century local historian. As he correctly reported, fueled in part by their hatred of local elites and eastern grandees who led the rebellion against Great Britain, many men who had been Regulators or who had sympathized with their movement later opposed the American Revolution. Caruthers's elderly interviewees remembered William Spurgin as someone who "had the confidence of the neighborhood for his integrity, and was regarded as being in every respect, an estimable man," at least before some local people parted ways with him politically during the Revolution. In addition, Caruthers also noted that, in 1772, Tryon's successor as governor, Josiah Martin, toured the backcountry, where he consulted with the "most competent and trustworthy" men, whom he later commissioned as military officers "in the service of his Majesty." As William was one of those men who received a military commission from Martin, he was also likely one of the backcountry men who persuaded the newly installed governor that local farmers had been—in Martin's words—"grievously oppressed by the Sheriffs, Clerks and other Subordinate officers of Government."[18]

Although some early chroniclers and later historians, unlike Caruthers, incorrectly romanticized the Regulators as protopatriots who would soon battle Great Britain to preserve colonial rights and liberties, most modern scholars agree that many, or even most, either remained loyal to the Crown or tried to remain neutral after 1776, though some, most notably Herman Husband, enthusiastically embraced the revolutionary cause. Conversely, although the notorious Edmund Fanning became an active and important loyalist, most of the local officials who tormented the Regulators in the backcountry became stalwart supporters of American independence.[19]

Of the twenty-three men whose names appeared on the list of Rowan County justices for 1771, at most four remained loyal to the king after 1776, compared with nineteen who actively supported independence and the war with Britain. A few Rowan County JPs became leaders in North Carolina's revolutionary movement. Matthew Locke, a longtime justice whose brother Francis was one of the local sheriffs who tangled with the Regulators and seized their livestock for nonpayment of taxes, was a colonel

FIGURE 1 | Alamance battleground monument. This obelisk, erected in 1880, incorrectly describes the Battle of Alamance in 1771 as a confrontation between "the British and the Regulators" and also as the "First Battle of the Revolution." Although led by Governor William Tryon, the troops who defeated the Regulators were North Carolinians. The monument's inscriptions celebrate the Regulators as America's foremost defenders of liberty and imply that their Confederate descendants were equally unrivaled as liberty-loving Americans. (Photograph by the author)

in the patriot militia and a member of every county-level revolutionary committee, and he also represented Rowan County in the state legislature for more than a decade after independence. By contrast, three of the four colonial justices who appear to have had loyalist leanings laid low after their initial altercation with local Whigs in the mid-1770s. Only William Spurgin remained relentlessly and actively committed to the king and thus opposed to the Revolution.[20]

North Carolina's last colonial governor, Josiah Martin, arrived in the province in August 1771, two months after his predecessor had overseen the Regulator executions and then departed for New York to assume the governorship of that colony. Although Martin initially believed the self-styled "friends of Government" who characterized the Regulators as unruly and treasonous, his tour of the backcountry the following summer convinced him otherwise. Appalled by the abuses he discovered there, Martin took steps to expose the corruption of local officials, removing the worst offenders from office. He also planned to reform the courts and strengthen the role of the governor in the appointment of sheriffs and local justices. As one Regulator leader observed gleefully, most backcountry magistrates "hate [Martin] as bad as we hated Tryon only they don't speak so free." Members of North Carolina's provincial assembly bitterly opposed Martin's reform efforts, which threatened to diminish their own power in their respective county communities. The legislature did, however, sanction the establishment of four new counties—Chatham, Guilford, Surry, and Wake—which opened more official posts to aspiring backcountry grandees while also addressing the Regulators' desire for smaller jurisdictions to make the county courts more accessible and to increase backcountry representation in the provincial assembly.[21]

Martin's arrival and the denouement of the Regulator crisis coincided with a lull in the imperial controversies that had begun with the passage of the Stamp Act in 1765. Preoccupied with local matters, between 1767 and 1770 backcountry people did not participate much in the colonial protests that occurred after Parliament passed the Townshend Duties Act—which imposed taxes on lead, paper, paint, glass, and tea—though during these years, resistance to imperial taxation and other policies became a mass movement, as people throughout the colonies mobilized to protest offensive measures by boycotting British imports, and by shaming those who did not comply with their nonconsumption efforts. In eastern North Carolina, local Sons of Liberty threatened to publish the names of certain "importers and purchasers" if they persisted in buying British goods, which they deemed "a practice so destructive in its tendency to the liberties of the people in this colony" as to warrant public punishment. These consumer boycotts were crucial in politicizing many people, including women, who did not typically engage in political activism.

Enforcing compliance was difficult, however, and the nonconsumption movement dissipated after 1770, when Parliament repealed all but the tax on tea.[22]

Although tensions remained high, more than three years passed before another major controversy aroused an even more potent colonial protest. In May 1773, Parliament passed the Tea Act, a law that gave monopoly privileges and tax breaks to the financially troubled London-based British East India Company; colonists condemned this measure as unfair to colonial tea merchants and, worse still, as a ruse to trick them to accept Parliament's tea tax by lowering the overall price of that much-loved imported commodity. Outraged colonists attacked British tea ships and, most famously, dumped ninety-two thousand pounds of tea in Boston harbor in December 1773. Parliament responded to Bostonians' destruction of the tea—which was worth nearly two million dollars in twenty-first-century money—with harsh disciplinary action, swiftly enacting four punitive laws known collectively as the Coercive Acts, which colonists dubbed "intolerable." Taken together, the Intolerable Acts closed the port of Boston, limited town meetings to one per year, made the upper house of the Massachusetts legislature royally appointed (rather than elected), exempted royal officials accused of criminal acts from prosecution in America, and required colonists to pay to house and provision British troops who might be lodged in private households.[23]

Although the Intolerable Acts aimed specifically to punish colonists in and around Boston for the destruction of the tea, news of Parliament's retaliation against Massachusetts galvanized resistance throughout British America. During the Townshend Duties protests in the late 1760s, many communities had organized committees of correspondence to coordinate intercolonial resistance efforts. On learning of these new laws in 1774, outraged colonists in Massachusetts and elsewhere again orchestrated intercolonial strategies, the most significant of which was their plan to convene a Continental Congress in Philadelphia in early September. In the meantime, North Carolina's first Provincial Congress, which met in New Bern in late August, called for the formal creation of local committees of correspondence throughout the province. Established to organize resistance to Parliamentary measures, in North Carolina and elsewhere these extralegal committees and congresses gradually assumed crucial political and judicial functions.[24]

In Rowan County, local Whigs anticipated the Provincial Congress's call to action, holding their first meeting in Salisbury in early August, during the county court's summer session. When the Rowan County committee was formally constituted in September, only four of the county's sitting justices—Matthew Locke, John Brevard, William Sharpe, and Christopher Beekman—were among the twenty-five men who became committee members. With its twenty-one nonjustices, the composition of this first Rowan County committee was indicative of how the imperial crisis ushered new men into positions of political prominence and influence, especially at the local level. As the crisis deepened and as North Carolinians moved toward declaring independence, the Rowan committee grew in size, and its membership came to include a few more justices. Of the thirty-seven men who constituted the membership of Rowan County's Committee of Safety in 1776, nine had been JPs who attended to their duties as royally appointed magistrates through February 1775, when the Provincial Congress abolished the king's courts and endowed local committees with temporary judicial powers.[25]

William Spurgin was among those justices who attended court sessions in 1774 and 1775, but neither he nor anyone else from Abbotts Creek served on any of the Rowan County committees. Regulators overall were also notably absent from the lists of committee members, perhaps because they felt loyalty or gratitude toward Governor Martin or because they could not fathom working together with their longtime local enemies.[26]

William was in Salisbury to attend court in August 1774, and, as he observed the proceedings of the county's Whig leaders, he must have surmised that it would be tough going for anyone who opposed them. Almost immediately, the group unanimously adopted seventeen strongly worded resolutions. Patriotic manifestos of this sort were common after news of the Coercive Acts reached America, and, like virtually all the others adopted throughout the colonies, the Rowan resolutions juxtaposed their authors' continuing "Obedience and Fidelity" to the king with an uncompromising opposition to what they considered to be unconstitutional Parliamentary taxes and the "late cruel and Sanguinary Acts of Parliament . . . upon our Sister Colony of Massachusetts Bay and the Town of Boston." More ominous was the committee's bold assertion that "it is the Duty and Interest of all the American Colonies, firmly to unite in an indissoluble Union and Association to oppose by every Just and proper means the Infringement of their common Rights and Privileges." For the time being at least, the resolutions' authors advocated peaceful protest via the resumption of nonimportation and nonconsumption, aided and abetted by the renunciation of "every kind of Luxury, Dissipation and Extravagance" and the promotion of local manufactures to replace essential British imports. They also singled out the importation of enslaved people as a particularly objectionable form of commerce, but not because of the horrors they endured during the Middle Passage or later as brutalized chattel in America. "The African Trade is injurious to this Colony," they opined, because it "obstructs the Population of it by freemen, prevents manufacturers, and other Useful Emigrants from Europe from settling among us, and occasions an annual increase of the Balance of Trade against the Colonies."[27]

Although there was nothing in these resolutions that directly violated William's official oath, the assumption of power by extralegal bodies, including the Congress that would soon convene in Philadelphia, was distressing to men like him, who, whatever their opinion of recent imperial measures, would not repudiate their loyalty to the institutions that the king's government established and sanctioned. Governor Josiah Martin denounced the resolutions that committees in Rowan and in other counties adopted as "derogatory to the dignity of His Majesty, and His Parliament, and tending to excite Clamour, and discontent among the Kings Subjects in this Province." Although many delegates to the Continental Congress took a more conciliatory stance, with a near majority supporting a plan that would have kept the thirteen rebellious colonies under British rule while affording them more autonomy within the empire, Martin nonetheless condemned that body as "unconstitutional [and] formed generally of men of the most inflammatory Spirits selected out of the several colonies for their democratical principles." In reality, Whig leaders were far from "democratical," but Martin and other like-minded men who believed that the king-in-Parliament rightly wielded sovereignty both in Great Britain and throughout its empire nevertheless concluded that "no loyal and dutiful subject of our most gracious sovereign can contemplate" the proceedings in Philadelphia "without feeling the most indignant revoltings."[28]

By September, delegates to the First Continental Congress were crafting an extensive program of economic sanctions that was designed to wrest concessions from imperial authorities. Known as the Continental Association, these measures mandated the resumption of nonimportation and nonconsumption and, eventually, also the cessation of all colonial exports. Congress charged local committees with enforcing the Association—by coercion, if need be—in their respective communities.

In Rowan County, the intimidation of dissidents began even before Congress's nonimportation measures went into effect in December 1774. At its very first formal meeting in late September, the Rowan County committee flexed its jurisdictional muscles by asserting the authority to discipline county inhabitants who opposed the Whig agenda by either words or actions. In particular, the committee denounced two Salisbury lawyers, John Dunn and Benjamin Booth Boote, for having circulated an "advertisement" denigrating the actions of local patriots. The men's statement does not survive, but they likely criticized the resolutions that Rowan County Whigs had adopted a month earlier, while also echoing Governor Martin's condemnation of all extralegal committees and congresses. Committee members condemned the men's statement as "in the highest Degree false and contemptible and even bordering upon Blasphemy" and resolved that Dunn and Boote "ought to be treated with the Contempt which the authors of so infamous a Performance deserve, and as Enemies to their Country." The committee also ordered a copy of its resolutions censuring Dunn and Boote to be nailed "against the two posts of the Gallows and the whipping post" in the Salisbury town square "to demonstrate the contempt in which the Committee" held these two offenders. Although Dunn and Boote escaped further prosecution at the time, both men were seized and sent to South Carolina as prisoners in 1775. Dunn eventually made his peace with local Whigs and returned to Rowan County, but Boote fought for the British and went to England after the war was over.[29]

William Spurgin's involvement in the Dunn-Boote affair in 1774 must

FIGURE 2 | Philip Dawe, *The Alternative of Williams Burg*, 1775. This satirical British print shows an angry mob forcing gentlemen in Williamsburg to pledge support for the local committee by signing the Continental Association. Although in most colonies, including both Virginia and North Carolina, prominent gentlemen actually led the patriot movement, intimidation and social ostracism were among the methods Whigs used to suppress and punish political dissent. (Library of Congress, Prints and Photographs Division [LC-DIG-ds-14481])

have raised his stature in the eyes of Governor Martin while conversely making him an irritatingly prominent adversary for local Whigs. As John Dunn later explained, an unnamed Rowan County magistrate had inspired him and Benjamin Boote to compose their statement by showing them a newspaper story about some New Yorkers who adopted resolutions condemning the Bostonians' rejection of Parliamentary authority. According to Dunn, it was this magistrate who persuaded Boote to draft the similarly anti-Whig document that outraged the Rowan County committee. The offending magistrate was almost certainly William. Local Whigs, who believed he was the culprit, summoned him to appear at the committee's November meeting "to answer a charge against his conduct relative to the protest and advertisement of Dunn and Boote."[30]

Although William claimed that he had not been involved in either drafting or signing the offending document, the committee's members did not believe him, and they accordingly adopted a strongly worded resolution to censure his alleged misconduct:

> Resolved, Therefore, that William Spurgin, Esqr., by disavowing all connection with his county in the present Measures, has as far as in his power relinquished the Rights of the people and opposed them, to be illegally and unconstitutionally taxed by the British Ministry, which has a tendency to spread sedition amongst his Majesty's Loyal Subjects in the County of Rowan. For which he is justly deemed by this Committee an Enemy to his Country, and should be treated as such by all his Majestys loyal subjects in America.

More than a mere rhetorical flourish, the committee's categorization of William as "an Enemy to his Country" was a public declaration that anyone who associated with him also risked being stigmatized as an "Enemy." This sort of social ostracism was an important tool of the Whig resistance movement, employed both to punish dissidents and to prevent their influence from spreading in the wider community. In November 1774, immediately after they censured William, the Rowan County committee adopted a second resolution in which they recognized him as a serious threat because of his influence in Abbotts Creek, where "the people of that Neighborhood . . . differ in Opinion from this Committee in the present unhappy dispute between America and the British Parliament." Consequently, the committee resolved to send its chairman, along with three or more additional members, to Abbotts Creek "to confer together for their mutual benefit."[31]

There is no way to know if that meeting took place and, if so, what its outcome may have been, but people in Abbotts Creek remained for the most part disaffected and at best lukewarm toward the revolutionary movement. Governor Josiah Martin, who overestimated the loyalty of the "Inhabitants of the Western Counties," including Rowan, nevertheless correctly attributed the reluctance of many to support the patriot committees to their recent experiences as Regulators, when they battled the same men who now led those committees, as well as to the "solemn Oath of Allegiance" they took when they received their pardons from Governor Tryon after the Battle of Alamance. Moreover, unlike the Baptists in Virginia, who aligned themselves with secular-minded Whig gentlemen— most notably Thomas Jefferson—in the hope of attaining religious liberty, in the mid-1770s most of North Carolina's backcountry Baptists saw no compelling reason to make common cause with the predominantly Presbyterian Whig elite.[32]

On 19 April 1775, the Battles of Lexington and Concord, in Massachusetts, began the final phase of the imperial crisis, propelling patriots in North Carolina and elsewhere toward mobilization for war and, ultimately, to declaring independence. In less than a month after these battles, delegates from thirteen colonies again gathered in Philadelphia. This Second Continental Congress established the Continental Army, chose George Washington as its commander, and charged local committees with recruiting, training, and equipping militia in their respective communities.

Meanwhile, in Rowan County, William and other local critics of the increasingly radical Whigs publicly avowed their continuing allegiance to the Crown and their staunch opposition to the colonial rebellion. In the spring of 1775, 195 men from the counties of Rowan and Surry (which had been part of Rowan until 1771) sent an address to Governor Martin in which they expressed "the warmest Zeal and Attachment to the British Constitution and Laws upon which our Lives and fortunes and the welfare of the Province now depend" and also their opposition to "meetings of people against the peace ... or anything which may give birth to sedition and insurrection." The signers reassured the governor of their determination "to continue [as] his Majesty's loyal subjects and to contribute all in our power for the preservation of the public peace and ... endeavour to cultivate such sentiments in all those under our care" so that "the malice of [the king's] enemies may be asswaged, [and] their wild designs confounded and defeated." Samuel Bryan composed this address, which William circulated in Abbotts Creek and also in the Moravian towns, where most inhabitants hoped to avoid allying with either side, at least for the time being.[33]

That summer, North Carolina Whigs, like most members of the Congress in Philadelphia, continued to affirm their loyalty to the king while disavowing the authority of his civil and military officials in America. In June 1775, the Rowan County committee asserted that "his Majesty George the third is lawful and rightful King of Great Britain and the Dominions thereunto belonging" but then called on militia to defend "that happy Constitution which . . . defends us from being taxed by any Man or set of Men without Representation and Consent," condescendingly adding that anyone "as may be of a different Opinion [ought] to consider the Bill of Rights and the Compact on which the [British] Constitution is founded, that you may see to what end different principles may lead." Rowan County committee members also tried to foster consensus among the county's white residents by warning that the British would incite deadly slave insurrections and Indian attacks to regain control of their rebellious provinces. Alluding to both the battles in Massachusetts and ongoing hostilities between Native Americans and white settlers who, despite the Proclamation of 1763, ventured beyond the Appalachians, the Rowan County committee accused the British of "letting loose upon our defenceless frontier a Torrent of Blood by the Savage rage of Indian Barbarity . . . Ripping Infants from the wombs of their expiring mothers, roasting Christians to Death by a slow fire." A year later, in July 1776, Thomas Jefferson and his colleagues in the Continental Congress made the same point, albeit with less graphic language, when they cited British encouragement of "domestic insurrections" and "merciless Indian savages" as the last of their long list of justifications for declaring independence.[34]

By August 1775, Rowan County's Whig leaders were also moving from persuasion to prosecution, seeking to stifle the most troublesome local dissidents. To that end, they summoned James Cook, a preacher associated with the Abbotts Creek Baptist congregation, to submit to their questioning. When they pressed Cook to supply them with "Information relative to the present unhappy disturbance," by which they meant the ongoing resistance to Whig authority in the Abbotts Creek neighborhood, he answered the committee's questions. At the committee's insistence, Cook also, "in the most explicit and humiliating Terms," expressed his regret for "signing the protest against the Cause of Liberty, which lately circulated in the fork of the Yadkin"—in other words, the recent address to Governor Martin in which 195 men had explicitly repudiated the authority of the Whig committees and congresses.[35]

The "Information" Cook provided, in turn, led to the committee's demand that three Abbotts Creek residents—Jacob Beck, Matthias Sappenfield, and William Spurgin—appear at their November meeting. Whig authorities jailed Beck for his "notorious contempt of this Committee and Opposition to American Measures," and then brought him forcibly before them "to give account of his political sentiments." Sappenfield, whom the committee condemned as an "incorrigible" enemy of the American cause, attended voluntarily. After being confronted by the committee, according to that body's minutes, both Beck and Sappenfield "cheerfully" signed the oath affirming both their loyalty to the king and "their approbation of the American Measures" undertaken by the authority of the Continental Congress and enforced by the local committees. The oath-taking ritual—and the idea that men might "cheerfully" see the error of their ways and undergo such dramatic political conversions—was an important means of publicly rehabilitating erstwhile enemies to the cause and ideally reassimilating them into the larger political community. Although Sappenfield later recanted, the committee discharged both him and Beck on this occasion, allowing them to return to their families after they had seemingly made their peace with local Whigs.[36]

By contrast, William Spurgin did not respond to the committee's summons. Perhaps a pivotal moment for him was when Governor Martin issued a proclamation on 15 August 1775 that included emphatically explicit instructions to all royal officials in the colony. "I do hereby strictly require and Command all His Majesties Justices of the Peace, Sheriffs and other officers . . . to exert themselves," he ordered, "in the discovery of all Seditious Treasons and Traiterous Conspiracies, and bringing to justice the principals and accomplices therein." In any event, to avoid the fate of Jacob Beck, whom the committee held prisoner until he accepted the patriot oath, William must have gone into hiding from November 1775 until early February 1776, when he began to recruit troops in response to the increasingly embattled governor's call to arms.[37]

What motivated William to take such a dangerous path, to make himself a pariah and eventually an outlaw in a community where he had previously been both respected and more than modestly successful? Perhaps it was an unwavering commitment to his official oath—and to his particular interpretation of what it meant to uphold the king's laws— though many of his contemporaries believed that allegiance could be conditional and that one oath, however solemnly sworn, could be renounced in favor of another.[38] William may have felt distrust or bitterness toward his colleagues on the county court because of their treatment of the Regulators, though there is no evidence of bad relations between him and the other justices. Governor Martin may have intimated that William and other men who supported him and the king against the increasingly unstoppable rebellion would reap significant rewards as a result of their continuing loyalty. Whatever his reasons, like so many others who ultimately did not support the Revolution, William concluded that remaining within the British Empire promised a better future for him and his family.

Jane's views and actions during these tumultuous years are unknown. The imperial crisis may have politicized Jane, but because women neither signed political manifestos nor swore oaths of allegiance, there is no surviving documentation of her political stance, if she had one, and no indication of what she thought about William's increasingly hazardous role in the unfolding drama. At home at Abbotts Creek, a relatively secluded and largely disaffected rural backwater, the hostility between Whigs and Tories may have been less palpable to Jane than the recent conflict between magistrates and Regulators because those earlier insurgents and their grievances, far more than those of the patriot movement, had been so central to the lives and interests of many members of her family and community. Jane likely experienced the imperial crisis most directly as an impediment to her usual domestic routine as imported goods—including salt, which was essential for preserving meat and fish—became scarce and expensive beginning in early 1775 as a result of nonimportation.[39]

Jane and William achieved stability and comfort at Abbotts Creek, where they had a substantial farm and a large and growing family. By 1775,

Jane was the mother of eleven children. The oldest, twenty-two-year-old John, had moved south with them from Virginia, but the others were born in Abbotts Creek, the youngest of whom was Israel Isaiah, an infant son. Added to these family mileposts was the prestige of William's appointment as a justice, which marked him as an influential man in Abbotts Creek and a de facto a member of the Rowan County elite. By late 1775, however, William was in hiding, a virtual outlaw in the eyes of his former colleagues on county bench. Whatever views she espoused in 1775, Jane's subsequent actions suggest that she had no influence on her husband's political choices. Separated from William, with armed violence surely on the horizon, she must have worried what the future would hold for her and her family.

3

William's War

FROM THE BEGINNING TO THE END of the American War for Independence, authorities on both sides of the revolutionary divide ranked William Spurgin as one of North Carolina's most prominent Tories. In January 1776, William was one of twenty-six men in the province whom Governor Josiah Martin authorized to form militia companies that would "repair to the royal banner" to suppress the spreading rebellion. In April 1782, six months after the decisive battle at Yorktown but still more than a year before the signing of the treaty that formally recognized the American triumph, William's name was included on a list of sixty-eight of North Carolina's most offensive enemies whose "lands, tenements, hereditaments, negroes, and other estates" were earmarked for immediate sale to raise revenue for the state, alongside those of wealthy merchants, landed gentry, and two former royal governors. Around the same time, former governor Martin, by then in London, commended William Spurgin and three other North Carolinians as men who had "real and great claims to the notice of the Government" as a result of their steadfast loyalty to the king and to the British Empire.[1]

In North Carolina and the other southern mainland British colonies, the war had three distinct phases, each of which posed different challenges. The first phase, which ended even before the Continental Congress declared independence in July 1776, featured early British efforts to muster support among white loyalists, enslaved people seeking freedom, and Native Americans hoping to shield their land from expanding white settlements. This initial phase resulted in a series of Whig victories and the subsequent withdrawal of British forces from the region. The war's second phase, which lasted more than two years, was a period of relative peace, despite continuing tensions—and intermittent violence—between local Whigs and Tories and attempts on the part of the new state governments to suppress and punish those who persisted in their loyalty to the king. During the war's third phase, by contrast, the southern states became North America's main military theater. From the British seizure of Savannah in December 1778 through Cornwallis's surrender at Yorktown in October 1781, the region would be the site of both partisan skirmishes between Tory and Whig militia and large-scale major battles.

Despite his prominence in the official records that defined and documented who were Tories and who were Whigs, and incentivized or punished adherence to one side or the other, the paper trail that verifies William Spurgin's actual wartime activities and experiences is remarkably thin. Between 1776 and 1782, William was a soldier, but, like most of his contemporaries in North Carolina and elsewhere on both sides of the revolutionary conflict, he served in a militia unit, not in a regular army regiment, though North Carolina loyalists formed at least four provincial units that served alongside regular British forces, and the state supplied multiple regiments of patriot troops to the Continental Army.[2] Major army campaigns were led by famous generals, centrally planned and organized, and often embraced wide expanses of territory and—for all of these reasons—they were usually well documented. With some notable exceptions, militia actions were typically local, reactive, and not the result of extensive coordination or planning among different military units. Although some officers in both Tory and Whig militia companies became widely admired—or feared—for their battlefield exploits, William's murkier military career as a loyalist militia officer was more typical. During the war, William engaged in combat only intermittently. In fact, he seems to have spent a significant amount of time at or near his home in Abbotts Creek, despite his official status as an "Enemy to his Country."

Thousands of Rowan County residents opposed the Revolution or at least tried to avoid involvement in the independence movement and in the war that followed. Scholars estimate that roughly 20 percent of all American colonists remained loyal to the king and to the British Empire after 1776 and that an additional 40 percent were neutral or apathetic. Despite strong Whig leadership in the area, the numbers in both of these latter categories were likely even higher in the North Carolina backcountry, where resentment toward eastern elites who led the revolutionary effort ran high just a few years after the defeat of the Regulators at Alamance. The patriot leader John Adams, who read the newspapers and knew North Carolinians as colleagues in the Continental Congress, believed that, as a result of this enduring bitterness, "the back part of North Carolina" was the only place in the thirteen rebellious colonies where the common people would rise up "in large bodies" to oppose the revolutionary cause. Governor Josiah Martin, who sympathized with the Regulators and had attempted to address their grievances, agreed; among North Carolinians, he believed that he could count on former Regulators, along with the numerous Scots Highlanders who had settled in and around Cross Creek, to oppose the rebellion. Wartime allegiances could be fluid. Still, in part because of these lingering animosities, a strong Tory presence persisted in Rowan County and elsewhere in the backcountry throughout the revolutionary era.[3]

Palpable evidence of those divisions emerged quickly, as partisans organized competing militias and engaged in hostilities in both Carolinas during the months between the commencement of armed hostilities at Lexington and Concord in April 1775 and the formal declaration of independence some fourteen months later. In late 1775, on learning of a Tory uprising in the Ninety Six District of South Carolina, patriots in North Carolina's Salisbury District, which included Rowan County, raised approximately five hundred men to help local Whigs to regain control of the area, despite the efforts of Tories in Rowan and Tryon Counties to derail their recruiting efforts. Then, in early 1776, several leading Rowan County Tories, one of whom was William Spurgin, gathered men from their communities to answer the governor's call to join Scots loyalists in recruiting men to fight for the king in eastern North Carolina.[4]

Among Rowan County's roughly seven thousand adult male "taxables,"

William's War

William was one of only three persistent loyalists who were singled out for both special praise from Governor Martin and special enmity from his Whig neighbors. The other two Rowan County residents who shared that distinction were Matthias Sappenfield and Samuel Bryan. The Sappenfields lived near the Spurgins in Abbotts Creek, and both William Spurgin and Matthias Sappenfield had previously drawn the ire of local Whigs. These two Abbotts Creek residents were among the very few men that the Rowan County committee compelled to appear before them to swear the oath of allegiance in late 1775. William managed to evade the committee. Sappenfield swore the oath. Nevertheless, the governor showed his faith in Sappenfield's continuing loyalty when he named him—along with William Spurgin and Samuel Bryan—as the three Rowan County men he entrusted with the task of raising troops to fight for the king in January 1776.[5]

Although William Spurgin and Matthias Sappenfield must have known Samuel Bryan, at least by reputation, there is no evidence that the three men were close friends or even that they moved in the same social circles. Loyalists came from all walks of life, and people chose to remain subjects of the king for a variety of reasons. One study based on loyalist claims submitted to the British government in an effort to obtain compensation for lost property after the war was over—a body of evidence in which obscure backcountry Tories were likely underrepresented—shows that, in North Carolina, 46.5 percent of all loyalists were farmers; 29.5 percent, merchants and shopkeepers; 11 percent, officeholders; 6.3 percent artisans; and 3.5 percent, professional people, such as physicians or lawyers. Like most men, and most loyalists, in Rowan County, Spurgin, Bryan, and Sappenfield all engaged in agriculture, but Bryan was a wealthy and powerful landowner, a member of a large and long-established Rowan County family who resided in the western part of the county, far from Abbotts Creek.[6]

Of these three Rowan County Tories, Sappenfield was the most obscure. Born in Germany, he migrated to America as a young man, settling in the North Carolina backcountry by 1753. He initially leased land in the Abbotts Creek neighborhood, where he owned at least 284 acres by the early 1760s, acquired more later, and eventually rose to the rank of captain in the county militia. Sappenfield appears to have signed at least one of the Regulators' petitions, and he may have been at the Battle of Alamance in 1771. He most likely came to the attention of Josiah Martin when the newly arrived governor made his conciliatory trip to the backcountry to meet with the Regulators in 1772. Four years later, Sappenfield responded to the governor's call by raising a company of seven men to go fight for the king, despite the fact that he had previously—albeit under pressure from the county committee—taken the Whig oath of allegiance and signed the Continental Association.[7]

Samuel Bryan's background, and the roots of his loyalism, was in many ways the antithesis of Sappenfield's. Bryan was born in Pennsylvania. His parents were English Quakers who moved their large family to Virginia in the 1720s and then migrated southward to the North Carolina backcountry some time before the establishment of Rowan County in 1753. Among the first white settlers in the area, the Bryans became important and prosperous landowners, and, like the vast majority of affluent backcountry people, they were opponents of the Regulators. Abandoning Quakerism, Samuel also became a vocal advocate for the Church of England, a minority denomination in the backcountry despite the controversial legal privileges it enjoyed as a tax-supported established church and one whose clergy in North Carolina were strongly disposed toward loyalism. Although at least one of his brothers supported the Revolution, Samuel Bryan was the lead signer—and also the likely author—of the notorious 1775 address to Governor Martin, which was signed by 195 men from Rowan and neighboring Surry County who averred their opposition to the Whigs and their own continuing "warmest Zeal and Attachment to the British Constitution." Bryan answered the governor's call to arms in 1776 and, over the course of the war, became a key loyalist militia officer in western North Carolina. Lord Rawdon, one of the British army commanders in the Carolinas, described him as "a shrewd man" who had "great influence" in his community.[8]

In terms of both his prewar social stature and his wartime exploits, William Spurgin fell somewhere between Bryan and Sappenfield. He was a substantial landowner who had been a long-serving justice of the peace in his county, where people remembered him decades later as having been "in every respect, an estimable man," one whom local Moravians trusted to be their liaison with the local magistracy when he sat on the county bench. Like Bryan and Sappenfield, William responded to the governor's summons to take up arms to oppose "the most horrid and unnatural rebellion that has been excited . . . by traitorous, wicked and designing men, [which] threatens the subversion of His Majesty's Government," and the Moravian merchant Traugott Bagge reported that William was "very active" in gathering "a company of good and bad, with wagons, horses, provisions and weapons," at a time when "many who sided with the King were driven from house and home . . . and . . . hiding in the woods" to avoid "persecution" by local Whigs. By early February 1776, both the Moravians and the Rowan County committee knew that William was working with one of his brothers and with some other area loyalists to raise a force to support the governor. Nevertheless, although he was a persistent Tory throughout the war, his military activities were more sporadic and less widely known than Bryan's.[9]

William seems to have fought in a total of two or three formal military engagements, the first of which was the Battle of Moore's Creek Bridge. This confrontation was the direct result of Governor Martin's efforts to organize two cadres of loyalist militia, one in the backcountry and another in the Scots Highlander settlements in Cumberland County, which would rendezvous at Cross Creek and then march southeast to Wilmington to join an expected British force of more than two thousand in the hope of restoring royal authority in North Carolina, at a time when the Continental Congress in Philadelphia was preparing for war and moving toward declaring independence. Although North Carolina's loyalist leaders hoped to enlist some six thousand men—five thousand former Regulators and one thousand Highlanders—their recruitment effort fell far short of that number, especially in the backcountry, and some of the men they did recruit left their companies rather than endure the long and arduous march to the coast. By the time the loyalists encountered Whig militia at Moore's Creek Bridge, roughly seventeen miles from Wilmington, on 27 February, their combined force of Highlanders and backcountry men numbered fewer than one thousand. At Moore's Creek Bridge, the loyalists fell to a rebel force of roughly the same number. As one of the Whig commanders, Colonel Richard Caswell, reported happily, "The Tories were totally put to the rout."[10]

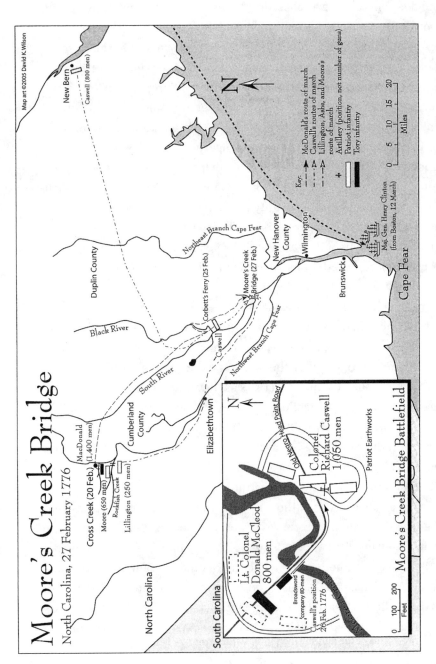

Moore's Creek Bridge

North Carolina, 27 February 1776

Map art ©2005 David K. Wilson

New Bern

Caswell (800 men)

North Carolina

MacDonald

Cross Creek (20 Feb.)
Moore (650 men)
Rockfish Creek
Lillington (250 men)

MacDonald
(1,400 men)

Cumberland County

Black River

Duplin County

South River

Caswell

Corbett's Ferry (25 Feb.)

Northeast Branch Cape Fear

Moore's Creek
Bridge (27 Feb.)

Elizabethtown

Northwest Branch Cape Fear

New Hanover County

Wilmington

Brunswick

Maj. Gen. Henry Clinton
(from Boston, 12 March)

Cape Fear

Key:
▲ MdDonald's route of march
▲ Caswell's route of march
▲ Lillington, Ashe, and Moore's
    route of march
+ Artillery (position, not number of guns)
▫ Patriot infantry
▪ Tory infantry

N

0   5   10   15   20
          Miles

Moore's Creek Bridge Battlefield

South Carolina

N

0   100   200
        Feet

Lt. Colonel Donald McLeod
800 men

Broadsword
company 80-men

Caswell's position
26 Feb. 1776

Old Negro Head Point Road

Colonel Richard Caswell
1,050 men

Patriot Earthworks

MAP 3 | The Battle of Moore's Creek Bridge. On 27 February 1776, Whig militia soundly defeated the Tory force of Scots Highlanders and backcountry farmers in the first battle of war that occurred in North Carolina. Although many Tories were taken prisoner after the battle, William Spurgin escaped capture. (*The Southern Strategy*, by David K. Wilson © 2005 University of South Carolina Press)

Whig commanders reported only one man killed and another wounded, whereas the loyalists' losses were heavy, with thirty dying and, according to Caswell, "850 common Soldiers taken prisoners, disarmed, and discharged" on the condition that they return to their homes, live quietly, and take the oath of allegiance to defend the rights and liberties of North Carolina. In a reversal of conventional European military practices, captured officers were treated far more harshly, initially confined in a "cold dirty jail" in Halifax with the twenty-six most influential—and therefore potentially the most dangerous—captives subsequently shipped off as prisoners to far-off Philadelphia. Some of these men remained incarcerated for a remarkably long time. Farquhard Campbell, a prominent Cumberland County legislator, stayed several months in Philadelphia before being transferred first to Baltimore and then to Frederick, Maryland; he was paroled only in April 1778, more than two years after he was captured. Norman McLeod, a backcountry Tory from Anson County, was held as a prisoner in Pennsylvania for nearly five years, during which local Whigs repeatedly pillaged his home, compelling his wife and children to flee. Governor Martin, who spent much of the war in British-occupied New York City, reported in 1778 that many Tories who had become prisoners after the battle at Moore's Creek Bridge "drop in here now and then by one's and two's as they find means to escape from captivity." Matthias Sappenfield was one of these North Carolina loyalists who, after being imprisoned first in Halifax and then likely in Philadelphia, spent the rest of the war away from his family in exile in New York, where he died in 1781.[11]

Others who escaped after the battle at Moore's Creek Bridge went into hiding to evade capture. Although Whig militia killed some Tories who sought cover in the vast expanses of nearby woods and swamps after the battle, other loyalists escaped and eventually found refuge in friendly Tory enclaves or quietly returned to their homes. Neighbors Soirle MacDonald and Donald McCrummin, both natives of Scotland who arrived in North Carolina in the 1770s, eluded capture but spent the next two years in hiding before making their way to Philadelphia, where they joined the British army in 1778. Major Alexander McLeod, another Scot, who had settled at Cross Creek in 1774, was "obliged to conceal himself for six weeks in woods & swamps until he made his Escape," finally sailing for England in 1778.[12]

Although there is no evidence of William's whereabouts during the months immediately following Moore's Creek Bridge, it is likely that he hid for several months during which Whig militias in Rowan County and elsewhere scoured the countryside to flush out Tories in order to consolidate the authority of the revolutionary regime in the wake of the Whigs' decisive battlefield triumph. Young Hugh McDonald and his father, both Tory privates who had been captured and released after the battle, were forced to flee to avoid recapture by Whig militia four months later. In March 1776, shortly after North Carolina's Provincial Congress, acting on the recommendation of the Continental Congress in Philadelphia, instructed local authorities to disarm all Tories, the Moravians reported that Rowan County Whigs were seizing guns and other weapons from loyalists in the Abbotts Creek neighborhood, where they also "took the young men" from Tory families into custody. There is no evidence that William and Jane's eldest sons—twenty-three-year-old John and fourteen-year-old William—were seized in these raids. The Spurgins' sons were likely protected by both their mother's need for their assistance on the farm and by the absence of their Tory father.[13]

Both William Spurgin and Samuel Bryan eventually returned to their farms and families in Rowan County. Spurgin and Bryan went home at least in part because they had large families for whom to provide—each left behind a wife and eleven children—and substantial property to pro-tect. Unlike their Scots comrades who were relatively recent arrivals to North Carolina, these men also had deep local roots and wide-ranging connections that they perhaps believed would help shield them from the wrath of their Whig enemies in their respective communities.

Although it is impossible to trace William's precise movements during this period, he was certainly home at some point during the winter of 1776–77 when his and Jane's twelfth living child was conceived. This child, the Spurgins' sixth son, who was born the following November, was called Josiah, a name that had not appeared previously in either the Spurgin or Welborn family, and one that William likely chose to honor the royal governor. William's time at home was likely brief, however, because, according to the Moravians, by early February 1777 local Tories and Whigs were "very hot against each other," and by the end of the month loyalists and other disaffected men from the Abbotts Creek neighborhood were "hiding in the woods most of the time for fear of being taken prisoner."[14]

Although Governor Martin continued to insist that many of the inhabitants of his province would rally to the king's standard, the resounding Whig victory at Moore's Creek Bridge proved to be a pivotal moment in the war in North Carolina and in the southern provinces generally. Two months before the engagement at Moore's Creek Bridge, in December 1775, Whig militia had defeated a combined force of loyalists and British regulars at the Battle of Great Bridge, near the Virginia port town of Norfolk. Moore's Creek Bridge was thus the second Whig triumph in the southern colonies, and a third was soon to follow. British forces under Sir Henry Clinton finally arrived in coastal North Carolina in March, but on finding that the province's loyalist militia already had been overpowered and dispersed, they left for South Carolina, where Clinton's attempt to capture Charleston in June ended in defeat at Sullivan's Island. At that point, the British withdrew their forces from the Carolinas and focused their military efforts farther north, where they had more success, their most notable victory being the seizure and occupation of the strategically important city of New York in August 1776.[15]

Despite occasional altercations between loyalists and "Liberty Men" and a major Whig offensive against the Cherokees in the summer and fall of 1776, the white residents of the Carolina backcountry were now technically at peace, and the main weapons that authorities there deployed against local Tories became legal rather than martial. In May 1776, North Carolina's Provincial Congress resolved that anyone convicted of taking up arms against America or giving aid or intelligence "to the open enemies thereof . . . shall forfeit all his goods and chattels, lands and tenements, to the people of the said Colony, to be disposed of by the Congress, or other general representation thereof." In November 1776, the state convention—North Carolina's de facto government before the adoption a state constitution in December—passed an ordinance pardoning those same offenders if they swore an oath of allegiance to the newly independent state, thereby explicitly renouncing the authority of the king and his government, "it being hoped that such Persons are now become sensible of the Wickedness and Folly of endeavoring to subject their Country to Misery and Slavery, and are penitent for the same." Known as nonjurors, those who failed to take the oath were subject to severe civil penalties. Nonjurors were barred from filing lawsuits or from defending themselves in court, nor could they buy, sell, or inherit property. In effect, the state barred nonjurors from collecting debts owed them, leaving them legally powerless to prevent their property from being summarily seized by their creditors. In an economy that traditionally ran on debt and credit, these state-imposed legal disabilities were especially onerous.[16]

Although William was obviously guilty of both providing information to British "enemies" of the state and taking up arms to support the king, neither county nor state authorities attempted to prosecute him under these early anti-Tory directives. In March 1777, the Rowan County sheriff summoned "all who were in hiding, and all who have shown themselves to be active Tories, to come forthwith and take the Oath of Allegiance to the Commonwealth, or else to remove themselves and their families from the land" and join the British in New York or elsewhere. There is no evidence either that William responded to this summons or that the sheriff or the Whig militia came after him to force him to swear the prescribed oath.[17]

A more concerted and comprehensive attempt to discourage, suppress, and punish loyalist activity in North Carolina began after the state enacted its first comprehensive anti-Tory legislation in April 1777. Whereas earlier mandates required men to subscribe to loyalty oaths and imposed penalties on those who acted against the state and its interests, after the formal declaration of independence in July 1776 states enacted laws to standardize their inhabitants' civic obligations and criminalize noncompliance. Oath-taking remained central to the process as states created more stringent pledges that explicitly renounced the authority of the king rather than merely avowing loyalty to the state. The dual purpose of this new and less potentially ambiguous oath was to expose enemies of the revolutionary regime and either to suppress dissent or to facilitate the political rehabilitation of the disaffected and of known Tories, whose conversion might serve as instructive examples to the general public.[18]

North Carolina's law was the aptly titled "Act declaring what Crimes and Practices against the State shall be Treason, and what shall be Misprision of Treason, and providing Punishments adequate to Crimes of both

Classes, and for preventing the Dangers which may arise from the Persons disaffected to the State." Beginning with the assertion that "all and every Person and Persons (Prisoners of War excepted) now inhabiting or residing within the limits of the State of North-Carolina, or who shall voluntarily come into the same hereafter to inhabit or reside, do owe, and shall pay Allegiance" to it, the statute then went on to define the crimes that the state sought to punish and the methods authorities would use to find and punish those who committed them.[19]

Following precedents in English law, the statute enumerated two crimes—treason and misprision of treason—and prescribed penalties for them. The statute defined treason as "knowingly and willingly . . . aid[ing] or assist[ing] any Enemies at open War against this State, or the United States of America, by joining their Armies, or by inlisting, or procuring or persuading others to inlist for that Purpose, or by furnishing such Enemies with Arms, Ammunition, Provision, or any other Article for their Aid or Comfort; or . . . form[ing] . . . any Combination, Plot, or Conspiracy, for betraying this State, or the United States of America, into the Hands or Power of any foreign Enemy; or . . . giv[ing] or send[ing] any Intelligence to the Enemies of this State for that Purpose." Anyone convicted of treason would "suffer Death . . . and his or her Estate shall be forfeited to the State." Persons who simply conveyed intelligence to "the Enemies of the State" or encouraged citizens "to favour the Enemy, or oppose and endeavour to prevent the Measures carrying on in Support of the Freedom and Independence of the said United States" were guilty of misprision of treason, and would be imprisoned for the remainder of the war and required to "forfeit to the State one Half of his, her or their Lands, Tenements, Goods and Chattels."

An express purpose of this new law was to rid the state of Tories. Although the law stated that "all persons" living in North Carolina were to take the new oath of allegiance, in practice county magistrates administered the oath only to white adult men, partly because the swearing of oaths typically coincided with militia musters, at least initially. The statute also mandated that local authorities particularly target suspect persons, such as erstwhile Crown officeholders and merchants who engaged in trade with Britain or who those who had acted as "as Factors, Storekeepers, or Agents" for British merchants. After paying their outstanding debts, these nonjurors had the "Liberty" to liquidate their property holdings in North Carolina, though any property they left behind unsold was subject to state appropriation after three months. Any person who returned to North Carolina after having been banished under the terms of this statute would be "be adjudged guilty of Treason against the State, and shall and may be proceeded against in like Manner as is herein directed in Cases of Treason."[20]

The passage of this law prompted the first significant exodus of loyalist families from North Carolina. In July 1777, the *North Carolina Gazette* reported the departure of a "large Vessel" from New Bern, "having on Board a great number of Tories, with their Wives and Families, chiefly Scotch Gentlemen who have refused to take the Oaths of Government to this State." Bound for British-occupied New York, these refugees were "mostly Gentlemen of Considerable Property" from the eastern part of the state. Martin Howard, the former colonial chief justice, was among the passengers, as were his wife and daughter. Other shiploads of Tories left for Britain, Nova Scotia, or the British West Indies during the summer and fall of 1777.[21]

As it turned out, however, the logistical difficulties of ridding the state of its enemies proved insurmountable. Orchestrating massive targeted oath-taking sessions was complicated, in part because loyalists defied the state mandate to attend militia musters. And though Tories who lived in port towns such as New Bern and Wilmington could flee fairly easily—as long as they could pay their passage aboard a ship—less affluent loyalists and those who lived far from the coast faced daunting obstacles if they sought to leave the state in compliance with the statute. As legislators conceded in their amended version of the law, enacted in November 1777, the "Penalties ordained by the [original April 1777] Act have been in a great Measure evaded by the Difficulty or Impossibility of procuring Vessels to transport all such Recusants beyond Sea, or from their being unable to pay the Expence of the Voyage, by which Means such Persons still remain within this State."[22]

The amended law addressed these problems by issuing precise new instructions to county justices about how, where, and when to administer the oaths and by giving those officials some discretion in imposing penalties on nonjurors. Counties were to be divided into districts, one for each justice, and magistrates were required to post written notices to inform citizens of the places and times they would be available to administer the oaths. In an attempt to persuade more of the disaffected to accept the Whig regime, this new legislation also stipulated that Moravians and Quakers, who objected to oath-taking on religious grounds, now had the option of affirming, rather than swearing, their allegiance to the state. Men who would accept neither the oath nor the affirmation would be brought before the county court, and, if they still refused to comply, they would be subject to expulsion, though the amended law empowered county justices to permit nonjurors who would not or could not leave to remain in the state subject to an array of stringent civil and economic penalties.[23]

In Rowan County, after the local magistrates worked their way through the statutorily mandated process of administering the oaths, the county court determined that at least 577 men still had "neglected or refused to appear to . . . take the Oath or Affirmation of Allegiance to the State agreeable to the Act of Assembly." Of the county's sixteen districts, the one in which Samuel Bryan resided had the most offenders with a total of 128 reported nonjurors. There were fifty nonjurors in the district that included William and Jane's Abbotts Creek neighborhood. William and his brother Samuel were among that group, as was William and Jane's twenty-five-year-old son, John, and Michael Hinkle, the husband of their oldest daughter, Rebecca; two members of the Welborn family; and three members of the Teague family, who had known the Spurgins for decades and who were related by marriage to Jane's family, the Welborns. All but seven of these fifty men, however, must have pragmatically acceded to the demands of Whig authorities because only William and six others were taxed at four times the normal rate—one of the other economic penalties the state imposed on Tories—a few months later. In 1778, the county taxed both Samuel Spurgin and William and Jane's son John at the standard rate, though both men seem to have avoided active military service for the duration of the war, most likely by hiring substitutes.[24]

In North Carolina, as in other states, every white male over the age of sixteen was required to attend militia musters and to heed the call to arms as needed to defend their local communities. During the War for Independence, states were also subject to periodic requisitions for troops to serve in the Continental Army, and, after soliciting volunteers and offering bounties to potential enlistees, they ideally filled out their ranks with drafts from county militias, though states routinely failed to meet their assigned allotments for soldiers. Serving in the regular army took men far from home; if they were paid at all, Continental soldiers received increasingly depreciated paper money. In these years when their own state was the site of no major battles, many North Carolinians resented persistent calls for men to join the Continentals. Indeed, in 1778, twenty-one Whig militia officers from Rowan County submitted a memorial to the state legislature in which they declared that residents of the backcountry "would willingly submit to any Tax that could be reasonably laid on us" to satisfy their portion of the state's obligation to support the Continentals. Forcing the "industrious yeomenry" to leave their families and farms to serve in the army, they maintained, caused "many inconveniences," including the "hindrance of Tillage and consequently a scarcity of provisions, which in our humble opinion we [patriots] may have more reason to dread than any reinforcements that may be sent" to aid the British army.[25]

Not long after the Rowan militia officers presented their memorial, however, the enemy was closer at hand, prompting increased urgency in Whig military recruitment and renewed efforts to suppress the local loyalist population. After fighting the war more or less to a stalemate in the Middle Atlantic states, the British withdrew the bulk of their forces from that region, though they continued to occupy New York City, an important port that served as headquarters for British military operations that, after the United States formalized an alliance with France in 1778 (and Spain entered the war as an ally of the French in 1779), expanded into the West Indies, the Gulf Coast, and even India. In terms of the continuing war in North America, the next step for the British was to invade the southern states. In December 1778, they handily captured Georgia's largest town, Savannah, and then marched to the interior, supported by white loyalists, some Native Americans, and thousands of enslaved people who flocked to the king's standard in the hope of securing their freedom.[26]

North Carolina's revolutionary leaders took a two-pronged approach to enhance the security of their state against an expected British invasion as enemy forces moved northward through Georgia and eventually into

South Carolina. To encourage Tories and other nonjurors to accept the authority of the state, however grudgingly, legislators and local officials took steps to enforce previously enacted laws that had authorized the seizure of dissidents' property. At the same time, Whig authorities also ramped up military preparations and more vigorously penalized those men who would not actively support the state's military efforts.

To punish Tories and produce much-needed revenue, the state legislature committed new resources to implementing the confiscation law that had been passed in 1777, appointing dedicated commissioners in each county who were charged with seizing the property of nonjurors and then selling all confiscated slaves, livestock, and other "chattel" and leasing any confiscated lands, with all of the proceeds accruing to the cash-strapped state government. The state also empowered its commissioners to collect commercial and personal debts due to loyalists by Whig inhabitants of the state, who now were to pay those sums to the state government rather than to their Tory creditors. Beginning in 1778, state land offices in the backcountry determined ownership of unsettled Granville District grants, and loyalists, including some members of the Bryan family, were dispossessed as a result. Finally, in January 1779, a new more stringent anti-Tory law enumerated sixty-eight persons whose property, along with that of "all others who come within the meaning of the confiscation acts," was to be relinquished absolutely and irrevocably to the state, and authorized local commissioners to divide confiscated property into tracts of no more than 640 acres to be sold at public auction. William Spurgin, Samuel Bryan, and Matthias Sappenfield were among the sixty-eight men explicitly named in this statute. Seizure of Tory properties began immediately, though enforcement was never complete and large-scale sales of confiscated acreage did not occur until after the passage of yet another law, in 1782.[27]

In January and February 1779, the North Carolina legislature also adopted policies designed to defend the state from an expected invasion, both by enhancing its military preparedness and by more forcibly suppressing dissent. A new militia law reorganized the state's armed forces to create a special State Regiment that would remain in North Carolina to thwart loyalist activity in advance of the British arrival. In addition, the legislature passed a resolution ordering all county magistrates to deploy their local militias to disarm and arrest "all disaffected persons, who, not satisfied with entertaining sentiments inimical to the Country may justly be suspected of a disposition of carrying those sentiments into execution." Altogether, these changes and the new resolve of the state to prosecute dissidents rigorously left William and his fellow loyalists little choice but to comply or to suffer gravely for their recalcitrance.[28]

While the actions of state and local authorities pushed committed Tories either to conform or to somehow evade the consequences of their dissent, the fall of Savannah to British forces commanded by Lieutenant Colonel Archibald Campbell in December 1778, followed by military successes in the interior aimed at restoring royal government in Georgia, lured Carolina Tories southward to support the expanding imperial offensive. For his part, Campbell desired—and expected—assistance from white Carolina loyalists, whom he hoped that he and others might recruit, as well as from Britain's Native American allies and from enslaved people throughout the southern states. One of Campbell's main recruiters was Colonel John Boyd, an influential loyalist resident of the Little River District in the South Carolina backcountry who had become acquainted with the British commander during his time as a refugee in British-occupied New York. In January and early February, Boyd traversed the western parts of both Carolinas, seeking recruits and local men who would use their own influence and connections to secure more troops from their communities. Two South Carolinians, Zacharias Gibbs and Christopher Neeley, were instrumental in this effort, as was apparently William Spurgin, who assumed the rank of major and became Boyd's third-in-command. Once assembled, Boyd's loyalist troops marched toward Georgia, attracting more recruits along the way. Boyd eventually amassed a corps of as many as eight hundred troops, which included at least thirty-five men from William's own Salisbury District in western North Carolina.[29]

Although William's exact movements as a recruiter and militia officer during this period cannot be traced, those of Captain Christopher Neeley are suggestive. Like William, Neeley was an officer in Boyd's army, and he later recounted his wartime activities to the Loyalist Claims Commission when he sought compensation for the losses he incurred as a result of his loyalism. Neeley's overall military career between 1776 and 1779 was likely akin to William's and to those of many other Tory militiamen whose combat experience was sporadic, though their loyalty to the cause was constant. A landowner in South Carolina's Ninety Six District, Neeley joined a local loyalist militia company in 1775 and fought in at least one engagement shortly thereafter, but he fled to "Cherokee Country" in 1776 when the Whigs took control of Ninety Six and its environs. When Neeley tried to return home later that year, he was "way laid by a Party of Rebels . . . and shot thru the Body with two Balls [and] left for dead." Despite being "Dangerously Ill" as a result of his wounds, Neely recovered and lived quietly at home until early 1779, when he heeded the British call to arms, "raised a Body of Men," and became a captain in the army that marched to Georgia with Colonel Boyd. Several years therefore elapsed between Neely's participation in formal military engagements, as was also the case for William. The fact that the combat experience of even Boyd's officers was so extremely limited and intermittent must have undermined their effectiveness against Whig militia who, whatever their shortcomings, mustered routinely and enjoyed relative stability among their corps of officers.[30]

Boyd's plan was to march his troops southward to Augusta, where he expected to join Campbell and his army of British regulars, who were supported by local Tories and others who had fled to New York or British East Florida and were now eager to help reinstate British rule in Georgia and beyond. Boyd's troops crossed the Savannah River from South Carolina into Georgia and then continued moving westward. By 14 February, they had set up their camp at a farm on the north side of Kettle Creek in present-day Wilkes County, where they were grazing their horses and eating fresh beef and parched corn after three days of marching with relatively little sustenance. At that point, the Tories sustained a surprise attack by a hastily assembled party of Whig militia from South Carolina and Georgia under the command of Colonels Andrew Pickens and John Dooly, and what one eyewitness called a "small skirmish" ensued. Although the Whig force of 340 men was less than half the size of Boyd's army, the Tories were thoroughly defeated. While the Whigs reported nine men dead and another twenty wounded, seventy Tories died at Kettle Creek, including Colonel Boyd, who with his dying breath avowed his loyalty to the king and prevailed on Pickens to inform his wife of his

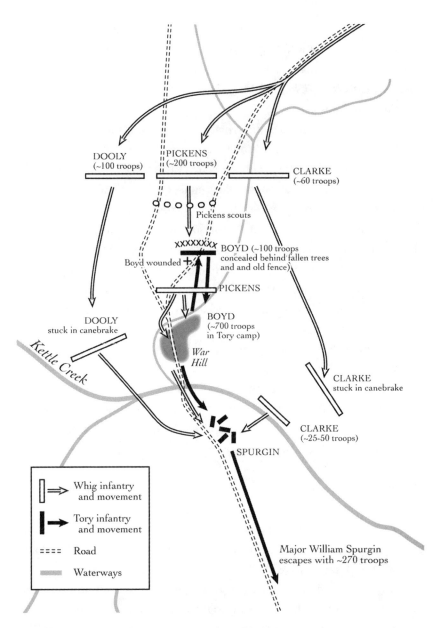

DOOLY
(~100 troops)

PICKENS
(~200 troops)

CLARKE
(~60 troops)

Pickens scouts

XXXXXXXX   BOYD (~100 troops
concealed behind fallen trees
and and old fence)

Boyd wounded

PICKENS

DOOLY
stuck in canebrake

BOYD
(~700 troops
in Tory camp)

Kettle Creek

*War
Hill*

CLARKE
stuck in canebrake

CLARKE
(~25-50 troops)

SPURGIN

Whig infantry
and movement

Tory infantry
and movement

Road

Waterways

Major William Spurgin
escapes with ~270 troops

MAP 4 | The Battle of Kettle Creek. This map shows the advance from the north of Whig militia, who surprised and defeated a much larger Tory force near Kettle Creek in Georgia on 14 February 1779. Although Kettle Creek was a small battle, it was significant as the first patriot victory of the Southern Campaign. Although Tory losses were heavy, William was able to retreat, leading his troops southward to safety. (Map by Nat Case, INCase, LLC, based on a map by Steven Stanley; courtesy of the American Battlefield Trust, www .battlefields.org)

death and to send her a few of his personal effects. An additional seventy-five Tories were wounded or captured. The battle took place less than a day's march from Augusta. While some sources say that the entire battle lasted roughly forty-five minutes, others estimate its duration at slightly less than two hours.[31]

Because of its small size and relatively short duration, Kettle Creek is generally regarded as a minor battle, and it is usually omitted from standard narrative histories of the war. This brief encounter between Whig and Tory militia was nonetheless consequential. The decisive Whig victory slowed the progress of the British reconquest of Georgia. The defeat of the Tory militia, and the imprisonment of so many in the battle's aftermath, also deterred other area loyalists from openly supporting the British offensive. As one early chronicler of the battle observed, had the Tories "successfully joined their [British] allies, there is no saying where the mischief would have ended . . . and the example of Boyd, might speedily have been followed up, on a more extensive scale of revolt, and with more decided effect." Equally important, though the British would eventually reoccupy Augusta and control most of Georgia for the remainder of the war, Kettle Creek was the first of a series of backcountry battles, fought mostly by Tory and Whig militia, and won mostly by the latter, that raised Whig morale and eventually shifted the momentum of the Southern Campaign in favor of the Americans. Although the British garnered more great triumphs on the coast with the occupation of Charleston in May 1780 and of Wilmington in January 1781, the war looked decidedly different farther west. The British never came close to securing control of the Carolina backcountry, where revolutionary armies won pivotal victories in larger engagements at Kings Mountain in October 1780 and at Cowpens in January 1781.[32]

Descriptions of what transpired at Kettle Creek, mostly by early nineteenth-century chroniclers who drew on oral histories and battlefield reminiscences included in soldiers' postwar pension applications and loyalist claims, provide the only extant evidence of William Spurgin's performance as a soldier. Hugh McCall, who wrote the first history of the Revolution in Georgia and who interviewed his uncle and other elderly veterans in part to compensate for a scarcity of archival records, penned the first and most substantive description of William's actions at Kettle

Creek. Although McCall's interviewees remembered Boyd's second-in-command, Lieutenant Colonel John Moore, as having "possessed neither courage nor military skill," they said that "the third in command, major Spurgen [*sic*] . . . acted with bravery, and gave some evidence of military talents." McCall recounted how, as Boyd led one segment of his army, which went down in crushing defeat, William moved his men to the other side of the hill and led at least some of them to safety, as the Whigs pursued them through the swamps and engaged them in close combat. Other historians have repeated McCall's positive assessment of William's performance, with one adding that the smaller Whig force was most in danger of losing the fight when "the Tories had gained the hill, and were re-formed under [Major] Spurgen." Nevertheless, even some knowledgeable historians have confused or conflated William Spurgin with his brother John, another Tory militia officer who died during a different skirmish with Whig militia in Georgia in March 1779.[33]

Most men who fought in small militia battles in remote places, far removed from city newspapers and other patriot communication networks, were, like William, obscure figures, and they remained so long after the war was over. Even more recent historians who have written about Kettle Creek, for instance, have described the Tories' three commanding officers there as "shadowy" and "mysterious" men. "There seems to be historical mystery surrounding each of the loyalists who fought at Kettle Creek," a leading modern authority on the battle has observed, so much so that there is even some uncertainty about Colonel Boyd's first name and about whether his second-in-command, Lieutenant Colonel Moore, was from Georgia or North Carolina. At Kettle Creek, the Whig commanders were only slightly less obscure, though Colonel Andrew Pickens— whose family, like the Spurgins and the Welborns, had traveled down the Great Wagon Road to settle in the Carolinas—became both well-known and widely admired for his later successes at the Battles of Cowpens and Eutaw Springs, and against the Cherokee Indians.[34]

The most thoroughly documented participants in the Battle of Kettle Creek were those men whom the Whigs made prisoners after it was over. Approximately twenty loyalist captives were forced to march in chains to Brigadier General Andrew Williamson's plantation near Augusta, where an additional seventy-nine men joined them in Williamson's bullpen, having surrendered voluntarily after Whig commanders deceptively promised to release them if they turned themselves in and then posted bond to ensure their future good conduct. To discourage future unrest, South Carolina's Whig leaders instead decided to make an example of the Kettle Creek Tories, who, rather than being treated as prisoners of war, were sent to Ninety Six, in Whig-controlled South Carolina, to stand trial for treason. By the time the trials ended in mid-April, some of the prisoners had been released or moved elsewhere, but of those who remained at Ninety Six, some fifty were found guilty of treason. Zacharias Gibbs, one of the men convicted, later recalled watching the erection of gallows and the digging of graves in preparation for a mass execution. In the end, however, only five men were executed at Ninety Six. Several others from Boyd's army who had been transferred to the Salisbury, North Carolina, jail, were found guilty and sentenced to death there in September.[35]

Fearing British retaliation, the Whigs reprieved most of the men they tried and convicted at Ninety Six but saved face by claiming that most "had been seduced and terrified into the fatal step, by Boyd, and a number of people who frequently came amongst them from North Carolina, under a variety of pretenses; and for want of proper information on the nature of our contest with Great Britain." Formal treason trials for soldiers—whom the traditional rules of war deemed enemies, not traitors—were uncommon, but treatment of prisoners of war by both sides became increasingly harsh as the war dragged on. The frequency of violence and even summary executions increased exponentially when more conventionally minded army generals were not around to police the behavior of bloodthirsty partisans. Whig treatment of Tory captives after the Battle of Kettle Creek was indicative of these trends and at the same time foreshadowed the increasing brutality of the war in the southern states and among militia in the backcountry in particular.[36]

William Spurgin evaded capture at Kettle Creek, just as he had done three years earlier at Moore's Creek Bridge. After the battle, according to the South Carolina Whig historian David Ramsay: "The tories were dispersed. . . . Some ran to North-Carolina, some wandered not knowing wither," while others "went to their homes, and cast themselves on the mercy of the . . . government." William likely tried all of these options, except for seeking clemency from the Whigs in Rowan County or else-where.[37]

In late 1779 and early 1780, William spent at least some time in and around Abbotts Creek. He was certainly at home with Jane at some point during the fall of 1779, when their thirteenth child, a son named Jesse, was conceived. The Moravians, who apprehensively recorded whatever violence or other disruptions they experienced or heard about in these troubled times, noted few incidents during these months, despite the seemingly constant arrival of soldiers, whom they described as mostly "deserters" fleeing northward and Whigs coming from the northern states to fight the British in Georgia and South Carolina. In late 1779 and early 1780, despite occasional robberies and rumors of Tory conspiracies elsewhere in the state, the main problems in and around Rowan County seem to have been smallpox, a mildew-infested wheat crop, and "an unusually long, hard winter, such as was remembered by no one in this country."[38]

That uneasy peace would end with the British capture of Charleston af-ter a six-week siege in May 1780. News of the fall of Charleston—a pivotal triumph that resulted in the surrender of General Benjamin Lincoln's entire army of more than five thousand men and put the fourth-largest American city into enemy hands—and of the subsequent victory of Brit-ish and loyalist troops over a combined force of Continentals and Whig militia at Camden in August energized North Carolina loyalists in the backcountry and elsewhere. Reports of the "good disposition of a con-siderable body of the inhabitants" pleased Lord Cornwallis, the British commander, who communicated with "the leading persons among our friends [in North Carolina], recommending in the strongest terms that they should attend to their harvest, prepare provisions, and remain quiet untill the King's troops were ready to enter the province," which he ex-pected would occur in late August or early September.[39]

Cornwallis's caution was to no avail. In June, immediately after hear-ing the news from South Carolina, North Carolina's backcountry Tories rallied at Ramsour's Mill on the Yadkin River, assembling a force of more than 1,300 men under Lieutenant Colonel John Moore, who had been one of Boyd's officers at Kettle Creek in 1779. Learning of the Tory encampment, a party of some four hundred Whig militia from the counties of Rowan, Mecklenburg, and Lincoln gathered and attacked the loyalists, who fell to their much smaller force after a brutal battle. Samuel Bryan may have been at Ramsour's Mill; soon after that engagement, he raised the king's standard and recruited more than eight hundred men to march southward, where they, too, suffered defeat at the hands of a smaller Whig force at Colson's Mill on the Pee Dee River in mid-July, though most of Bryan's army escaped capture. Many of Bryan's men, who came from "the forks of the Yadkin and that neighborhood," which included Abbotts Creek, had joined his group because local authorities would have otherwise forced them to serve in the Whig militia. These conflicts pitted North Carolinians against each other, as would be the case in so many later backcountry battles.[40]

On 30 June 1780, between the engagements at Ramsour's Mill and Colson's Mill, forty-four-year-old Jane Spurgin gave birth to her thirteenth and final child. Just three days earlier, the Moravians had nervously observed the growing "Tory camp" at Abbotts Creek and noted that loyalist militia were "out in force" throughout the area.[41] Where was William? Was he with the British commander in Charleston? Was he with Bryan and their fellow-loyalists in battle at Colson's Mill? Was he among the Tories patrolling—some would say terrorizing—the Abbotts Creek settlement? Was he at home with Jane and their newborn child?

There is no way to know for sure, but whatever modicum of stability and safety the Spurgins may have enjoyed previously would soon be compromised as the Carolina backcountry became the site of seemingly unending partisan violence and civil war. The Whig historian David Ramsay's summation of the impact of the "calamities of the years 1780 and 1781" on his own state of South Carolina applied equally to its northern neighbor. "There was scarcely an inhabitant of the State," he wrote, "however obscure in character or remote in situation, whether he remained firm to one party or changed with the times, who did not partake of the general distress."[42] The war, which had been an intermittent presence in Abbotts Creek since 1776, now became a daily fact of life.

4

Jane's World

IN EARLY 1781, with both British and American armies in the area and their respective generals planning for a major confrontation, divisions among the Spurgins of Abbotts Creek became emblematic of the civil war that ravaged Rowan County and its environs. From his militia camp at Abbotts Creek, William Spurgin—with the likely encouragement of Josiah Martin, the former governor, who had returned to North Carolina to drum up loyalist support for the British offensive—furnished horses and supplies to the army commanded by Lord Cornwallis, who arrived in Salisbury on 3 February after a long march in driving rain that had swelled the Yadkin River to near-flood levels. At exactly the same time, the able new commander of the Southern Army of Continentals, General Nathanael Greene, was receiving Jane Spurgin's hospitality at the family's Abbotts Creek home. As the Rowan County native and early North Carolina historian E. W. Caruthers noted, for two to three days Greene made his headquarters "at the house of Col. Spurgen [sic]," whose wife was "as true a Whig as her husband was a Tory." While one son, eleven-year-old Joseph, brought provisions to William at the nearby Tory encampment, one of his older brothers tried to persuade their father to give up the fight and return home.[1]

When the war was over, Jane Spurgin would describe herself as "a good Citizen and well attached to the government."[2] Although her reception of

Greene at Abbotts Creek can be interpreted as evidence of her allegiance to a cause diametrically and violently opposed to William's, her wartime activities and experiences are otherwise nearly undocumented. Unlike William, who was mobile, if elusive, during the war, Jane stayed at Abbotts Creek, where she attended to her children and to the family farm. Like most of her neighbors, she experienced the war mainly as a series of material hardships and uncertainties, amid persistent threats of violence. Jane and her children suffered as a result of William's political choices, which jeopardized their family's property holdings and required the payment of punitive extra taxes. Because loyalty and allegiance were gendered attributes, moreover, Jane's professed patriotism did not protect her. At least in ordinary times, men owed loyalty and allegiance to their country, but women owed both to men. In Jane's world, law and custom presumed that the politics of a Tory's wife—if she had any interest in politics at all—would be compatible with her husband's.

Although the Revolution in the southern backcountry was unusually bloody and divisive, that conflict was a civil war that fractured families of all sorts throughout British North America. Some divisions were generational. One particularly notorious example was the famed patriot leader Benjamin Franklin and his Philadelphia-born son William, the last royal governor of New Jersey, who became one of America's most active loyalists and emigrated to Britain after the war was over. A similar but much less famous case was that of the Hadden family of Newark, New Jersey, in which the son fought for a loyalist regiment while his father, an ardent Whig, prosecuted local Tories. Conversely, Joshua Campbell, a North Carolina loyalist, disinherited his son and namesake for supporting the Revolution.[3]

Siblings, too, took different sides in the revolutionary conflict. John Randolph, a friend of Thomas Jefferson's, was a prominent loyalist who fled Virginia in 1775, whereas his brother Peyton was one of the most vocal and influential Whigs in the Old Dominion. George Robert Twelves Hewes, a Boston shoemaker who participated in the destruction of the tea in Boston in 1773 and later served as both a soldier and a privateer in support of the Revolution, had a Tory brother. Moses Dunbar, the only

Connecticut loyalist convicted of treason in a civil court and executed as a result, had two brothers who served in the Continental Army. Maria DePeyster Bancker Ogden of New York had five sons, four of whom actively supported the Revolution, whereas the fifth was a loyalist who remained in occupied New York City for the duration of the war.[4]

Although disagreements between wives and husbands may have been less common, or perhaps only less well-documented, Jane and William were far from being the only married couple for whom the Revolution created political divisions that were seemingly irreconcilable. When Samuel Quincy, a Massachusetts-born royal appointee, remained loyal to the king and left for England in 1776, his wife, Hannah, who supported the Revolution, stayed with her Whig brother in Boston and never again saw her estranged husband. Jane Bartram was a Philadelphia woman who professed "a friendly and warm desire for the Liberties and rights of the United States of America" and likewise remained at home when her Tory husband fled to New York in 1778. Annis Boudinot Stockton of New Jersey, an avid patriot, saved the papers of the local Whig Society from enemy troops and participated in fund-raising efforts to benefit the Continental Army, whereas her husband, Richard, an erstwhile Whig, repudiated the revolutionary cause when, after being captured by the British, he swore allegiance to the king in exchange for his freedom.[5]

Some women who were loyal to the king were married to men who supported the Revolution, but law and custom worked in tandem to obscure these sorts of domestic political conflicts. On the one hand, the common practice of requiring only men to swear oaths of allegiance spared Tory women from the sort of public reckoning that county committees and magistrates imposed on William Spurgin and other loyalist men. On the other hand, the English common-law doctrine of coverture, which governed property relations within marriage, determined how states enforced the anti-Tory laws, giving loyalist women in predominantly Whig families significant incentives to keep their dissenting views from becoming public. Because coverture vested control of all marital property in the hands of husbands, the state viewed family property as belonging to men, rendering wives' political allegiance immaterial in matters of confiscation. Both the common law of marriage and the widespread practice of exempting women from oath-taking derived from the presumption that wives were wholly domestic and dependent, and that women lacked political consciousness.[6]

Revolutionary politics confounded such assumptions as women expressed political views and sometimes engaged in activities that belied contemporary gender conventions that limited their concerns to household tasks, child-rearing, and other aspects of domestic life. From the earliest days of the imperial crisis, public-spirited women resisted British tyranny, most notably during the various efforts, beginning with the Stamp Act protests, to secure the repeal of offensive acts of Parliament by forgoing the consumption of goods imported from Britain. Leaders of colonial nonimportation and nonconsumption initiatives sought—and received—support from women far beyond the main urban centers of Boston, New York, and Philadelphia. In 1774, fifty-one North Carolina women from in and around the town of Edenton signed a manifesto in which they approved of both the ongoing tea boycott and the more general nonimportation agreement that the Continental Congress had recently adopted, and one disapproving Scottish visitor reported that women in the coastal town of Wilmington had "burnt their tea in solemn procession" as part of a patriotic protest. Women also penned newspaper essays to promote the nonconsumption efforts and otherwise express their commitment to the patriot cause. Once the war began, many traveled with the armies, whom they served as nurses, cooks, and laundresses. A few—most famously Deborah Sampson of Connecticut—dressed as men and saw combat as soldiers.[7]

Other patriotic acts were more uniquely female, derived from white women's socially prescribed roles as amiable companions and virtuous wives and mothers. In 1776, as both sides steeled for war, the Whig press praised "young ladies, of the best families" in various locales, who resolved that "they will not receive the addresses of any young gentlemen . . . except the brave volunteers" who went off to fight the Tories, and whose actions thereby displayed "that brave, manly spirit, which would qualify them to be the defenders and guardians of the fair sex." When some "young ladies" from Rowan County composed and adopted a series of resolutions to that effect, the county committee thanked them for their "spirited performance" and declared that such

A SOCIETY of PATRIOTIC LADIES,
AT
EDENTON in NORTH CAROLINA.
Plate V.

FIGURE 3 | Philip Dawe, *A Society of Patriotic Ladies*, 1775. Women in Edenton, North Carolina, were among the many who became politicized by the imperial crisis and supported Whig nonimportation and nonconsumption efforts. This British print satirized the "ladies" of Edenton, variously portrayed here as mannish, sexually promiscuous, and neglectful of their maternal duties. Real ladies, the artist suggests, would not engage in politics; legitimate political activities, in turn, would not include women. (Library of Congress, Prints and Photographs Division [LC-DIG-ppmsca-19468])

"sensible and polite" resolutions were "worthy of the imitation of every young lady in America."[8]

As mothers, women also received accolades for instilling patriotic virtues in America's next generation. One example from rural North Carolina was Ann Ryan, whose daughters Martha and Elisabeth, aged eleven and nine respectively in 1776, adorned their cipher book with images of American flags and ships—including one called the *Yankee Hero*—and patriotic slogans such as "Liberty or Death." Like most girls, especially in rural areas, the Ryan sisters learned their lessons from their mother at home, just as Jane Spurgin likely taught her younger daughters—Agnes, Jane, and Elizabeth—basic reading, writing, arithmetic, and Bible verses at Abbotts Creek during the war years. Although teaching one's children may have seemed like a low-risk political act, the teachings of a politically outspoken mother could be profoundly consequential. William Gipson, who served as a young man in Rowan County's Whig militia, later remembered that his mother had been "tied up and whipped by the Tories, her house burned and property destroyed" for having "committed no other offense than that of earnestly exhorting her sons to be true to the cause of American liberty." The potential influence mothers wielded as their children's first teachers became an important impetus for improving female education in postrevolutionary America.[9]

During the war, however, women's most common and far-reaching service to both their families and their country was the more tangibly productive work they did on the home front, where many did double duty by assuming their absent husbands' agricultural and business responsibilities in addition to their usual household labors. In Jane's case, that would have meant overseeing the production and sale of the family's crops, and tending to horses, cattle, sheep, and other livestock, all of which were essential to her family's prosperity and, as sources of provisions and supplies for revolutionary forces, also critical to the war effort. At least two of the winters during the war were unusually severe, according to the Moravian diarists who carefully recorded details about the weather and other challenges of wartime farming. In running the farm, Jane may have had some occasional assistance from William—who came home from time to time—and from their adult son John, who resided nearby, as well as from the other older children who still lived with her at home. The Spurgins also benefited from the labor of either one or two enslaved men, who had been acquired by the family sometime after 1768 and who were at some point during the war either confiscated by the state or left Abbotts Creek, either to join the British or for other some other unspecified reason. The loss of this bonded labor must have been a profound blow to Jane as she struggled to maintain both the farm and

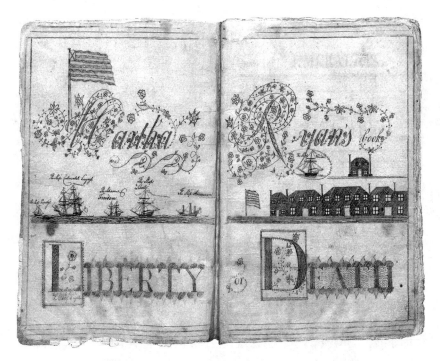

FIGURE 4 | Martha Ryan's cipher book, 1781. Martha Ryan and her sister learned their lessons at home from their mother. During the Revolution, those lessons likely included information about the war and its causes. These beautifully illustrated pages depict an American flag, six named ships, a fort, and perhaps the Ryan family home, as well as the revolutionary slogan "Liberty or Death." (Southern Historical Collection, Louis Round Wilson Special Collections Library, University of North Carolina at Chapel Hill)

her household while raising many young children in a time of seemingly continual dearth and crisis.[10]

Women's routine domestic work also became more demanding as a result of wartime scarcities. Revolutionary boycotts and British naval blockades severely curtailed Americans' access to imported commodities, the most important of which were mass-produced British textile products. Although people in Rowan County could still purchase some finished cloth from local Moravian weavers, wartime disruption limited their access to the other ready-made textiles typically used for better clothing, bed linens, and various household articles. During the prerevolutionary nonimportation efforts, production of homespun cloth had become a symbol of female patriotism, and the evidence suggests that women did, in fact, increase their domestic production of textiles during both the imperial crisis and the war that followed. Travelers noted the presence of looms in many of the houses they visited. Women who showed "frugality and industry, at home . . . in manufacturing our own wearing" won encouragement and praise from the patriot press. Even affluent women were mending, patching, and refashioning worn or outdated clothing and other items—or having their servants or enslaved domestics do so for them—unable to replace tattered stockings and outgrown children's clothes until after the war was over. In the backcountry town of Hillsborough, the proprietors of a fledgling paper mill, who aspired to produce a locally made alternative to scarce imported paper, also called on women to save rags, fabric scraps, and "old Handerkerchief[s], no longer fit to cover their snowy Breasts," which they hoped to use as raw materials for this "necessary Manufacture."[11]

During the war years, the economic challenges civilians faced escalated as inflation soared and governments called on citizens to pay increasingly higher taxes. Like the other states, North Carolina financed its war effort mostly by printing paper money. Unbacked by gold or other tangible assets, state-issued paper currency was essentially a promissory note whose real value (and purchasing power) declined as the war dragged on—as governments incurred more debt and printed more paper money—and overall confidence in the state's ability to repay its debts diminished accordingly. One North Carolina historian summarized the inflation of the state's revolutionary currency as follows: "The depreciation of currency was such that while in December 1778, the decline in value was only 5 per cent [from the previous year], a year later it was 30 percent. During the following year it went by leaps and bounds, until in December 1780, it fell by 200 percent, and the next December its value had declined by 725 per cent." Farmers and others who were required to accept this depreciated currency as payment for whatever goods and services they provided also paid high taxes to help pay for the war, but by 1780 the state was shielding itself from the ravages of inflation by mandating that citizens pay all or part of their taxes in provisions, such as corn or pork. Because William, not Jane, was listed as the property owner on the Rowan County tax rolls, and because he was a Tory, the Spurgins were taxed at four times the normal rate. Jane must have been unable to meet this obligation because her husband was listed among the county's "Tax Delinquents" when the war was over.[12]

As the wife of an avowed and notorious Tory, Jane also faced other economic pressures that were potentially much more devastating than spiraling inflation and high taxes. The most immediate threat to the welfare and status of her large family came in the form of the various directives that authorized state confiscation of loyalist property. William's entire estate had been vulnerable to confiscation since May 1776, when the Provincial Congress resolved that anyone who was "convicted of taking up arms against America," as William and his loyalist comrades had done at Moore's Creek Bridge, "shall forfeit all his goods and chattels, lands and tenements." Pressures to conform and the likelihood that the state would enforce the confiscation laws increased once the British shifted their military offensive to the southern states, as North Carolina authorities prepared for an enemy invasion by redoubling efforts to administer the oath of allegiance and to punish those who still refused to support the revolutionary cause. Such efforts obviously posed grave threats to the Spurgins' livelihood and, in the longer term, jeopardized whatever material legacy Jane and William had hoped to provide for their many offspring.[13]

On the issue of gender, the provisions of the anti-Tory laws were decidedly ambiguous. Despite prevailing assumptions that a woman's political allegiance was either nonexistent or determined by her husband's, revolutionary-era statutes used language that explicitly defined both treason and misprision of treason as crimes that could be committed by both men and women. North Carolina's foundational anti-Tory law, enacted in 1777, sought to define and punish all "Persons disaffected to the State" and stipulated that one of the penalties imposed on such offenders would be the loss of all or part of "his or her Estate." Although the statute instructed those local authorities charged with administering loyalty oaths to target certain categories of inhabitants who were likely exclusively male—"late Officers of the King . . . [and] Factors, Storekeepers, or Agents . . . for Merchants residing in Great-Britain or Ireland"—the law went on to give those authorities "full Power to issue Citations against Persons" in those categories and compel them to swear the oath of allegiance. State legislators continued to use this sort of gender-neutral language in subsequent amendments and additions to the anti-Tory laws.[14]

At the same time, in other ways the confiscation statutes perpetuated the cultural assumptions and legal prescriptions of the English common law of marriage, which afforded widows a dower portion, typically a one-third share, of their deceased husbands' property. Just as the common law generally aimed to protect widows by preserving the dower rights of even those whose husbands were executed for committing heinous crimes, the confiscation laws extended this protection to the wives of Tories if those women remained in America after their husbands left, either because they had been formally banished or had fled to avoid prosecution or because they were engaged in combat against the revolutionary cause. Although North Carolina's earliest anti-Tory laws employed gender-neutral language in empowering magistrates to preserve "so much of the Traitor's Estate, as . . . may appear sufficient, for the Support of his or her Family," the statute enacted in 1782 included updated verbiage that tacitly acknowledged the reality that only the wives of Tories—whom the state viewed as de facto widows because their husbands were both physically distant and politically dead—benefited from this policy. In orchestrating the sale of confiscated estates, in 1782 the state expressly ordered its agents to "set apart so much of the personal property, including all the household goods of every estate liable to be sold as aforesaid, as will be sufficient for the reasonable support of the wives, widows and children, of any person whose estate is, or may be confiscated, and one third of the lands . . . in the same manner as lands in dower are directed by the common law."[15]

All of this meant that Jane's gender, not her patriotism, was the better weapon to be deployed in any effort to shield a portion of her family's property from confiscation. Although the earlier confiscation statutes had left to the discretion of county magistrates the amount of property to be retained by the "Traitor's" family in each particular case, the prior experience of such men with a legal system based on common-law precedents likely predisposed them toward preserving the traditional dower share—the so-called widow's third—a provision that, in any case, was explicitly specified later by law. Legislators and county magistrates alike likely sympathized with the plight of frail women and innocent children rendered vulnerable by the indefensibly bad political choices made by the very men who were supposed to be their protectors and providers, or at least they recoiled from being seen as needlessly persecuting dependent women and children, who, deserted by their domestic governors, were now beholden to the benevolence of state. At least equally important, however, was the reluctance of authorities to make women and children public charges, dependent on their neighbors for financial support and burdensome to their overtaxed and increasingly war-weary communities.

Beginning in 1778, with the threat of confiscation looming, Jane began navigating the complicated legal processes that could help her to retain ownership of the family land. The 1777 anti-Tory law authorized the confiscation and sale of "vacant" lands, which the state defined as property belonging to the king and to the absentee Earl of Granville, but also acreage owned by anyone who refused to sever their ties to the Crown by taking the state's loyalty oath. The seizure and reallocation of such lands in Rowan County, which eventually should have included William's, began in early 1778. For aspiring landowners, securing title to these so-called vacant lands was a multistep process. After ascertaining that a particular tract was, indeed, officially vacant, the prospective grantee had to "make an entry," which meant recording their intent to claim the property, with the county land office. After a three-month waiting period to allow for the filing of any potential objections to the land transfer, the next steps were for the tract to be surveyed and, eventually, for the land office to issue a new land warrant to the successful claimant. At every stage of this transaction, official fees were levied. The law also required land recipients to take the oath of allegiance to the state before formally receiving their deeds, a provision aimed at preventing Tories from reclaiming their property or from acquiring new acreage to replace what they had lost to confiscation.[16]

State land records and county deed books suggest that Jane initiated, but did not complete, the process necessary to secure legal title to a portion of the land on which she and her children resided. In 1778, Charles Hinkle, a neighbor of the Spurgins whose politics were sufficiently Whiggish to make him a target of Tory violence, entered a claim for 400 acres "on waters of Abbots Crk," which he then "Made over" to John Groff, who, in turn, transferred the claim to Jane. Although neither Jane nor anyone else appears to have taken the additional steps—or paid the additional fees—necessary to complete the process that would have resulted in her procuring the land warrant that would have established her legal title to this tract, this truncated transaction marked Jane's first effort to become a landowner in her own right. It was also the first stage in a quest that eventually led to her petitioning the state legislature after the war was over.[17]

Another tactic simultaneously pursued to save the Spurgin land from state appropriation followed a different trajectory. William clearly expected his children to inherit his land eventually. When he made his will in 1806, even after years of being estranged from his family, he stipulated that any remaining property he owned in North Carolina "Be Divided as the Laws of that Province Directs" among the offspring he left behind there. As it turned out, the Revolution and the enactment of the confiscation laws effectively expedited the movement of some of William's property from one generation to the next. According to the Rowan County deed books, in May 1778, Jane and William conveyed 396 acres on Abbotts Creek—which they had purchased on 1767—to their oldest child, John, their only adult son. (Although two daughters, Rebecca and Margaret, had also reached adulthood by 1778, daughters were less likely than sons to inherit land, especially in large families.) The common law gave husbands control of marital property, but another customary provision required a wife's approval when her husband chose to sell or otherwise alienate a portion of his estate. In 1778, William was technically an outlaw, and it is unclear whether he actually appeared to register the new deed or whether Jane—in a reversal of the typical common-law practice—acted as William's surrogate for this transaction. Whatever legal steps they took, later that year, twenty-five-year-old John Spurgin appeared for the first time as a landowner on a Rowan County tax list, his new status attained earlier than planned as a result of his parents' efforts to shield the property they had accumulated over the years from state confiscation. Significantly, the state outlawed this stratagem for saving loyalist property by deeding it to a relative in 1781.[18]

Although Jane's subsequent public statements in her petitions may suggest otherwise, this legal maneuvering, along with the timing of the births of their two youngest children, suggests that she and William re-mained on relatively cordial terms in the late 1770s, despite their political differences, and that they cooperated with each other in these efforts to save the family property. Scholars have found that wives who took charge of their family's business and financial interests during the war showed growing confidence in their own competence and that, unlike women who followed their husbands into exile, they could also draw on family and neighborhood networks to help them to negotiate their new terrain as de facto heads of households. In Jane's case, Charles Hinkle and John Groff were part of a support network that also included other neighbors and fellow members of the Abbotts Creek Baptist Church who would later support her efforts to reclaim her property when she petitioned the legislature. Although hindsight reveals that Jane's actions in 1778 con-stituted her first efforts to supplant William as both property holder and household head, her decision to stay at home in Abbotts Creek and her attempts to retain the property there also clearly served not only her own financial interests but also those of the entire family, including William, who may have still contemplated returning to Rowan County once the war was over.[19]

The state did not immediately move to confiscate William's property, but the legal steps Jane took in 1778 were nonetheless prudent, as shown by the losses of some other women in situations similar to hers who were not as fortunate. For instance, Barbara Hamm was the wife of An-drew Hamm, who owned 250 acres, plus a sawmill and a gristmill, in the Abbotts Creek neighborhood. Like William, Andrew planned to fight for the king in 1776, but his capture by the Whigs prevented him from going to Moore's Creek Bridge. After his release, Andrew Hamm returned home, where he remained "quiet" until early 1780, when he joined Cornwallis's army at Charleston rather than obey the summons of local authorities to serve in the Whig militia. Shortly after Andrew's departure for South Carolina, however, Barbara—who was the mother of one young child and pregnant with another—was driven from the family's property, which the state confiscated. Andrew, who was perhaps unaware of the fate of his wife and child, stayed with the British army through the siege of York-town, while Barbara fled to Pennsylvania and eventually reunited with her husband in Canada.[20]

Unlike Barbara Hamm and her family, Jane and her children were able to remain at home in Abbotts Creek, but whatever comfort and security they enjoyed there during the war's early years dissipated once news of the British invasion of South Carolina reached Rowan County. Whigs had relentlessly hunted local Tories in the aftermath of Moore's Creek Bridge, leading many loyalists to refrain from overt opposition to the Revolution, at least in the short term. William may have lived at home quietly during that period, at least intermittently; Samuel Bryan resided unmolested on his land in Rowan County in the years following that ill-fated battle. The arrival of the British, however, led worried Whigs to press even quiescent loyalists to conform, forcing them to take the state's oath of allegiance and to serve in the local militia. These demands, coupled with the arrival of the British, mobilized disgruntled Tories, many of whom were eager for revenge. William Spurgin left to serve with Colonel Boyd in February 1779, and Samuel Bryan raised a large force to fight for the king in the summer of 1780. Local Whigs retaliated in kind. Rowan County and the Carolina backcountry in general was in a state of civil war even before the arrival of the main armies commanded by Cornwallis and Greene in early 1781.[21]

Moravian diarists chronicled the comings and goings of troops, as well as the violent acts perpetrated by partisan militia on both sides. In mid-June 1780, within weeks of learning of the British occupation of Charleston, the Moravians observed that local Tories were "out in force in the Abbots Creek settlement," where they established a camp in which as many as two thousand men were reportedly gathered. During the summer of 1780, the horrified Moravians observed that the "bitterness between the two parties was almost unbelievable," as "Liberty Men on horseback" hunted Tory men in the woods and traumatized the wives and children they had left behind at home. In August, several women from the Abbotts Creek neighborhood passed through the Moravian community of Bethania, where they told the townspeople that "their husbands joined those in favor of the king, and now [they] have been driven from their farms and told to go to their husbands." At this point, it is unclear whether William was with the Tories in Abbotts Creek or with Cornwallis, who was in Charleston planning his invasion of North Carolina and optimistically savoring reports of the "undoubted fidelity" and "good disposition of a considerable body of the inhabitants" whom he expected would rally to support him on his arrival in that state.[22]

During the fall of 1780, the situation in and around Rowan County worsened, as the Moravians reported more violence and plundering, along with the arrival of more soldiers, as some of Bryan's Tories stumbled home in defeat and South Carolina Whigs under General Thomas Sumter came north to prepare for the expected British invasion. In early October, the Tories took the offensive, though the Moravians believed they were mostly assaulting Whigs who had previously attacked either them or their families. Most historians agree that, as the violence escalated, the Whigs were the more vicious, terrorizing soldiers and civilians alike. One group of Rowan County residents complained that Whig militia "unlawfully and feloniously plundered and robbed sundry peaceable people . . . of their property under the pretence of their being Tories and Enemies to their Country, and converted the same to their own use in open violation of the Law." Some other county residents petitioned for relief from the violence of Whig militia by whom "Women and Children have been tortured, hung up and strangled, cut down, and hung up again, sometimes branded with brands or other hot irons in order to extract Confessions from them." The overall brutality of the region's partisan warfare shocked General Nathanael Greene, a seasoned military officer. "The whole Country is in Danger of being laid waste by the Whigs and Tories," he wrote, "who pursue each other with as much relentless Fury as Beasts of Prey."[23]

Greene and other regular army commanders were relatively unaccustomed to these sorts of violent altercations between partisans and civilians—often between neighbors—that could sometimes escalate into deadly skirmishes or battles. A case in point began with the Tories' attack on the home of Frederick Goss, a Whig who lived on a farm near Abbotts Creek. A group of Tories from the nearby loyalist encampment plundered the family's house, taking "all of the bed clothing, about seventy yards of homespun cloth, with whatever else they could find that was worth carrying away," and then moving on to the field where Frederick Goss and his teenaged son, Jacob, were harvesting flax to be used to make more cloth. The Tories seized Jacob and brought him to their camp, but he later escaped and made his way home. The Gosses then roused their sympathetic neighbors to pursue the Tories in retaliation. Although the Tories had left their camp, the Whigs found them, and the opposing forces clashed in a fight that one nineteenth-century chronicler described as "severe but short." None of the Whigs died in the encounter, though several Tories lost their lives, either by gunshot wounds or by drowning as their defeated force tried to escape the charging enemy by crossing the Yadkin River.[24]

Small-scale and often deeply personal confrontations of this sort do not appear on even the most comprehensive lists of revolutionary-era battles. Nor do continual partisan militia offensives to hunt down local enemies count as actual battles, even when deadly violence ensued as a result of those efforts. But such encounters—genuine violence and rumors of it—were facts of life for backcountry residents even before the arrival of the thousands of troops that constituted the main armies, commanded by Greene and Cornwallis, in early 1781. In addition to these smaller raids and altercations, by one count there were also fourteen bona fide battles or skirmishes in the North Carolina backcountry counties in 1780, compared with only five during the entire period from 1776 through the end of 1779. That number increased to thirty-nine in 1781. Local men in Whig and Tory militia units participated in all of these engagements, and they alone fought most of the earlier skirmishes and battles.[25]

For civilians, the presence of so many soldiers posed an array of serious problems. Armies brought diseases with them; smallpox, which first passed through the area in 1779, returned with a vengeance in 1780–81, carried mostly by Tory prisoners taken after the Whigs' victory at Kings Mountain and by Cornwallis's invading army. The presence of so many soldiers also made food, fuel, and everything else even more expensive, and, in this year of subpar harvests, civilians faced potentially ruinous demands for supplies and provisions from both sides. One Rowan County woman, Sylvia Whitlock, who had "eight children to provide for," worried that the "20 bushels of corn demanded from me for the use of the public . . . if taken, will cause distress." Jane Spurgin later recalled that she "was almost Continually harassed from the military who took from her grain, Meat, and many other Articles without the least recompense" and that during the war's harshest years "she and her family of Small Children enjoyed hardly any of the of the produce of her plantation."[26]

Although military officials or their agents could be threatening or rude when they canvassed the countryside in search of provisions, blurring the distinction between requisitions and plunder, civilians also weathered confrontations with robbers, who were often soldiers or men masquerading as soldiers. As early as 1777, Waightsill Avery, North Carolina's first state attorney general, delivered a speech in a Salisbury courtroom denouncing the "many Acts of baseless Violence . . . committed in this State by our Friends, as well as by our Foes," adding that some "wanton Violations of private Property . . . have been committed under a mistaken Notion that there was no Law" to punish them. In fact, it was difficult to eradicate and punish robbers, especially in the war's final phase as local men mobilized and as more armed strangers flooded into the region. Years later, Eliza Wilkinson of South Carolina recalled her harrowing encounter with "banditti" who stormed her house, plundered its contents, and insulted her and her female companions, and then returned the next day to carry off more household goods, clothes, jewelry, and shoe buckles. "They took care to tell us, when they were going away," she wrote, "that they had favored us a great deal—that we might thank our stars it was no worse." After that encounter, Wilkinson remembered, "We could neither eat, drink, nor sleep in peace. . . . The least noise alarmed us. . . . In short, our nights were wearisome and painful; our days spent in anxiety and melancholy."[27]

As Wilkinson's comments suggest, women and children were particularly vulnerable to robbers and other predators. Worst of all was the possibility of rape. Though rarely prosecuted either in peacetime or during wars, rape has been one way in which victorious armies historically have shown their contempt for the vanquished, and it was a fate some American women are known to have suffered during the Revolution. One such incident occurred in April 1780 at Monck's Corner, South Carolina, where loyalist soldiers in Lieutenant Colonel Banastre Tarleton's British Legion physically assaulted and raped, or attempted to rape, several local women. American leaders and the patriot press used such stories of actual and rumored rapes perpetrated by British soldiers and their allies to good effect, inspiring men to assert their manhood by rising up to defend their frail and virtuous women against such abhorrently vile predators.[28]

Elizabeth Steele, a Whig tavern owner who also hosted General Nathanael Greene in 1781 and who was one of the wealthiest residents of the town of Salisbury, described the British mistreatment of local civilians when they arrived in her community. "I was plundered of all my horses, dry cattle, horse forage, liquors, and family provisions," she explained to her brother in Pennsylvania, "and thought I escaped well with my house furniture and milch cattle, when some in this county were stript of all these things."[29]

Jane Spurgin may have been thinking about the general peril that surrounded her and her children when she welcomed General Greene to her house in February 1781. The fact that her husband was a well-known loyalist who was by then encamped with his comrades not far from home should have shielded her from assault or intimidation from Tory militia, as well as from harsh treatment at the hands of British soldiers once Cornwallis's army arrived in the area. At the same time, however, Jane's status as the wife of a prominent local Tory rendered her particularly vulnerable to Whig attacks. By the logic of the times, when it came to families and property, any violence or damage inflicted on Jane or her home was also an emasculating attack on William as both patriarch and property owner. Greene's presence at the Spurgin residence at Abbotts Creek was a powerful deterrent to local Whigs who might have felt inclined to harass the Tory's wife either because of their hostility to William or because they did not fully believe that Jane, unlike her husband, was truly on their side. Extending hospitality to the Continental commander therefore provided Jane with physical protection while also enabling her to show her own distinct political allegiance to the revolutionary cause. Not that Greene's arrival guaranteed her and her children's safety. Indeed, the general cautioned Jane that a battle could possibly occur on her land as a result of his presence. In the event that Cornwallis's army discovered his location and prepared to attack, Greene advised, "she must go into the cellar with her children, and remain there until the conflict was over."[30]

Although no military engagement ensued on the Spurgin property, fragmentary evidence indicates that Jane did more than simply offer food and shelter to the Continental general. Casper Hinkle, a young man from

Abbotts Creek who saw active service in the Whig militia in 1780 and 1781, recalled seeing "the camp of General Green who was then encamped at one Sperguiss [sic], a Colonel of the Tories," which suggests that at least some of Greene's soldiers were also staying on or near the Spurgin property. In addition, according to the local historian E. W. Caruthers, "having no other means of information, and knowing Mrs Spurgen's patriotic spirit," Greene asked her to recommend some trustworthy person "for the purpose of procuring some information respecting the movements of Cornwallis." Jane offered him the services of one of her sons, who went on horseback to gather intelligence, supplying Greene with valuable information at a "critical juncture," thereby helping him to prepare for the eventual confrontation with Cornwallis at Guilford Courthouse (present-day Greensboro) on 15 March 1781.[31]

At Guilford Courthouse, Greene led a combined force of some 4,500 Continentals and militia against Cornwallis's much smaller army of approximately 2,100. Although the British technically won that battle—because they held the ground while Greene retreated—their costs were heavy, as nearly one-quarter of Cornwallis's men were killed, wounded, or captured. Greene's losses were proportionately much lighter. After the battle, Cornwallis took his army first to Cross Creek and then to Wilmington to recruit and regroup, effectively ceding control of the backcountry to the Americans.[32]

The British commander later unfairly attributed the failure of his North Carolina campaign to a lack of loyalist support. "Our experience has shewn that their numbers are not so great as had been represented," Cornwallis wrote from Wilmington in April, "and that their friendship was only passive, for we have received little assistance from them since our arrival in the province." In fact, during the more than two years between the British seizure of Savannah and the battle at Guilford Courthouse, more than three thousand North Carolina loyalists had fought a series of mostly ill-fated engagements without the support of the British army. These repeated battlefield losses, along with ongoing persecution at home, help explain why North Carolina's exhausted Tory population sent fewer than three hundred volunteers to fight with Cornwallis's army at Guilford Courthouse in March 1781.[33]

Although the evidence is at best sketchy, it seems likely that William

Spurgin was one of those North Carolina men who turned out to support Cornwallis in this pivotal battle but that he and the British commander separated not long after the battle was over. In a 1794 statement in which he summarized his wartime service and experiences, William began by averring that "at the commencement of the American War he was an inhabitant of North Carolina and always opposed the Revolters in their endeavors to subvert the British constitution, and ever has adhered to that Government under which he experienced every security." He then went on to describe his military activities in 1781 specifically, presumably believing that his associations with important British military officers would carry more weight with the imperial officials who evaluated his requests than would his connections with various Carolina Tories (many of whom were by then, at any rate, dead, dispersed, or reintegrated back into their prewar American communities). In 1781, William recalled, he "left his property and Joined Lord Cornwallis [and] marched with him through the Carolinas near the Line of Virginia; [and] was then sent back to forward an express to Lord Rawdon, which he completed, but could never join him again."[34]

This statement suggests that William accompanied Cornwallis on at least part of his march northward from South Carolina, which ended in Salisbury, not far from Abbotts Creek, and that he also was part of the force that engaged with Greene's army at Guilford Courthouse, a tiny village not far from the border—or, to use a more contemporary term, the dividing "line"—between Virginia and North Carolina. Although William must have known that the battle occurred in Guilford County, which was adjacent to his own home county of Rowan, he likely believed that a less specific geographic descriptor would have been more meaningful to his petition's addressee, John Graves Simcoe, a British general whose wartime service had been mostly in the northern states and who, in 1791, became the first lieutenant governor and commander in chief of the province of Upper Canada.[35]

The "express" William carried for Cornwallis was a message for Lord Rawdon, a British officer who commanded a small force of men in South Carolina. Written two days after the engagement at Guilford Courthouse and sent in quadruplicate via different couriers to ensure its eventual safe arrival, the purpose of the message was to inform both Rawdon and Sir

Henry Clinton, the British commander in chief, of the recent battle and to present its outcome in the best possible light. "I attacked [Greene] . . . after a very sharp action and routed his army and took his cannon," Cornwallis reported, adding that "the great fatigue of our troops, the number of wounded and want of provision prevented our pursuing the enemy." Cornwallis did not disclose the fact that his losses had been ruinous and that Greene's prudent withdrawal had inflicted damage that would prove decisive in determining the ultimate outcome of the war in the Carolinas. After the battle, Greene himself confided, "I am now perfectly easy, persuaded that it is out of the enemy's power to do us any great injury." A month later, trying to save face with an irate Clinton, Cornwallis glumly observed, as he contemplated invading Virginia, "North Carolina is of all the provinces in America the most difficult to attack (unless material assistance could be got from the inhabitants, the contrary of which I have sufficiently experienced)."[36]

After successfully delivering Cornwallis's message to Rawdon, William neither rejoined the British in Wilmington nor returned home to Abbotts Creek in the months following the battle. After the departure of the main armies, Whig and Tory militia continued their intermittent hostilities against each other. At the time, Captain William Bostick's militia company was one of several Whig forces patrolling the area. John Quillin, one of the soldiers in Bostick's company, described its activities after the battle at Guilford Courthouse, when he applied for a federal pension in 1833. His company's chief objective, he recalled, "was to rout the disaffected persons or Tories, and march from Surry Courthouse . . . down the Yadkin River some times one side & some time the other to Abbots Creek & [Uwharrie] River & about the Mountains of the same name in pursuit of a Tory Captain Spurgin but we fail'd to Take him, but found & took a number of Guns from disaffected persons."[37]

During the long, hot summer of 1781, Whig authorities bemoaned the persistent violence and disorder caused by William's band of Tories and other unrepentant loyalists, especially the Tory militia company commanded by Colonel David Fanning, who was leading his troops in a series of mostly successful skirmishes and battles across central North Carolina. These Tories were so troublesome, General Greene surmised, because "they act in small Parties, and appear in so many different shapes, and have so many hiding places and secret springs of intelligence that you may wear out an Army, and still be unable to subdue them." Greene believed that the expulsion of the British from Wilmington would squelch loyalist activity throughout the state. "Strike at the root of the evil by removing the British," he advised North Carolina's governor, Thomas Burke, "and offer these poor deluded Wretches some hopes of forgiveness, and you will feel little injury from this class of People." In September 1781, a month after Greene penned this letter, Fanning raided the town of Hillsborough, where the state legislature had convened, and took Governor Burke and some two hundred others prisoner.[38]

Nor would Cornwallis's surrender at Yorktown on 19 October 1781 or the British evacuation of Wilmington a month later end the violence in North Carolina. In early 1782, Tories in Bladen County, in the southeastern part of the state, were doing "mischief such as robbing and stealing, and . . . shot at some men and cut and abused some with their swords." More than three months after Yorktown—a British defeat that effectively, if not officially, determined the war's outcome—these loyalists refused to surrender, and at least one local Whig believed that they would not admit defeat "till they can be beaten or killed." In June, a Continental Army lieutenant warned some Moravians to avoid a nearby swamp because "there were probably more than three hundred Tories in it, and while they would probably not kill us, they would rob us of everything we possess." Nor were loyalists the only armed men harassing civilians. One Whig soldier recounted his experience in "a house really Crowded with young Women" near the town of Tarboro, where he saw "several officers each with a Girl in his arms." He, too, "took a Girl, also following their patron, which was rather homely and who, I thought, began to cry, so as soon as I could get off conveniently, I quit."[39]

As the war was winding to a close, the issue of what to do with the loyalists became a priority for government officials on both sides. In March 1782, former governor Josiah Martin, who was by then in London, lobbied government ministers on behalf of the North Carolina loyalists, mentioning William Spurgin by name—along with Samuel Bryan and two other backcountry Tories, William and Robert Fields of Randolph County—as having "real and great claims to the notice of the Government" as a result of the sacrifices they made "from principles of Loyalty." A month later, in April 1782, the state of North Carolina listed William's estate as one of only three in Rowan County—and one of only sixty-eight in the entire state—that would be confiscated and sold immediately to raise essential revenue.[40]

In 1782, after Yorktown but before the signing of the treaty that officially ended the war in September 1783, Jane's world was clearly in a state of flux. She was forty-six years old and had been married to William for roughly three decades, though she had seen little of him over the past six years. She had given birth to thirteen living children, the youngest of whom was only two years old, and had a total of six offspring aged twelve or younger living with her at home. The security of that home was precarious. The fact that the state had not confiscated William's property, while fortunate overall, left Jane's future uncertain. Although formal confiscation would have deprived her of most of the family property, official implementation of the penalties against William also would have afforded her the legal status of widowhood, which, in turn, would have enabled her to claim the dower portion of his estate. Would William return to Abbotts Creek? Would Jane and her children become homeless and impoverished? Resolving these vexing issues would be the focus of her efforts for nearly a decade after the war was over.

5

The Tory's Wife

ON 20 JANUARY 1783, representatives of the United States and Great Britain signed a preliminary peace treaty that recognized the independence of the United States and ended the war in North America. By mid-April, that momentous news from Paris had reached North Carolina, where the state's governor designated the fourth day in July as a public day of thanksgiving. Not yet routinely observed as a civic holiday commemorating the anniversary of American independence, in 1783 the Fourth of July would be special in North Carolina, the only state to officially choose that day to collectively mark the impending peace. "By order of the government of this State," the Moravians at Wachovia reported, "we celebrated a day of thanksgiving on July 4th, for the re-establishment of peace, and with all our heart we rejoiced before the Lord our God with instrumental music and songs." Some other communities in North Carolina and elsewhere organized militia parades and celebratory dinners and speeches. Meanwhile, back in Paris, on 3 September 1783, the negotiators signed the final treaty, which the American Congress ratified on 14 January 1784.[1]

This simple chronology of peacemaking and celebrations belies the true complexity of the transition from war to peace, a protracted process that occupied governments, communities, and families for a decade or more after the Treaty of Paris. While state governments

wrestled with transcendent issues ranging from the appropriate relationship between Church and State in an independent republic to the
role that slavery and the slave trade would play in the postrevolutionary
world, other, more mundane, matters were of more immediate concern
to the Spurgins and to many other Americans once the war was formally
over. While state authorities debated how to deal with the Tories, loyalists like William considered whether they would try to stay in the United
States or begin anew elsewhere. So, too, did the spouses and offspring of
Tories have to weigh the prospect of bidding farewell to banished or disaffected family members against the option of following them into exile.
For some families, including the Spurgins, property-related issues were
equally fraught. Might William's property escape confiscation entirely,
or could Jane obtain title to at least part of his estate? How would the
state's decisions regarding William's property affect the family's short-
and longer-term plans? Meanwhile, returning soldiers and prisoners on
both sides of the recent conflict confronted harsh economic realities
born of years of wartime inflation, debt, and taxes. If the triumph of 1783,
in the words of Governor Alexander Martin, brought "the power of
United America to the summit of her wishes" and secured "the fruits
of uninterrupted Constitutional freedom" for its people, the return of
peace nonetheless brought many new uncertainties and challenges.[2]

In the same address in which North Carolina's governor celebrated
the news of the peace treaty in 1783, he also urged the state assembly
to show clemency toward loyalists, "who through ignorance & delusion
have forfeited their lives, but are endeavouring to expatiate their crimes
by new proofs of their fidelity," adding that the state should enforce the
penalties of the "Treason Law" only against the "principal offenders."
Acting on this recommendation, the assembly passed a law that clari-
fied the state's the policy toward North Carolinians who had refused to
support the Revolution, explicitly acknowledging that the recent conflict
had been, in fact, a civil war. "Whereas, it is the policy of all wise states
on the termination of civil wars, to grant an act of pardon and oblivion
for past offenses," began the preamble to the statute, the state was now
"disposed to forgive offences rather than punish where the necessity

for exemplary punishment has ceased." A section of the law granting a general pardon, however, was followed by another specifically exempting "persons who have taken commissions, or have been denominated officers, and acted as such under the King of Great Britain, or . . . are named in any of the . . . confiscation laws." Although William was not one of the three North Carolinians—Peter Mallett, David Fanning, and Samuel Andrews—whom the state now explicitly excluded from pardon as a result of their involvement in "deliberate and wilful murder, robbery, rape, or house burning" during the war, his military service and his having been named in several earlier anti-Tory laws put him beyond the scope of this new statewide offer of clemency.[3]

What the statute said, however, was not an accurate guide to what was happening in communities throughout the state. Although as many as one in forty residents of the United States fled the country as a result of their loyalism, many more decided to stay, even if it meant leaving home to seek a fresh start in some other American community. As early as July 1783, Governor Martin complained that "divers ill disposed persons" were flooding into North Carolina, making it difficult to distinguish between those who truly merited pardons under the law from those who did not, thereby contributing to "the great uneasiness and disturbance of the good and virtuous Citizens." The governor issued a proclamation prohibiting more Tories from entering the state without his express permission and ordering all those who had arrived since 1 May to leave immediately. But this proclamation was difficult to enforce, especially against people who were not well known or whose postwar conduct was modest and unassuming. This situation was by no means unique to North Carolina. In fact, one recent study of neighboring South Carolina found that the vast majority of former loyalists there cultivated the goodwill of their neighbors and were peaceably reintegrated into society. A similar process likely occurred in North Carolina during the postwar era. Of more than 5,000 claims for compensation filed by loyalist exiles in Britain after the war, only 142 came from former residents of North Carolina, and native North Carolinians submitted only a small subset of those applications.[4]

Some men whose active wartime service to the king was, if anything, more widely known and more consequential than William's were not among these aid-seeking exiles. Those who returned home after the war included Samuel Bryan, who had accepted the royal governor's commission and fought in the Battle of Moore's Creek Bridge in 1776 and raised another force to fight in the Carolinas in the early 1780s, a man whom British military commanders considered to be the most influential Tory in Rowan County, and who, like William, had been named as one of the sixty-eight North Carolina loyalists whose property was subject to immediate seizure and sale. After Yorktown, Bryan had left the state, traveling to the British province of East Florida along with many other southern Tories who intended to settle there as loyal subjects of the king after the war was over. In 1783, however, he returned to North Carolina once it became clear that under the terms of the peace treaty Spain was to reclaim Florida, which had been a Spanish colony before its transfer to the British in 1763 as a result of their victory in the French and Indian War. Bryan therefore was one of those Tories whom North Carolina's governor denounced in his proclamation, and who should have been expelled from the state as a result of his executive order. Nevertheless, Bryan returned to his old community in Rowan County, where he died, in 1798, still owning at least 100 acres and one enslaved man and apparently well regarded by his neighbors.[5]

Perhaps William Spurgin, too, considered staying in North Carolina. William likely heard of Bryan's return, and he must have been aware of the fifth and sixth articles of the Treaty of Paris, by which the United States government promised protection to loyalists and to allow them to return to their prewar communities. By the terms of the treaty, Congress also was bound to "earnestly recommend" that the state legislatures "provide for the Restitution of all Estates, Rights, and Properties, which have been confiscated" from loyalists, while also mandating that there would be "no future Confiscations made nor any Prosecutions commenced against any Person or Persons for, or by Reason of the Part, which he or they may have taken in the present War."[6]

Though William would not have known it in 1783, however, North Carolina's state government (and governments of other states) mostly ignored these treaty provisions, which Congress lacked the authority to enforce under the Articles of Confederation. For most states, selling confiscated loyalist property was a significant source of much-needed revenue. Although some of North Carolina's more conservative political leaders emphasized both the sanctity of property rights and the ethical and practical need to comply with the terms of the treaty—which in most other respects was extremely favorable to American interests—the state continued to sell confiscated property after the treaty was signed and ratified. By 1787, the state of North Carolina had netted some £600,000 from the sale of confiscated land, slaves, and livestock and from the appropriation of loyalist debts. Ultimately, seizures in Rowan County were among the heaviest in the state, mostly due to the confiscation of the vast holdings owned by Henry Eustace McCulloh, an absentee landlord who lost a total of 60,000 acres in seven counties, including nearly 5,000 acres in Rowan. The seizure and sale of loyalist property in North Carolina continued thorough 1790; the last sales of confiscated land in Rowan County, in November 1787, included two tracts totaling 285 acres that had belonged to Matthias Sappenfield, the Spurgins' deceased Abbotts Creek neighbor.[7]

In all, fifty-four men from Rowan County ultimately lost all or part of their landholdings as a result of state confiscation and sale. According to the official records, however, William Spurgin was not one of them. Although two land office entries (other than Jane's) appear to have targeted presumptively vacant Spurgin land in 1778, that acreage was never seized. Indeed, the only evidence of William's having lost property of any sort as a result of state confiscation is a vague entry in the Guilford County court records for February 1782, when the court ordered "William Spurgin's former property to be returned to the state from the hands of the Comm[issioner] of Confisc[ated] E[states] in [the] Co[unty] of Rowan." This ruling, however, referred not to land, but rather to specific "items" that had been part of William's personal estate: "1 feather bed, 2 sides of tanned leather, 1 axe, 1 hoe, 2 waggon loads of corn, 2 sheep, 1 pewter plate." It is not clear whether the state, in turn, disposed of these items or allowed Jane to reclaim them.[8]

But state appropriation was not the only way that Tories lost property in the postrevolutionary era. In 1792, in a carefully worded communication William addressed to the Canadian governor, John Graves Simcoe, he explained that that he had "Lost all my Property [which was] taken and Soald from me by ye Reabils, my Land, my Negroes, my Stock and houshold goods," yet he never attempted to secure compensation for these losses from the Loyalist Claims Commission, a body established in London in 1783 expressly "to enquire into the Losses and Services of all such persons who have suffered in their Rights, Properties, and Professions, during the late unhappy Dissensions in America, in Consequence of their Loyalty to His Majesty, and Attachment to the British Government." William, indeed, lost his estate, and he lost it to "Reabils," but those men received his property not as a result of his loyalism but rather in payment for his outstanding debts.[9]

Beginning in 1782, William's creditors initiated a series of lawsuits against him. Despite the undoubtedly sorry state of the Spurgins' finances in 1782, debt did not in itself connote poverty; in normal times at least, debt signified creditworthiness and solvency insofar as when people offered goods or services on credit, they were showing faith in the recipient's eventual ability to repay what they owed. Merchants, artisans, and farmers tracked long-term business relationships in account books or ledgers that detailed specific exchanges of goods, services, and sometimes cash over time, with the respective overall status of creditor and debtor often changing with each newly recorded exchange. Compared with bonds or promissory notes, this sort of "book debt" was a more personal form of credit and one that was pervasive as a way of conducting business in cash-poor eighteenth-century America, with payment in full and the zeroing out of an account typically occurring only when two parties ended their business relationship. Nor was being sued for debt necessarily a source of shame or a sign of insolvency. Debt litigation was the main business of the courts in colonial America, and creditors continued to use the courts extensively to enforce their claims against delinquent debtors in the postrevolutionary era.[10]

The disruption of trade, armies' seizure or destruction of crops and other commodities, and high wartime taxes meant that many Americans experienced unprecedented debt in the 1780s, but the state also burdened loyalists such as William with additional and uniquely harsh legal disabilities that complicated the normal workings of economic life. Although account books for neither William nor his creditors have survived, the men who sued him had been supporters of the Revolution, and, as such, they were citizens of North Carolina who had the right to file suits in court. Because William had been a substantial property owner in Rowan County before the war, there must have been people who were indebted to him, too—people who bought his crops, for instance—but the state's anti-Tory laws, which made him an outlaw, also took away his civil and economic rights. Not only was William's property under threat of confiscation by the state, then; he also lacked the ability to defend himself in court or, more importantly, to use the courts to collect whatever sums others may have owed him, which, in turn, would have helped him to address the demands of his creditors.

According to family tradition, William spent much of the 1780s "laid out in the woods" because there was supposedly "a price on his head," though it is unclear exactly why. Although William had been officially banished from the state and its officials were vigorously pursuing the sale of Tory property, local authorities had stopped imprisoning loyalists and demanding their attendance at county militia musters after the British left the state. Whether or not William was truly hiding in the woods in and around Rowan County, Jane later stated that he had "not . . . lived with her Since the war." Whatever his feelings toward Jane and his children, William must have known that his economic situation was nearly hopeless because when, in November 1782, the Rowan County court summoned 160 local loyalists, including him, "to appear . . . to shew Cause under the Act of Assembly why their Estates Should not be Confiscated," he did not respond, perhaps because he knew that litigation was already underway to liquidate his holdings to satisfy his creditors.[11]

According to Jane, before the war, William owned a total of roughly 700 acres in two Abbotts Creek tracts. In November 1782, four men filed suits against him in two counties, Rowan and Guilford (which had been formed from parts of Rowan and Orange Counties in 1771), to assume ownership of that property as payment for outstanding debts. In the Rowan County lawsuit, the plaintiffs were William Davis, Barney (or Johan Bernhardt) Idol, and Nathaniel Moore. Davis was a county justice who lived in the Abbotts Creek neighborhood; in fact, the area that had been called "Spurgin's district" before the war was known as "Davis's district" after William left the county bench. Davis was a captain in the

Whig militia, where Barney Idol's son Jacob served under him, "marching about through the County to keep the Tories in check" in 1780 and 1781. Nathaniel Moore is more difficult to identify, but a man by that name appeared in the first federal census in 1790, situated among names of other Abbotts Creek householders, which suggests that he, too, lived in the area. The plaintiff in the Guilford County case was Charles Bruce, an influential Whig who was a justice of the peace and also a member of the convention that drafted North Carolina's first state constitution in 1776. In 1783, Bruce would win election to the state assembly, and he became the commissioner for confiscated property—the state official charged with selling loyalist property—for the Salisbury District in 1787.[12]

Although the paper trail is sparse and confusing, it is clear that the courts decided both cases against William, almost certainly in absentia, and that by November 1782 the Rowan County sheriff was poised to sell the Abbotts Creek tracts to the highest bidder at auction to repay the "execution against Wm Spurgin for £435.4 which Barney Idle, Wm Davis, Nathaniel Moore & Charles Bruce recovered for debt and damages, also £11.16 [court] costs," for a total of £447. The two Abbotts Creek properties included 396 and 310 acres, respectively, and the family's house was situated on one of these tracts. Charles Bruce purchased the entire 706 acres for £240 at a public vendue on 21 December 1782. By virtue of that sale, the Spurgins should have lost their land and their home without recouping funds sufficient to satisfy fully the demands of William's creditors.[13]

At that point, on the verge of being both penniless and homeless, Jane acted boldly to prevent, or at least to delay, the loss of the family land. In March 1783, she appealed the county court's judgments in favor of Bruce, Davis, Idol, and Moore to the Salisbury District Superior Court, which, in turn, ordered the lower court to "bring up the Papers relative to the Judgment obtained in the Said Court . . . against the Estate of William Spurgin" for review in its next session. At the same time, the district court suspended the enforcement of the lower court's ruling, which voided both the county's impending seizure of the Spurgin property and its subsequent sale to Bruce, at least for the time being. Equally important, by referring to the "Estate of William Spurgin," the court acknowledged William as a politically dead noncitizen and Jane as a de facto widow, possessing legal rights as a result of her no longer being a wife who was subject to the strictures of coverture.[14]

Because the records of the Salisbury District Court are a "broken series," with many papers missing, it is unclear whether the county court complied with the higher court's order, but it seems unlikely that any court ever formally reversed the initial rulings in favor of William's creditors. In 1784 and 1785, the status of the property was therefore in a state of limbo. In both years, despite the fact that he was a noncitizen and not living at home with Jane, William Spurgin's name still appeared on the Rowan County tax lists, though the tax collectors reported him as owning no land or other taxable personal property, such as slaves or livestock. In 1785, the tax collectors also included William's name on a separate list of "Tax Delinquents and Insolvents." Jane's name appeared nowhere in the county tax rolls, though she and her children still lived on the family land at Abbotts Creek.[15]

In the fall of 1785, two pivotal events led Jane to take her appeal beyond the courts to the state assembly, which was due to convene in New Bern in November. On 18 October, Charles Bruce went to court to prove, or certify, his purchase of the 706 acres at Abbotts Creek three years earlier, thereby effectively finalizing that transaction. Around the same time, William Spurgin, whose whereabouts had been uncertain since 1781 or 1782, resurfaced when he was arrested for horse-stealing somewhere in Rowan County and then tried for that offense in the Salisbury District Superior Court.[16]

In September 1785, a grand jury in Salisbury indicted "William Spurgin late of the county of Rowan, yeoman" for stealing with "force and arms . . . one mare of a bay colour, of the price of five pounds, of the goods and chattels of Peter Custer" the preceding March. The court's designation of William's place of residence—"late of the county of Rowan"—acknowledged both the impending loss of his land and the fact that he had spent much of the past several years away from home. Its use of the descriptor "yeoman" was both a compliment and an insult. On the one hand, as a tax delinquent and a landless insolvent, William's current status was far below that of a respectably middling yeoman farmer. On the other hand, he had been an "esquire," perhaps even a gentleman, as recently as ten years ago, so even the generous designation "yeoman" denoted his remarkable decline in status and power.[17]

In court, William pled not guilty, but he was tried and convicted of the crime of horse stealing and then sentenced to death. The court ordered that, on Friday 14 October, sometime between ten and four o'clock, he and another convicted horse thief were to be taken from the Rowan County jail "to the Place of Execution, [and] that there they be hanged from the Neck until they be Dead." The gallows was the preferred method of executing white people who were convicted of felonies in early America, and North Carolina classified no fewer than thirty crimes as capital offenses in the 1780s. That long list included many crimes against property, including burglary, theft, and also the more specific offense of horse-stealing, which was a problem of epidemic proportions after the war, leading the state legislature to enact a law to better prosecute the "banditti of rogues . . . [who] confederated to steal horses" and to conceal their crimes by "pass[ing] them through many hands so suddenly and secretly that when one is detected with a stolen horse they have witnesses among themselves to enable the possessor to prove a purchase from a second, and he from a third, and during the time necessarily taken up in proving the pretended past purchases, the confederated villain who first stole the horse has notice from the others to make his escape and elude justice." By fencing and then selling horses, such "banditti," many of whom were likely renegade loyalists or other propertyless men, were making money in a difficult postwar economy.[18]

Whether or not one of these larger horse-stealing operations included William, he did not escape conviction, though the court's death sentence was never carried out against him. Several factors may have saved him from execution. First, despite the severity of the written law, North Carolina authorities typically did not execute white people for property crimes, reserving that maximum penalty mostly for those convicted of murder or rape, both before and after the Revolution. Second, the ideals of the Revolution (and, more generally, of the trans-Atlantic Enlightenment) impelled at least some Americans to push for humanitarian legal reform in their respective states. Although North Carolina never undertook the wide-ranging reforms spearheaded by Thomas Jefferson in Virginia or by Benjamin Rush in Pennsylvania, some of the state's leaders advocated formally decreasing the number of capital crimes and imposing other penalties on persons convicted of property-related offenses. Indeed, in 1787, two years after William's conviction, North Carolina's state legislature enacted another law specifically related to the crime of horse-stealing, which changed the prescribed punishment for a defendant's first offense. If convicted, the amended statute declared, the offender "shall stand in the pillory one hour, and shall be publicly whipped on his, her or their bare backs with thirty-nine lashes well laid on, and at the same time shall have both of his, her or their ears nailed to the pillory and cut off and shall be branded on the right cheek with the letter H of the length of three-quarters of an inch and of the breadth of half an inch, and on the left cheek with the letter T of the same dimensions as the letter H in a plain and visible manner." Under the new statute, however, the state retained the death penalty as punishment for a horse thief's second offense.[19]

The preamble to this 1787 law helps explain why William was spared execution and seemingly any other form of punishment for his crime in 1785. Despite the gruesomeness of the newly prescribed corporal penalties, the legislators believed that the amended law was both more humane and, at least equally important, more palatable to magistrates and jurors alike. Beginning with the observation that "it is inconsistent with the policy of a well regulated government" for horse thieves to receive the same punishment as murderers, the lawmakers went on to lament that in such cases when "the punishment in its nature and gradation" did not fit the crime committed, courts and plaintiffs "from compassion forebear to prosecute, juries from the same motive too often acquit, and if convictions are had, pardons are extended to the guilty." In other words, because such an extreme penalty repulsed so many judges and juries, convicted criminals often received no punishment at all for their transgressions, and that appears to have been the case with William. Although no surviving records indicate that he received an official pardon or commutation of his sentence, he was not executed or otherwise punished.[20]

Jane had no way of knowing that William would survive the court's judgment against him when she made her first appeal to the state legislature for assistance in late 1785. Moreover, even if the authorities spared her husband's life, as she explained in her petition, she did not expect him to return "to assist in the Maintenance of herself & and eight Small children" because he had not lived with them in the years since the war had ended. Like the state itself, Jane regarded William as a noncitizen rendered "politically dead" as a result of his Toryism, and, indeed, now doubly "dead" because convicted felons lost their civil personhood, even if they managed to keep their corporeal lives. With no husband to represent her and her children in the public sphere, Jane approached the state as a de facto widow, who, in her words, was now reduced to "relying on the humane & upright disposition of the General Assembly" for protection and help.[21]

When she chose to petition the legislature, Jane availed herself of a process, and a right, that had existed for centuries in the English-speaking world. From medieval times, people throughout the realm of England, regardless of their status, could petition the king and Parliament to request favor or assistance, or to seek redress of grievances. Petitioners appealed for relief from debts or taxes, settlement of private disputes, enactment of special laws, and an array of other actions. Following English practice, governors and legislators accepted petitions from residents of the colonies in America. State governments (and the federal Congress) continued to do so after independence. For most women, the right to petition was the only political right that they formally possessed under Anglo-American law.[22]

Wartime disruption and the comparatively egalitarian rhetoric and ideology of the revolutionary era changed the practice of petitioning, at least in the short term, in three key respects. First, petitions became more numerous, as citizens flooded their legislatures with requests for tax relief, soldiers' arrears, payment for military provisions, and resolution of other war-related issues; additional petitions came from loyalists or their families who hoped to recover confiscated property and from enslaved people seeking formal emancipation because they had been manumitted by their masters or had fought for the Whigs during the war (either on their own or as paid substitutes for white men) unlike the thousands of enslaved people who instead flocked to the king's standard to win their freedom.[23] Second, both proportionately and in terms of absolute numbers, women submitted more petitions to the legislature than they did during the colonial era because they found themselves confronting unprecedented war-related challenges. Finally, because petitioners were, by definition, supplicants seeking the favor of their superiors, some adapted the rhetoric of these highly ritualized appeals to better suit the political sensibilities of a revolutionary age. Some North Carolinians described their requests as "memorials," not "petitions," a subtle difference that connoted the sending of a message or even an instruction to their legislators rather than a plaintive "prayer" for help. The distinction between "petitions" and "memorials" was both ill-defined and evolving, but the more assertive tone of some of these documents seemingly reflected an increasingly democratic understanding of the relationship between legislators and their constituents in revolutionary America.[24]

The minutes of North Carolina's general assembly for the two-month session in 1785 during which Jane submitted her first petition illustrate these three trends. Between 1750 and 1776, North Carolina's colonial assembly received a total of 239 petitions, with female petitioners accounting for only 11 (or less than 5 percent) of that number. By comparison, in November and December 1785 alone, North Carolinians submitted 101 petitions or memorials to their state assembly, of which 9 (or 9 percent) came from female petitioners. In that 1785 session, 24 of the requests the legislature considered came from men, individually or in groups, who called themselves "memorialists." Those who submitted "memorials," and who likely saw themselves as equals or near-equals to the legislators who considered their requests, were mostly men bearing military or professional titles—such as Dr. or Esq.—or men in groups seeking civic improvements or public policy initiatives rather than a redressing of a personal grievance, such as the "sundry of the Inhabitants of the Town of Edenton" who asked the legislature to empower their town commissioners to "convey part of the Town common to the Trustees of Smith's Academy."[25]

During that 1785 session, the legislature considered requests from nine female petitioners, each of whom sought to neutralize or lessen the war's destructive impact on their respective families. Martha Dixon, the widow of a man who "died in Service to his Country in July 1782," requested and received a state pension to support herself and her children.

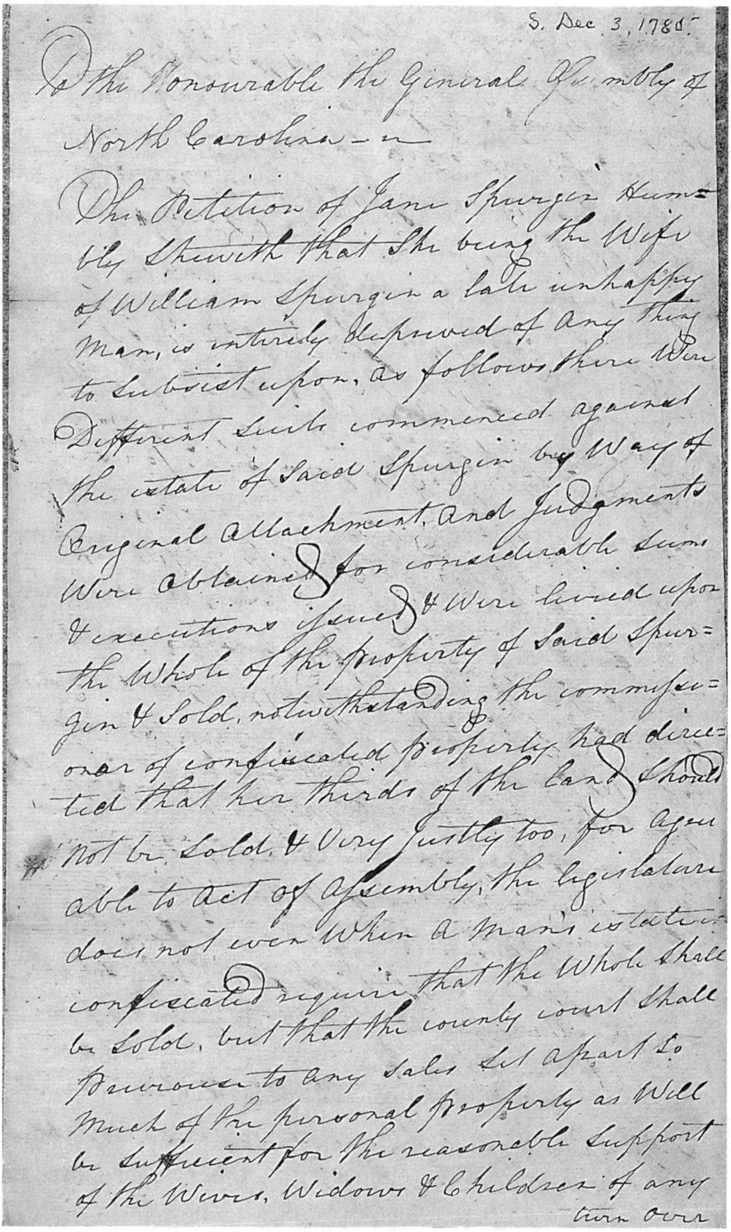

S. Dec 3, 1785

To the Honourable the General Assembly of
North Carolina — in

The Petition of Jane Spurgin Humb=
bly Sheweth that She being the Wife
of William Spurgin a late unhappy
Man, is entirely deprived of any thing
to Subsist upon, as follows there were
Different Suits commenced against
the estate of Said Spurgin by Way of
Original Attachment, and Judgments
were obtained for considerable Sums
& executions issued & were levied upon
the Whole of the property of Said Spur=
gin & Sold, notwithstanding the commissi=
oner of confiscated property had direc=
ted that her thirds of the land should
not be Sold, & Very Justly too, for agree
able to act of Assembly, the legislature
does not even When a man's estate is
confiscated require that the Whole shall
be Sold, but that the county court shall
Pruvious to any Sale Set apart So
Much of the personal property as Will
be Sufficient for the reasonable Support
of the Wives, Widows & Children of any
                                         turn over

FIGURE 5 | Jane Spurgin's first petition, December 1785. With this petition, Jane joined the growing numbers of Americans, including many women, who sought legislative assistance in resolving various war-related problems. Jane described William as both absent and "politically dead." She unsuccessfully requested the restoration of property that her family had lost during the Revolution. (Courtesy of the State Archives of North Carolina)

Margaret Balfour petitioned as the executrix of the estate of her brother, Colonel Andrew Balfour, who had been "murdered by the Tories," to collect wages owed to him for his past service as a member of the state assembly. The remaining seven, including Jane Spurgin and the widow and daughter of North Carolina's last colonial chief justice, who had left for New York as part of the first mass exodus of Tories in 1777, petitioned to recover property that had been lost during the war. In keeping with the common-law doctrine of coverture, none of these nine petitioners were married in the conventional sense. Two were single women, four were widows, and three—Mercy Bedford, Hannah Davis, and Jane Spurgin—were de facto widows of men who were, in Jane's words, "politically dead" as a result of their loyalism.[26]

Both during and after the war, the wives of Tories were instrumental in mitigating the impact of state appropriation of their families' property. Although most of these women presented themselves as weak and humbly apolitical, and thus dependent on the goodwill of the state in their husbands' absence, some sought to distance themselves from the misconduct of their spouses. In 1778, when Margaret Cotton of Anson County asked the legislators to verify her right to the dower portion of the estate of her husband, James, who was one of the state's most prominent Tories, she assured them that though he "imprudently took part with the enemies of America . . . she and her children have been hitherto conformable, and are willing to bind themselves by every tye to any rule that the Honorable . . . Legislature shall think proper to devise and require of them." Cotton, who was herself the member of a well-known loyalist family, assumed correctly that the legislators would never test the veracity of her statement by forcing her to swear an oath of allegiance to the state. Elizabeth Torrence of Dobbs County told a different sort of story when she attempted to reverse the sentence of banishment against her husband, Thomas, in 1783. Torrence attributed her spouse's misguided loyalty to the king to "the persuasion and instigation of the enemies of his country," portraying Thomas as a weak and "passive offender" whose pardon would be welcomed by his "his distressed . . . unhappy family," which included "seven helpless infants," while "not inconsistent with the policy and good government of the State."[27]

In her own first petition to the state legislature, Jane combined these approaches, both distancing herself from William and his "Trespasses during the late Warr" and painting a sympathetic picture of herself and her suffering children as being "entirely deprived of Any thing to Subsist upon" as a result of their ongoing financial and legal troubles. In fact, Jane overstated the size of her family, if not the severity of her financial woes, claiming that she alone was responsible for "the Maintenance of herself & eight Small children," though she had only four children under the age of twelve by 1785. Nevertheless, unlike the appeals submitted by many of her female contemporaries, Jane's petition was overall less an emotional appeal than a careful recounting of her current situation and an assertion of the state's self-imposed obligation to provide for, in her words, "the reasonable Support of the Wives, Widows & Children of any person whose estate is, or may be, confiscated."[28]

Submitting a petition was a collaborative effort, making it difficult to distinguish the petitioner's voice from those who offered advice and assistance in the process of composing and presenting the request. Like most petitioners, Jane certainly relied on a clerk or scribe to write the document that the legislators eventually read. We know this because she ultimately presented three petitions in all, each of which was written in a different hand—which meant that the writing was not her own—and which referenced her variously as "Jane," "Jean," or "Jennet." If Jane needed assistance articulating and explaining the particulars of her case, she may have turned to family and friends. She surely had the sympathy of many of her neighbors in Abbotts Creek, seventy-eight of whom publicly declared their support for her as cosigners of the second petition she submitted in 1788.[29] Yet whatever roles other people played in preparing Jane's petitions, her voice is nonetheless distinctive among women's petitions for its legalism and clarity, as well as for her growing exasperation at the state's apparent unwillingness to fulfill its self-proclaimed protective role.

In 1785, Jane began her first petition to the legislature by owning her ambiguous status as "the Wife of William Spurgin a late unhappy Man" before succinctly recounting her legal travails and their material consequences. She and her children were suffering, she asserted, because "Different Suits commenced against the estate of Said [William] Spurgin . . . And Judgments Were Obtained for considerable Sums & executions issued & Were levied upon the Whole of the Property . . . & Sold . . . for the purpose of Satisfying Some individuals Who had a Claim against her Husbands estate." Although she did not question William's status as a debtor, Jane forcefully argued that the liquidation of his property violated the confiscation statutes, which stipulated that the authorities would "Previous to any Sales Set apart so Much of the personal property as Will be Sufficient for the reasonable Support of the Wives, Widows & Children of any person Whose estate is, or may be confiscated & one third of the lands if Sufficient for their Support," boldly adding that they might also "at their discretion Assign the Whole of the land" to the offender's family.[30]

In Jane's view, whether the sales were undertaken to penalize William or to satisfy his creditors, the state's obligation to her and her children remained unchanged. Indeed, she somewhat audaciously invoked the most generous interpretation of the confiscation laws as they pertained to loyalists' dependents, asking for either "an indefeasible right to Seven hundred & four acres" at Abbotts Creek—in other words, all of William's land—or, barring that, "her thirds" of that property, as well as "a Negro fellow named Simon" whom William had also owned. Trusting the law, Jane concluded her petition with a conventional declaration of her reliance "on the humane & upright disposition of the General Assembly," adding, "Your Petitioner waits with Great expectation." She must have been both surprised and angry when the assembly's Committee on Proposition and Grievances rejected her petition without explanation or comment.[31]

Some months later, in the summer of 1786, as Jane likely planned her next move, a transaction that would have been of great interest to her came before the Rowan County court. In August 1786, the court certified that Catherine Sappenfield, the widow of Matthias Sappenfield—the Abbotts Creek loyalist who had been captured and imprisoned after the Battle of Moore's Creek Bridge, died in New York in 1781, and was posthumously attainted for high treason in North Carolina in 1782—had officially received title to "1/3 of his planta[tion] whereon the Widow then lived, as her Dower, agreeable to Law." Catherine's one-third dower portion of her husband's property was roughly 142 acres because the state claimed an additional 285 that had belonged to Matthias, which it sold to Edward Scarborough in November 1787. For Jane, Catherine Sappenfield's case was a compellingly concrete local example of how the authorities should have implemented the confiscation laws to punish only those individuals whose activities had been truly treasonous without unduly victimizing their innocent dependents.[32]

If knowledge of the relatively successful settlement of the Sappenfield estate did not impel Jane to redouble her efforts with the legislature, two other events likely did. After her initial failure to reverse the courts' rulings and the subsequent auction of the Abbotts Creek acreage, Jane and her children continued to live on the property, despite their being, by her own account, "threatened every day to be turned out." In October 1786, one of William's creditors, William Davis, received a grant for 100 acres that the county's recorder of deeds described as being "adjacent to that of William Spurgin," suggesting that Davis may have taken possession of at least part of the disputed acreage, leaving an anxious Jane to wait for the other claimants to seize additional portions of the property, including the house in which she lived. By this time, it is clear that Jane and William were living entirely separate lives. In November 1787, William became a father yet again, but Jane was not the mother of this new infant son. Aaron Spurgin was born in either North Carolina or nearby Virginia to Ann Bedsaul Ruddick, a married woman more than two decades younger than William, who had previously lived with her husband, Solomon, in the southern part of Montgomery County, on the Virginia side of North Carolina's northern border. The Bedsauls and the Ruddicks were among those Quaker families who had fled North Carolina and resettled in Virginia after the suppression of the Regulators in 1771. It is unclear whether their families were acquainted before the war, but it seems likely that William and Ann's relationship began while he was on the run and in hiding during the 1780s.[33]

Whatever else she felt about William's continual absence and eventual infidelity, Jane may well have been pleased to terminate her relationship with her husband, who was both a traitor and a horse thief in the eyes of the state and who had done little to make her life easier for more than a decade. Jane's second petition, which she submitted to the legislature in

November 1788, bristled with indignation and exasperation born of both her deteriorating circumstances and the conviction that she had suffered years of unfair treatment from men—at home and in the public realm— whom both law and custom deemed her patriarchs and protectors. Jane complained that state troops had "Continually harassed" her during the war, and she now sought payment for the "grain, Meat, and many other Articles" they had commandeered from her farm "without the least rec- ompense." In this second petition, she also reiterated her claim to her rightful widow's portion of William's property, which "was by Law allotted to her and had been laid off according to Law for the Subsistence of her and her Small Children" but which had been instead "Seized and lays under ejectment" rendering her and her children "worse Situated than a Widow and Orphants."[34]

Even as she recounted the "Callamities and hardships" she and her children endured, which she attributed mostly to William's "mistake and bad Conduct," Jane also took a more critical view of the state, this time demanding—rather than expecting—that the legislators act honorably toward her. Likely thinking of the comparatively happier fate of Catherine Sappenfield, she pointedly informed the legislators that "Other Women under the Same Circumstances are not treated in so hard a manner," adding, "nor can Your Petitioner believe it to be the meaning of the Law . . . to make the Wife and Children entirely miserable on account of the Husbands and fathers transgressions." Although she employed the conventionally subservient petitioner's rhetoric when she described her- self as "imploring [the] Mercy" of the legislators, Jane ended her petition by forcefully urging them to "give to her and [her children] Such releif as by Law originally intended."[35]

In 1788, Jane also collected signatures from seventy-eight men from Rowan County who supported her claims against the state. Although she must have deeply appreciated the willingness of these men to endorse her petition publicly, it is worth considering whether they supported her cause on its merits or because they hoped to prevent her and her children from becoming impoverished public charges. Whatever their motives, in offering their support, these men neither contrasted Jane's patriotism with her husband's Toryism nor restated the provisions of the confiscation laws. Instead, they simply appealed to the legislature to offer relief to a suffering woman and her family. "We the Subscribers do join with the aforesaid Jean Spurgin," they declared, "and pray that her distresses may be considered and Redress granted her and her Children."[36]

In garnering support for her petition, Jane drew on members of long-standing overlapping personal networks in and around the Abbotts Creek community. Church and family connections were especially important. Of the seventy-eight men who signed her petition, at least thirty were associated with the Abbotts Creek Baptist Church, where Jane and her family were longtime worshipers.[37]

Over the years, families within these Baptist circles had intermarried with the Spurgins and with each other. William Ledford, whose daughter Sarah was married to William Spurgin's brother Samuel, signed Jane's petition, as did Sarah's three brothers. Jane's brothers, James and Isaac Welborn, signed, and so did James's four sons, as well as five members of the Teague family, who had intermarried with both the Welborns and the Ledfords, and who had lived in Virginia near the Spurgins before moving to North Carolina. Those who endorsed Jane's petition also included her son-in-law Aquilla Jones and one of his brothers, along with Tilman Creadlebaugh, whose sister had married John Spurgin, Jane's oldest son. Four members of the Hinkle family signed Jane's petition, including Michael Hinkle, who had married Jane's oldest daughter, Rebecca. (Charles Hinkle, who had assisted Jane in 1778, died in 1783.) The three Klinert brothers who supported Jane's petition all married Hinkle women, but the Klinerts also had another connection to the Spurgins because William was one of two men who provided security to the local court when the brothers' father, Peter, received a license to operate a tavern in Rowan County in 1774. As all of these intricate and somewhat confusing interconnections suggest, Jane was able to call on a strong network of family and friends whose charitable impulse toward her and her children would have been amplified by their shared membership in the closely knit Abbotts Creek Baptist community.[38]

The support of these men was not politically motivated. While at least nine men who had been either Tory or disaffected nonjurors in 1778 signed Jane's petition, so, too, did some men who had fought on the American side during the recent war. William Ledford Jr. served three three-month stints in the local militia. Daniel Motsinger spent parts of 1780

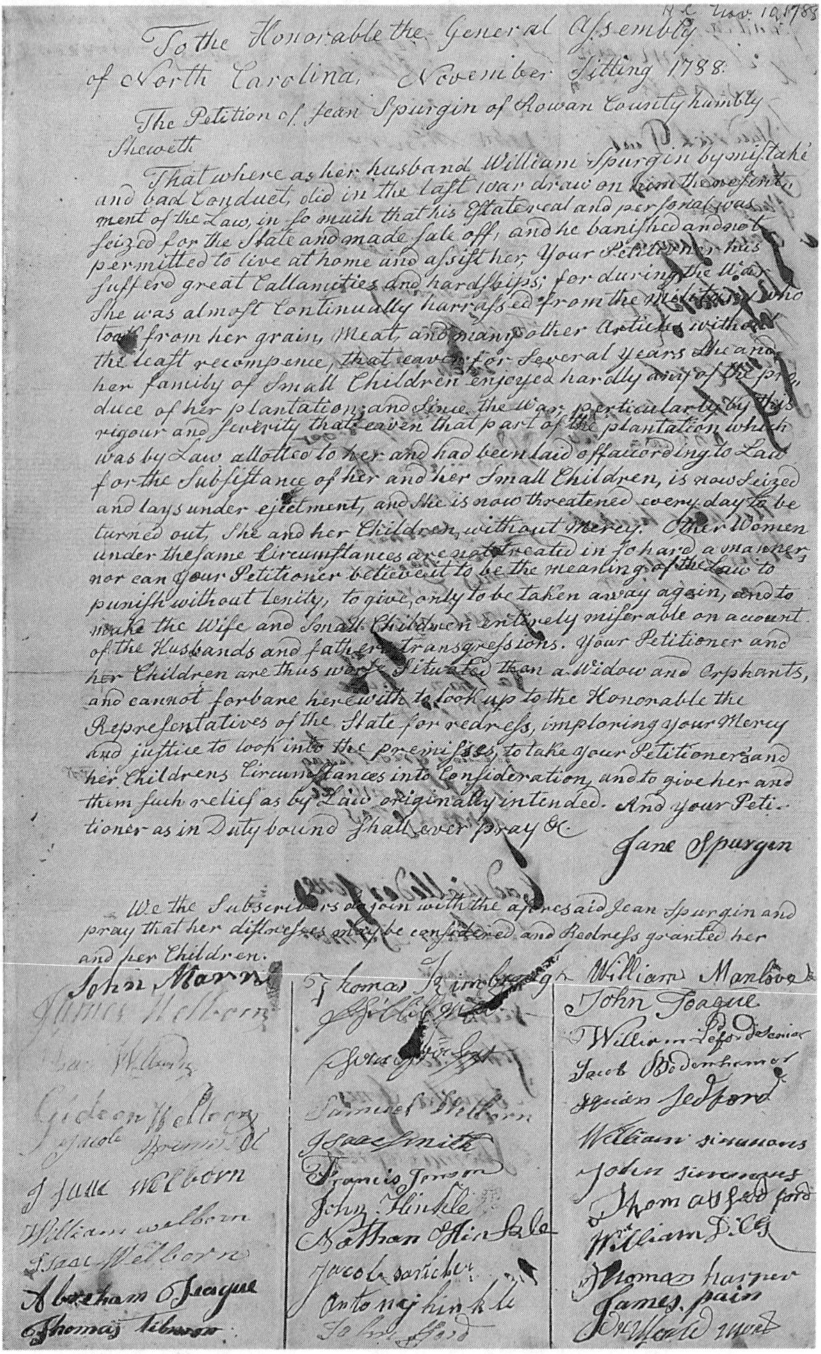
To the Honorable the General Assembly of North Carolina, November Sitting 1788.

The Petition of Jean Spurgin of Rowan County humbly Sheweth

That whereas her husband William Spurgin by mistake and bad Conduct, did in the last war draw on him the resentment of the Law, in so much that his Estate real and personal was seized for the State and made sale off, and he banished and not permitted to live at home and assist her, Your Petitioner has suffer'd great Callamities and hardships; for during the War She was almost Continually harrassed from the Military who took from her grain, Meat, and many other Articles without the least recompence, that eaven for Several years She and her family of Small Children enjoyed hardly any of the produce of her plantation, and Since the War, perticularly by this rigour and Severity that eaven that part of the plantation which was by Law allotted to her and had been laid off according to Law for the Subsistance of her and her Small Children, is now Seized and lays under ejectment, and She is now threatened every day to be turned out, She and her Children, without Mercy. Other Women under the same Circumstances are not treated in so hard a manner, nor can your Petitioner believe it to be the meaning of the Law to punish without Lenity, to give, only to be taken away again, and to make the Wife and Small Children entirely miserable on acount of the Husbands and fathers transgressions. Your Petitioner and her Children are thus worse Situated than a Widow and Orphants, and cannot forbare herewith to look up to the Honorable the Representatives of the State for redress, imploring your Mercy and justice to look into the premisses, to take your Petitioners and her Childrens Circumstances into Consideration, and to give her and them such relief as by Laid originally intended. And your Petitioner as in Duty bound Shall ever pray &c

Jane Spurgen

We the Subscribers do join with the aforesaid Jean Spurgin and pray that her distresses may be considered and Redress granted her and her Children.

William Manlove
John Teague
Jacob Bodenhamer
William Simmons
John Simmons
Thomas Stafford
Thomas Harper
James pain
Isaac Smith
Francis Jonson
John Hinkle
Nathan Hinkle
Antoney Hinkle
Abraham Teague

FIGURE 6 | Jane Spurgin's second petition, November 1788. In this second attempt to attain satisfaction from the legislature, Jane collected the signatures of seventy-eight men who supported her efforts. Jane's own signature appears on the right side of the page,

John avary
William bain
Joseph Wilson
Shudrick Dial
Samuel petty
Jacob wier
Joab Sprague
Richard Cox
John Cox
John Carol
John pirkens
John yonoley
Michael hinkel
Moses Smith
John Swim
Samuel Harper

John Ledford
Dannel Klinert
Loranee Klineit
John McEnory
James Anderson
Peter Clinard
Henry Klinert
Felix Motsinger
Jacob foe
woolwich Richerd
Jacob Motzginger
William Smith
Daniel Morkginger
John Sarichar
Adam harmon
James Evens
Isaac Sprague
Nathan pike
John fo X
Tilmon gridolbarg
William blair
John Mores
Cad Walleder jones
William Tilmon
Moses teague
Nicholess been
John Clonch
Aquila Jones
Thomas Jones

at the end of the body of the document, before the men's signatures. (Courtesy of the State Archives of North Carolina) and 1781 "employed in defending the lines and property of the Citizens of Rowan & the adjacent Counties against the depredations of the Tories who . . . were laying waste the Country & murdering its inhabitants" until he himself was wounded in an altercation with Tory militia. Nathan Hinkle enlisted in the Continental Army in his native Pennsylvania and spent three years fighting there and in New York and New Jersey before moving to Rowan County, where he married into the Ledford family. The vast majority of the seventy-eight signers, however, seem to have spent the war years quietly at home. Their desire to help Jane owed less to her spirited support for the Revolution than their desire to assist a distressed and potentially homeless neighbor, a woman whom many had known for years and who was now, seemingly through no fault of her own, left alone to care for a large and needy family.[39]

Despite this significant outpouring of sympathy and support from the men of her community, Jane's second petition was not successful. The assembly's Committee on Propositions and Grievances rejected her request for compensation for the supplies she advanced to the army because she did not present the necessary vouchers to prove the legitimacy of her claim. At the same time, however, the committee's members endorsed the passage of a law "Securing the Said Jean [*sic*] and all others in Similar circumstances the Lands so assigned them under the [confiscation] act." While this ruling appeared to be a significant victory, the full assembly neither responded to the advice of the committee nor acted on its recommendation.[40]

In November 1789, as Jane likely considered her very limited remaining options, North Carolina became the penultimate state to join the federal union by ratifying the constitution that had been drafted two years earlier in Philadelphia. Ratification came just in time to have the state included in the first federal census, in 1790, which listed "Jean Spurgin" as the head of a nine-person household that consisted of three males (likely her youngest sons) and six females (herself, her unmarried daughters, and two granddaughters whose parents, Rebecca Spurgin and Michael Hinkle, died in 1787 and 1790, respectively). Jane's oldest son, John, was missing from the Rowan County census because he was among those North Carolinians who had migrated west, hoping to establish a new state called Franklin in a distant part of North Carolina, which in 1790 instead became the eastern edge of the newly formed Tennessee Territory. ⸲ too, had Jane's estranged husband apparently left the area, though a William Spurgin was listed in the census. Although this William was likely Jane's second son, who was born in 1762 and married sometime before 1787, the census-takers erred in assigning his household a head count identical to Jane's.[41] Nevertheless, the inclusion of two Spurgin-headed households in the 1790 census shows that Jane and her family remained in their house at Abbotts Creek and that her case against the state to preserve her home had not reached its final resolution. To that end, she submitted her third and final petition to the legislature in 1791.

The Common Rights
of Other Citizens

WHEN WILLIAM SPURGIN and Ann Bedsaul Ruddick left with their young son, Aaron, they joined a wave of Americans who deserted their spouses, sometimes exchanging old partners for new ones, in postrevolutionary America. North Carolina's legislators, alarmed by the fact that so many "evil disposed persons, going from one part of our country to another, and into places where they are not known, do marry, having another husband or wife still living, to the utter destruction of the peace and happiness of families," enacted a statute in 1790 to address the problem. The law had three provisions. First, it reminded potential offenders that bigamy was, and would continue to be, a capital offense. Second, it permitted remarriage by "any person or persons whose husband or wife shall continually remain beyond sea for the space of seven years together, or to any person or persons whose husband or wife shall absent him or herself in any other manner for the space of seven years together, such person or persons not knowing his or her said husband or wife to be living within that time," in effect establishing the possibility of common-law divorce. Third, the law recognized other cases in which a marriage could become legally void, including by divorce "according to the mode established, or which hereafter shall be established by law." Although no one had ever received a legal divorce in North Carolina, the state's legislators had come to believe that divorce might be an option in the future and that minimizing the social and economic disorder caused by broken marriages was a matter of public policy.[1]

Postrevolutionary Americans were on the move. Although historians generally interpret postwar migration as evidence of a widespread pursuit of landownership and upward mobility, for some people geographic mobility promised a different sort of opportunity. Political choices either caused or facilitated the breakup of the Spurgins' marriage, while the disruptions of war created a space in which Jane and William—and Ann Ruddick and her husband, Solomon—could effectively end their marriage discreetly and without the usual social stigmas or legal or financial penalties. Moreover, given the peaceful return of Samuel Bryan and so many other banished Tories, it is worth considering whether financial and marital woes, even more than politics, impelled William to leave North Carolina after the war was over. There is no way to know for certain whether the Revolution was the main cause of the demise of the Spurgins' marriage or if its dissolution constituted liberation or loss from Jane's perspective. Nevertheless, their story, like their state's pragmatic legislation, shows that the Revolution that upended monarchy in America also could destabilize, and in some cases destroy, established domestic relationships and family hierarchies.

North Carolina families and communities were built on the mutually reinforcing foundations of patriarchy and white supremacy. The English common law enshrined the prerogatives of men over wives and children, and the slave codes established the near-absolute power of masters over the people they enslaved. The Revolution introduced no systemic changes to these arrangements: both patriarchy and slavery thrived in the postrevolutionary era, and neither white domestic dependents nor enslaved people categorically won new legal or civil rights. Nevertheless, the libertarian rhetoric of the Revolution and the disruptive experience of war destabilized both the patriarchal family and chattel slavery as institutions, at least in the short term. Throughout the war, African Americans took advantage of every opportunity to seize their freedom, and Black resistance persisted in the postrevolutionary era. Traditional family relationships, too, were challenged, as children defied their fathers—or moved away from home to begin their adult lives beyond the reach of their elders—and marriages strained and sometimes ended. While the Spurgins' marital woes produced no official documents that verified the disintegration of their decades-old union, other unhappy couples took the novel step of attempting to sever their conjugal bonds formally by seeking a legal divorce.[2]

Revolutionary ideals of liberty and autonomy encouraged at least some Americans to view the ability to end abusive or otherwise unhappy marriages as a republican right. In the early 1770s, lawyer Thomas Jefferson posited a "liberty to divorce," though even his political allies seemingly rejected this notion, and Jefferson's unhappily married client died before he could submit what would have been Virginia's first divorce petition for the legislature's consideration. Nevertheless, one North Carolina couple sought that same "liberty" when they asked the state assembly to end their marriage in 1787, explaining that they had wed as teenagers, stayed together for "three long years" until their "Reason approached the state of Maturity," and then lived separately for twelve years "deprived of all those blessings which arise from the happy Union of Kindred Souls." James and Mary Garret sought the liberty to escape from a marriage that they described as "the Source of all their Miseries and Misfortunes." In 1791, a South Carolina man used language that was even more pointedly reminiscent of the thirteen colonies' Declaration of Independence when he petitioned to sever the bonds of wedlock. "Since Marriage was instituted for the purpose of promoting the happiness of individuals and the good of society . . . when mutual wretchedness must be the consequence of their continuing connection," he asserted, that union "should be dissolved and . . . the parties should be left free to form such other domestic connections as to contribute to their felicity." All of these petitioners were unsuccessful, however, because, though divorce was theoretically possible in most states after independence, its purpose, as one historian has aptly noted, "was emphatically not to make both individuals happy, but to eliminate sources of social disorder."[3]

Enacted in 1785, Pennsylvania's divorce statute, the republic's first general divorce law, made the case for divorce less on the basis of liberty than as a means for preserving a "well regulated" social order. "Whereas it is the design of marriage, and the wish of parties entering into that state that it should continue during their joint lives," the law's preamble stated, "yet where the one party is under natural or legal incapacities of faithfully discharging the matrimonial vow, or is guilty of acts and deeds inconsistent with the nature thereof, the laws of every well regulated society ought to give relief to the innocent and injured person." Pennsylvania's divorce law established the business of deciding when and if a marriage might be terminated as a function of the state, making the process (if not always the desired outcome) more accessible by delegating divorce cases to the courts, which convened comparatively frequently across the state, instead of the legislature. With the sole exception of South Carolina, where no divorce was granted until after the Civil War, other states gradually enacted comparable divorce laws of their own, with North Carolina doing so in 1814.[4]

Before the adoption of these general divorce statutes, people used various informal and largely unregulated ways of ending their marriages, but those who sought the formal legal dissolution of marital unions petitioned their state legislatures, which saw dramatic increases in such requests during the revolutionary era. North Carolina's legislature received only one divorce petition during the entire colonial period (in 1766), but the state assembly considered fourteen such requests between 1779 and 1800, of which they granted only one, in 1794. Individual petitions for divorce continued to increase in the coming years, with twenty-two submitted in 1813 alone—the year before the enactment of the state's divorce law—though only four of these petitions were successful. Despite its rarity, divorce became a legitimate possibility in postrevolutionary North Carolina, though dissolving an abusive or dysfunctional marriage was by no means a simple process, and the overwhelming majority of attempts to do so failed. That remained true even after the state enacted its general divorce statute, which codified potentially admissible grounds for divorce: chiefly adultery or impotence but also, in some cases, abandonment or cruelty. In response to growing demand and the resulting increase in the legislators' workload, the law also followed the national trend of transferring jurisdiction in divorce cases from the legislature to the courts, though the statute mandated that the state assembly confirm any divorce a court granted before its decree would be final.[5]

Notwithstanding the steep odds against obtaining a divorce, the war gave rise to circumstances that for some made it worth trying. The experience of a long conflict, fought by thousands of soldiers moving across huge expanses of territory, undermined some existing marriages and resulted in new ones that were doomed from their inception. One of the earliest divorce petitions that came before Virginia's state assembly—and the very first submitted by a woman—came in 1786 from Susannah Wersley, whose predicament was a direct result of the war's intrusion into her Hanover County community. In early 1781, a wounded Continental soldier from North Carolina was convalescing in her father's house when he "paid his addresses" to Susannah, whom he married—"activated by a principle of convenience and deception alone," she later surmised—and then promptly abandoned her. Over the next five years, Wersley heard that her estranged husband had been in North Carolina and then in Boston. By the time she sought a divorce in 1786, she had concluded that she would never see him again. The legislature nevertheless rejected Wersley's petition, perhaps because after her husband fled, she continued to live with her parents and, at least equally important, she had no dependent children. As a result, Susannah Wersley was unlikely to become either a source of disorder or a financial burden to her community.[6]

Although women were more likely than men to seek divorces on the grounds of desertion, husbands also suffered wartime abandonment born of infidelity. In his successful effort to secure a divorce, James Martin of Pennsylvania complained that his wife, Elizabeth, had "resorted among the British soldiers," when they occupied Philadelphia in 1778, taking "one Serjeant Havell . . . into his [Martin's] . . . house and bed, and cohabited" with him. When the British left the city, Elizabeth Martin departed with them, posing as Havell's wife and absconding with much of her husband's "effects," while leaving him to pay her debts. When North Carolinian Ezra Bostick returned home to Anson County after being "called forth in defence of his Country" in 1781, he found that his wife, Sarah, had sold his property, abandoned their children, and run away with another local man, Timothy Haney, with whom she had five additional children before Ezra petitioned to have their marriage dissolved in 1791. And in 1796, Solomon Ruddick petitioned Virginia's state assembly, seeking to divorce his wife, Ann, who had taken up with William Spurgin. According to Solomon, Ann had "eloped" with William six years earlier, abandoning her family and leaving him and their five "small and helpless" children in a "Deplorable and Distrest Situation."[7]

In his petition, Solomon Ruddick invoked morality and prevailing gender conventions, not politics, in hopes of swaying the lawmakers who assessed the merits of his request. Like approximately one-fifth of all American Quakers, Ruddick had eventually abandoned the pacifist stance of the Society of Friends and sided with the Whigs during the Revolution. In 1779, a Baptist named Flower Smith formed a militia unit to fight the Tories in and around the Ruddicks' Chestnut Creek neighborhood. Under pressure to support the war effort and aware of the approaching British forces, Solomon Ruddick and at least thirty-four other members of the local Quaker meeting joined Smith's militia company, which fought in both Virginia and North Carolina in 1781, though it is unclear whether Ruddick himself actively participated in any battles. In seeking his divorce, it would have been easy for Solomon to note his own patriotism and to discredit Ann by revealing that she had left him for a reviled Tory, but he did not. By choosing that strategy, Solomon would have implicitly advanced the potentially distasteful idea that Ann made an independent and consequential political decision—and a reprehensible one at that. Acknowledging Ann's status as an unruly political actor would have cast doubt on his own fitness and probity as both a husband and a citizen. Solomon chose a seemingly safer approach, stressing Ann's lack of womanly virtue and her resulting shortcomings as a wife and mother. By contrast, he described himself as "a Friend to Virtue and Enemy to Vice" and appealed to the "Justice [and] Magnanimity" of the legislature to end his twelve-year marriage to a woman who, he claimed, had been "abandoned by Virtue & Divested of all Conjugal affection and Matrimonial Tenderness." Although the legislators deemed his petition "Reasonable," they never enacted the legislation that would have dissolved his union with Ann, who was by then residing with William in Canada.[8]

Some petitioners did cite politics either as a pretext or a justification to bolster their arguments in favor of obtaining a divorce. Although on occasion male petitioners described their estranged wives as having consorted (socially or sexually) with enemy soldiers, it was more common for female petitioners to mention their husbands' political offenses, especially if they sought divorces when the war was still raging and when Whig legislators were understandably more embittered toward their British and Tory foes. At the same time, some marriages survived political differences that were seemingly unreconcilable. Benjamin Almy was a Rhode Island state official and a Continental Army officer; his wife, Mary, was a committed loyalist who spent the war years in British-occupied Newport, where she may have hosted a Tory spy ring. The couple reunited and continued to live together after the war was over. When Mary died in 1808, Benjamin was "overwhelmed with sorrow," according to her obituary.[9]

Divorce petitions from New Hampshire, a small state with complete records, illustrate the increasing demand for divorce and the changing rationales for the dissolution of marriages in the colonial and revolutionary eras. Between 1681 and 1765, New Hampshire's legislators received a total of six divorces petitions, and eight more residents of the province sought to end their marriages between 1766 and 1775. In the following decade, which more or less coincided with the war, however, twenty-three New Hampshirites requested divorces, including thirteen women, and the legislators granted eight of those women's petitions. At least four of the eight women who obtained divorces in New Hampshire between 1775 and 1784 claimed that their husbands had—in the words of petitioner Rebekah Davis—"voluntarily joined the Enemies of America," either by enlisting in the British army or navy or, in one case, by fleeing to British-occupied New York. Significantly, none of these four female petitioners described themselves as patriots or as being in any way politically engaged or motivated, though their continued presence in New Hampshire signaled at least a tacit acceptance of the new regime and their dependence on the state in their husbands' absence, much as Jane Spurgin had appealed to the North Carolina legislature for protection and support in her first petition. Equally significant, however, was the fact that at least two of these four New Hampshire women had been unhappily married, by their own accounts, for years before the war, making their husbands' Toryism more a convenient justification for divorce than the root cause of their estrangement from their absent spouses.[10]

Although divorce petitions yield telling insights into how the Revolution disrupted marriages—or, in some cases, provided an opportunity to end unions that were already strained or ruptured—relying on these documents alone would severely undercount the number of marriages that dissolved after the war or even as a result of it. Some couples presumably went their separate ways amicably, leaving no paper trail to document their change in domestic arrangements. Some women whose husbands abandoned them, and who managed to acquire property or earn wages to support themselves in their absence, petitioned the legislature for release from the strictures of coverture and to be granted, in the words of one petitioner, "the Privilege of enjoying the fruits of my Labour and [to] Secure my Smal Estate . . . free from any and all Claims of my dissipating husband." And, of course, some wives of absent loyalists, including Jane Spurgin, petitioned not for divorce but rather to recover a share of their family's confiscated property, fully aware that their marriages were effectively over.[11]

In her third and final petition, composed in December 1791 and presented to the legislature a month later, Jane again sought compensation from North Carolina's state government for losses she and her family incurred during the recent war. This time, however, her approach changed in two critical respects. First, in addition to disparaging William's political choices, she presented herself as a bona fide separate political actor, distinct from her Tory husband in both belief and conduct. Second, though Jane still played the gender card—noting that she was old, infirm, and "had six Children to provide for"—she now primarily stated her claim to compensation as a right to property, which she construed as an essential right, one that had been at the heart of colonists' quest for independence from Great Britain and remained central to Americans' understanding of citizenship in the postrevolutionary era.

Jane began her petition by reiterating her story, informing the legislators that "during the late war She furnished the regular Troops and Militia of this State with Provisions and Forriage some part of which, the officers that took it gave her certificates for," though more often the soldiers simply confiscated goods from her farm "owing to her husbands being disaffected to the government and owing to the same reason, the vouchers She did obtain would not be received and audited by the auditors of Salisbury District to whom they were presented for that Purpose." In other words, Jane asserted that because she had the "misfortune to be married to a man who was Enemical to the revolution[,] . . . an evil that was not in her power to remedy," the state had doubly wronged her, first by allowing its soldiers to seize her property and then by refusing to compensate her for her losses, including those for which she had vouchers to prove what the government owed her. She also appended to her petition an affidavit, which she swore before a Rowan County magistrate, to underscore the validity of her claim. The state's refusal to repay this debt was especially unfair, Jane argued, because she had "always behaved herself as a good Citizen and well attached to the government." In this petition, therefore, Jane asserted—unambiguously and more forcefully than any other North Carolina woman during this period—a political identity and a pattern of public conduct that was distinct from and, indeed, emphatically opposed to that of her husband.[12]

Describing herself as a "Citizen" was one of three striking rhetorical flourishes that distinguished this third petition from its predecessors. Another was Jane's irate observation that she thought "it extreamly hard to be deprived of the Common rights of other Citizens." The third was her decision to call herself not a petitioner but a "memorialist," adopting the more egalitarian descriptor increasingly used by men, though not by women, in the postrevolutionary era.[13]

What did Jane mean when she called herself a "Citizen"? Although modern Americans use that term mostly to denote a legal status synonymous with nationality—to refer, for example, to which country's passport a person carries—to eighteenth-century Americans the principal definition of a "citizen" was a person who was a member of the political community and as such possessed certain obligations and rights. Even so, there were at least two competing popular understandings of the notion of citizenship. On the one hand, there was the republican ideal, which emphasized disinterested service—especially military service—to the polity. Although Jane may have cautiously alluded to that ideal when she mentioned her own allegiance to and sacrifices for the patriot cause, the appeal of selflessness as a precondition for citizenship had waned even before the war was over. On the other hand, postrevolutionary

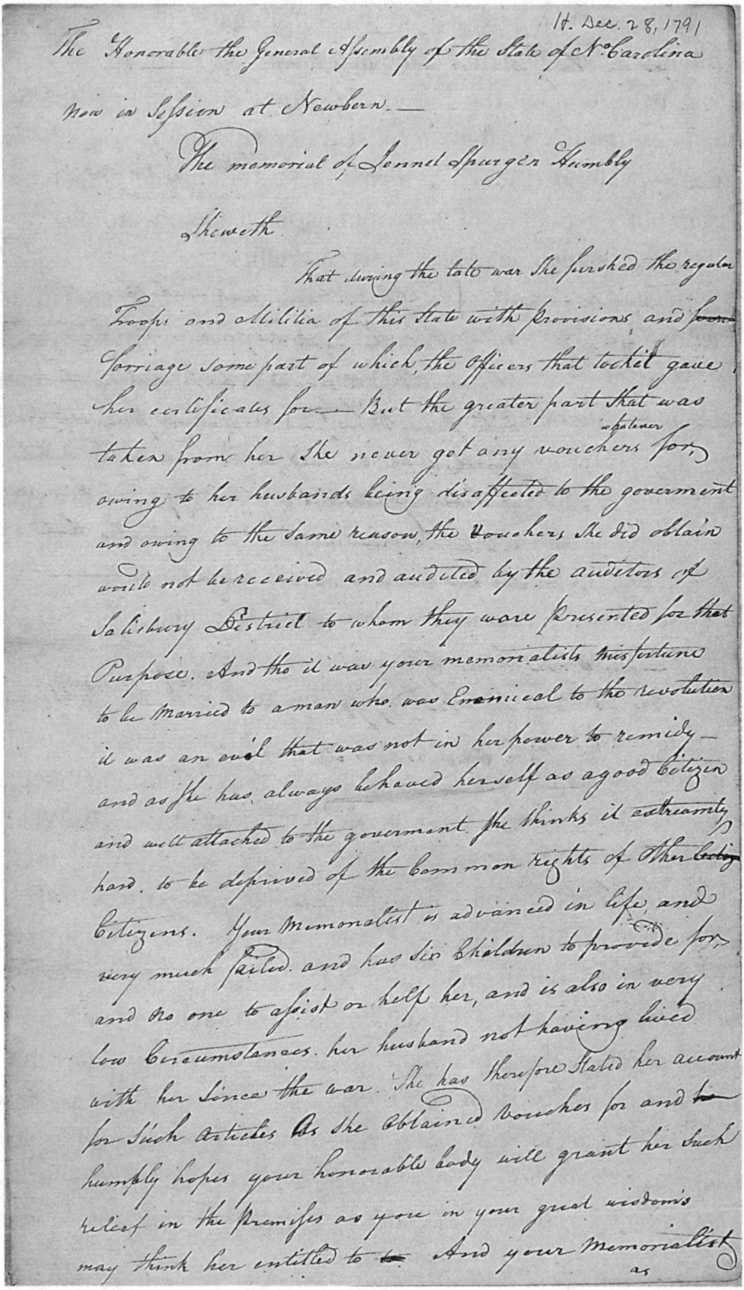

The Honorable the General Assembly of the State of No. Carolina

now in Session at Newbern.—

The memorial of Jennel Spurgen Humbly

Sheweth.

That during the late war She furnished the regular Troops and Militia of this state with provisions and Carriage some part of which, the Officers that took it gave her certificates for — But the greater part that was taken from her She never got any vouchers for whatever, owing to her husbands being disaffected to the government and owing to the same reason, the vouchers She did obtain would not be received and audited by the auditors of Salisbury District to whom they were presented for that Purpose. And tho it was your memorialists misfortune to be married to a man who was Enimical to the revolution it was an evil that was not in her power to remidy — and as she has always behaved herself as a good citizen and well attached to the government, she thinks it extreamly hard. to be deprived of the common rights of other body Citizens. Your Memorialist is advanced in life, and very much failed. and has six children to provide for, and no one to assist or help her, and is also in very low Circumstances. her husband not having lived with her since the war. She has therefore Stated her account for such articles as she obtained vouchers for and humbly hopes your honorable body will grant her such releef in the premises as you in your great wisdoms may think her entitled to — And your Memorialist as

FIGURE 7 | Jane Spurgin's third petition, December 1791. In this final petition—which she called a "memorial"—an exasperated Jane took the unusual step of asserting her claim to "the Common rights of other Citizens." No one commented on the boldness of her rhetoric. (Courtesy of the State Archives of North Carolina)

Americans' more explicitly legal or constitutional understanding of citizenship was at best ill-defined and in a state of flux. The newly adopted federal constitution left the matter of defining citizenship in the hands of the states, though most state constitutions did not include the word "citizens"—preferring alternate terms such as "persons," "inhabitants," or "residents"—and none of these foundational documents clearly enumerated all of the people's obligations and rights.[14]

Significantly, the authors of North Carolina's first state constitution did use the word "citizen," but they did so only once, in Article XL, which stated "That every foreigner, who comes to settle in this State having first taken an oath of allegiance to the same, may purchase, or, by other means, acquire, hold, and transfer land, or other real estate; and after one year's residence, shall be deemed a free citizen." By choosing to enshrine this common-law precedent in their constitution, North Carolina's Whig leaders defined property ownership as the preeminent mark of inclusion in the state's political community. This same logic guided the authors of New Jersey's first state constitution, who declared that "all inhabitants," regardless of gender or race, "of full age, who are worth fifty pounds proclamation money, clear estate in the same," would have the right to vote.[15]

It is noteworthy that Jane, too, framed her own claim to citizenship in terms of the right to own and protect her family's property. Whereas elite and educated women in the salons of Philadelphia might cite their intellectual accomplishments and informed civic engagement as grounds for their membership in the polity, Jane based her case for inclusion on a more traditional understanding of citizenship as deriving from one's material stake in society. If the state considered Jane a widow, her property rights were unassailable, according to both the common law and the statutes that set aside a dower portion of a Tory's property for a wife who remained in North Carolina. Recovering debts and reclaiming her dower portion was a "common right" enjoyed by other "citizens" who were the real or fictive widows of banished Tories, women such as Catherine Sappenfield, her Abbotts Creek neighbor.[16]

Just as the Revolution gave rise to some early and powerful critiques of slavery, so, too, did it occasion the first serious consideration of the issue of women's rights. Because they envisioned the sexes as playing dissimilar roles both in the family and in society, however, even those Americans who conceded that women were equal to men in terms of their status or significance saw the sexes as fundamentally different and therefore possessing different sorts of rights. Men's most important and widely celebrated rights were political—voting, officeholding, jury service—whereas women's were not. "Put simply," one historian has argued, "men's rights involved liberties that allowed choices, while women's rights consisted of benefits that imposed duties." Those duties were first and foremost domestic and familial. Honorable women were duty bound to be virtuous wives and mothers, in return for which they would receive the benefits of men's respect, protection, and material support. In this case, the benefit Jane requested derived from her long-standing effort to fulfill her obligation to act as steward of the family land to safeguard her children's interests in both the short and longer term. Above and beyond whatever legally sanctioned dower or other property rights she might recoup, these gender-based benefits were among the "Common rights" that Jane sought in her third and final petition.[17]

This last encounter with state authorities was ultimately more satisfying, though not because of Jane's bold assertion of citizenship and rights. From the state's avowed commitment to protecting widows and orphans to her male neighbors' expression of support for her petitions, Jane's gender, not her politics, was always the most promising point in her favor, and though the politicized rhetoric of her third petition was unique, no one commented on it at the time. Statutes that recognized married women's property rights were decades away throughout the United States, and when nineteenth-century legislators adopted these laws, they were often motivated less by the desire to empower wives than to preserve the estates of indebted men—and, by extension, the patrimony of their sons—by transferring property to women to shield it from men's creditors. Perhaps a higher court had, indeed, reversed the judgments against William, though no surviving records show that to have been the case. A far more likely scenario was that state officials simply returned a portion of William's lost property to Jane so that she could pass the acreage on to one or more of her many landless sons. Like the married women's property laws that eventually provided blanket protection to the heirs of insolvent planters by vesting property temporarily in the hands of wives and mothers, the state's action in this case enabled a younger generation of Spurgin men to become property-owning "citizens" and members of the polity.[18]

Although she was no protofeminist, Jane clearly resented legal customs and social conventions that penalized good women who were married to bad or imprudent men. In that sense, the state's morphing of women who had lost their husbands to politics, not death, from wives to fictive widows was entirely appropriate. Jane became indignant only when the state refused to afford her the rights assured to her by its own statutes, the rights that widows customarily enjoyed under the English common law, and other benefits that constituted the putative rights of women in postrevolutionary America.

Although it seems unlikely that Jane's assertiveness impelled state legislators to recognize the validity of her claims, her memorial was nonetheless significant because few women of her era presented themselves so plainly as rights-bearing citizens, at least in public. It is true that Mary Willing Byrd, a widowed Virginia plantation mistress, employed the rhetoric of the imperial crisis and the rights of citizens when she protested being forced to pay taxes imposed by a state legislature in which she had no representation, and that Abigail Adams famously pressed her husband John to "remember the ladies" and be mindful of men's potential for tyranny when Congress debated the nature of America's new republican government. These elite women, however, took their stands in private letters, not public forums. By contrast, Jane dictated her grievances to a male clerk, and her petition was read aloud, in public, to the prominent men who constituted the membership of North Carolina's most powerful political institution, the state legislature.[19]

In this third petition, for reasons that are unclear, Jane did not reiterate her claim to the dower portion of William's property, which surely counted as one of the "Common rights" of female citizens, and the legislature once again rejected her request for compensation. The Committee on Propositions and Grievances, which reviewed her current requests, conceded that Jane, indeed, had presented vouchers to verify some of the transactions for which she sought reimbursement, but they also determined that she had no documentation to prove "the greater part" of what she believed the state owed her. More important still was the fact that the legislature had delegated the responsibility for settling all war-related accounts to district-level boards of auditors, and that the legislators proved unwilling to reverse the decision made by those lower-level authorities. Because the state-appointed auditors for the Salisbury District were charged with deciding such cases, the committee concluded, approving Jane's expenses was "improper for their present decision . . . as the same account has been exhibited to the auditors . . . who refused to grant them, owing in all probability to the want of proper Vouchers."[20]

Several months after the legislators considered her petition, however, the state land office issued a grant, in Jane's own name, for 400 acres in Abbotts Creek, and her deed to that land was officially recorded in the Rowan County records. Although those records are incomplete, it seems likely that a recent court decision caused the state to intervene finally to address Jane's ongoing efforts to prevent the loss of her family's home, which was by far her most important grievance. On 10 May 1792, Charles Bruce, who had purchased the Spurgins' property at auction a decade earlier, won a lawsuit against Jane, who still occupied the land, in the Rowan County court. The court issued an order of ejectment against Jane, who planned to appeal that ruling to a higher court. At that point, the state stepped in and verified her title to 400 acres in Abbotts Creek, while Bruce retained the remainder of the property, which was adjacent to Jane's.[21]

Whatever satisfaction Jane received from this outcome, her hard-won victory did not negate all the material losses that the war inflicted on her and her family. She never received payment for the goods she supplied to the state's soldiers; though the 400 acres she received was more than her widow's third of William's property and the state's grant included the house where she and her family had resided for decades, the Spurgins had possessed nearly twice that amount of land before the war, and county deed books refer to several tracts as "formerly belonging to" William that were finally liquidated to satisfy creditors in the postwar era. Perhaps even more objectionable was the fact that Jane had to pay fees to register her title to her newly granted acreage. The county deed book shows that she paid fifty shillings per hundred acres to register her tract "on Abbotts Creek adj[acent to] John Motzinger, Barny Wire, and [formerly] William Spurgin."[22]

This land title effectively dissolved the economic ties between Jane and William, though they remained legally bound as husband and wife. There is no evidence to suggest that either she or William ever sought a formal dissolution of their marriage. William procured a de facto divorce by moving with Ann to Canada. But why did Jane not divorce William? Did Jane know about William's relationship with Ann? If not, was her decision to stay in Rowan County when William left mainly a determined effort to reclaim part of his estate for their children, a strategy that was fairly common among dispossessed loyalist families?

If Jane knew about William and Ann, she also might have known about the 1790 law that would have effectively ended her marriage seven years after William's departure, and she also may have known that she was unlikely to receive a formal divorce from North Carolina's legislators, who had not granted one to date. Even if Jane was unaware of the extremely daunting odds against her obtaining a legal divorce in North Carolina, she likely did know that even a successful divorce petition did not typically confer the right to remarry, and that women who requested divorces mostly did so primarily to shield any property they had—or would acquire—from the claims of their estranged spouses. At least with regard to the family's house and its surrounding acreage, the state's land grant to Jane, in her own name, in 1792, solved that potential problem.

By then, despite years of frustration and failure, several factors increased the likelihood that Jane's efforts to attain security for herself and for her children finally would be successful. Perhaps most important was the legislative committee's pronouncement, in response to Jane's second petition in 1788, that she and other real or fictive widows of loyalist men should receive dower portions of their husbands' confiscated property as specified in the state's anti-Tory laws, a matter that the full assembly left unresolved by never directly addressing the committee's recommendation, either as it pertained to Jane specifically or to dispossessed women generally. Jane's deteriorating circumstances may have been another contributing factor. By 1792, she was fifty-six years old and, as she informed the legislators, "had no one to assist or help her," and she described herself as "being in very low Circumstances her husband not having lived with her Since the war." In addition, as the legislators from Rowan County likely knew, by 1792 William had left the state, so there was absolutely no possibility of his eventually reclaiming his role as head of (and chief breadwinner for) the Spurgin household.

At the same time, settling Jane's case also constituted part of the state's more general agenda of resolving outstanding claims and issues from the revolutionary years, particularly those involving loyalists and their families. The final sales of confiscated property in North Carolina occurred shortly after the legislature enacted the last laws pertaining to the loyalists in 1784 and 1787, which respectively mandated the sale of their real and personal property. During this same period, however, in response to petitions from loyalist men or their wives, the state legislature also passed numerous private bills permitting individual Tories to return to their prewar homes and, in some cases, to reclaim all or part of their lost property, either for themselves or for their children. Jane's memorial appears to have been the last individual request that the legislators received either from a loyalist or from a member of a loyalist's family seeking to resolve war-related issues, though the courts continued to hear cases arising from the confiscation statutes, with at least one case remaining unresolved at the turn of the new century.[23]

So, too, did the British government move to settle its postwar accounts with loyalist exiles in London and elsewhere. Beginning in 1783, thousands of loyalists submitted their applications to the Loyalist Claims Commission in the hope of recouping at least a portion of the value of their lost American property. Although the commission's original rules required claimants to apply for compensation by March 1784, Parliament later extended that deadline to 1786. The resolution of outstanding claims continued into the late 1780s, with the commission presenting its final report in 1789. William Spurgin never submitted an application to the Loyalist Claims Commission in London, though he did join the diaspora of dispossessed Tories who resettled in Britain, the British West Indies, Nova Scotia, India, and virtually every other corner of Britain's still extensive empire.[24]

By September 1792, William was in Upper Canada (present-day Ontario), where he petitioned the newly arrived royal governor, John Graves Simcoe, informing him that he had lost all his property as a result of his loyalism, that the British government still had not repaid him for horses and provisions he provided to Cornwallis's army in North Carolina, and that he had "nothing to Subsist upon" now that he was in Canada. William also explained that his "famuley"—by whom he meant Ann and their now-five-year-old son, Aaron—were stranded in Pennsylvania and that he lacked the necessary funds to finance the remainder of their journey north. William ended his petition by gently inquiring "Wheater there Could be Any Assistance Alowed to poor People at ye furst Settling heare As I And A maney Others Are Reduced So Lowe I Cant tell how we Could Rase Sum [Small] Crop" to feed themselves. Although Simcoe's response to William's petition is not extant, it is clear that Ann arrived in Canada some months later, and her and William's second child, Samuel, was born there in February 1794. Two daughters followed in 1795 and 1799.[25]

William apparently severed ties completely with his family in North Carolina. When he wrote his will in Charlotteville, Upper Canada, in 1806, he did not mention Jane, and he bequeathed only a token "five Shillings Starling money of Great Britan" to each of his American children, whom he listed by name, unaware that three of them—John, Elizabeth, and William—had died since his departure. In his will, William also stipulated that his North Carolina offspring should equally share whatever "property Rail and personal Lying and Being . . . in Roan County Recovered or to be Recovered Thereafter," though, perhaps also unbeknownst to him, he now had no claim whatsoever to that property, ownership of which had been transferred to either his creditors or to Jane.[26]

William was one of thousands of so-called late loyalists, who were residents of the United States who flocked to Upper Canada after 1790 in response to Simcoe's offer of cheap land and low taxes. Largely as a result of this migration, the population of Upper Canada grew from fourteen thousand in 1791 to seventy thousand by 1811. Unlike the first loyalist émigrés who became exiles in Canada during and immediately after the war, most of these settlers who came later sought economic opportunity, and, unlike William, they had no true allegiance to the British Empire. As William emphasized repeatedly in his correspondence with Simcoe, however, his own loyalty was steadfast, and his prior service to king and empire entitled him to more than the basic land grant of 200 acres, at a nominal cost of only six pence per acre—much less than the going rate in Ohio or upstate New York—that the governor offered to all comers in the hope of increasing the population and productivity of the king's remaining dominions in North America.[27]

Although it took six years, and four petitions, for William to get what he deemed appropriate compensation for "his former Surcomstances and Sacrifices done to His Majestey and for his Armeys . . . during ye Late Rebellious War," Simcoe's government eventually granted him 1,200 acres, free of charge, in a part of Norfolk County on the north shore of Lake Erie known as the Long Point settlement. The order issued to the surveyor general to allot and record William's land grant was the first official document in which he was called "Colonel Spurgen," a rank bestowed on him either by Cornwallis during the war or later by imperial authorities in Canada. William planned to build a distillery and a gristmill on his new property, part of which was situated on a "fine Spring of Water." Although these tracts needed to be cleared and improved, his Canadian landholdings were nearly twice what he had owned in North Carolina.[28]

Written in his own hand with his own idiosyncratic spelling, William's communications to Simcoe revealed a political worldview that was markedly different from Jane's. Jane used increasingly demanding language when she addressed North Carolina's state legislature, politely but forcefully seeking satisfaction as a "Citizen" who legitimately claimed certain "rights." By contrast, William was consistently, even obsequiously, deferential when he addressed the Canadian governor. In 1796, four years after he arrived in Upper Canada and after he had told Simcoe on multiple occasions of his loyalty to the king and his military service in the recent war, William still was "humbly beg[ging] that your Exolencey would take the Whole matter of his Grevances Under your Wise and good Consideration" and "imploar[ing] and pray[ing] ye Governers Gratious goodness to alow me What Land he thinks right to do." This rhetoric of abject dependence had some basis in reality insofar as William and his new family were both homeless and impoverished when they arrived in Upper Canada and therefore truly dependent on the largesse of the king's government. At the same time, however, William's petitions also conveyed a respect for hierarchy and a near-reverence for the prerogative that Simcoe wielded by virtue of his status as the king's representative in North America. William still very much embraced the monarchical political culture that most Americans—including his estranged wife—discarded when they declared independence and constructed republican governments that derived their sovereignty from the people.[29]

William's Canadian sons apparently did not share this unshakeable attachment to the monarchy or to a future in the king's dominion of Upper Canada. When he made his will shortly before his death in 1806, William divided his Canadian landholdings equally among the four children of his second family, while reserving the tract in Charlotteville, where he and his family resided, along with his personal property, for his "Loving wife" Ann. Although both of William and Ann's daughters married sons of loyalist settlers and spent the rest of their lives in Canada, their two sons moved to Indiana sometime after 1820, and Ann went with them. She died in Jackson County, in southeastern Indiana, sometime between 1835 and 1838.[30]

Just as North Carolina's backcountry attracted land-hungry farmers in the 1750s, Indiana and other parts of the region that Americans called the Northwest Territory (or later the Old Northwest) became magnets for white settlers in the postrevolutionary decades. The new federal government aggressively promoted the westward expansion of white settlement and agriculture as a means of establishing control of this territory, which the Treaty of Paris recognized as belonging to the United States though it was still claimed (and occupied) by Native Americans. Although Michigan, not Indiana, was the main destination for Canadian farmers seeking cheap land and longer growing seasons, many people from North Carolina and Virginia settled in southeastern Indiana after 1800. In 1810, the Indiana Territory had a white population of 23,890. By 1816, the territory had become a state with a reported white population in 1820 of 145,758, a number that included a strong contingent from the Spurgins' extended family.[31]

In 1799, Ann Bedsaul Ruddick Spurgin's estranged husband, Solomon, having failed in his attempt to secure a divorce from the Virginia assembly, gave his power of attorney to his friend Joshua Hanks and prepared to leave the state. According to the Ruddick family history, by 1797 Solomon had "married a woman by the name of Amy," which may have been true, given that Virginia, like North Carolina, had enacted a post-revolutionary law that exempted anyone whose spouse had been absent from the United States for more than seven years from prosecution for bigamy. Ann left for Canada with William in 1790, and, though there is no evidence that their Virginia neighbors ostracized Solomon and Amy, the couple must have known that no one would question the legal status of their union if they relocated elsewhere. Amy and Solomon, who apparently reaffirmed his Quakerism after the war, were among the first settlers in what grew to be a thriving Friends community near Chillicothe, Ohio, though they left Ohio for Kentucky in 1803. They later followed the path taken by many former residents of the southern backcountry when they left Kentucky for southeastern Indiana, where they arrived by 1814. Solomon and Amy made their new home in Jackson County, where Solomon and Ann's sons also settled, and where William and Ann's Canadian sons would eventually arrive with their widowed mother.[32]

But even before the Ruddicks and the Canadian Spurgins migrated into the Northwest Territory, Jane and William's three youngest sons—Isaiah, Josiah, and Jesse—had left North Carolina and acquired land in Washington County, Indiana, which was located adjacent to Jackson County, where the Ruddicks and their Spurgin half siblings would later settle. Although the Ruddick family history states that Solomon and Amy "made their home with William's family" in Indiana, it is unclear the extent to which these three groups of half siblings interacted with each other. Jane's sons Isaiah and Josiah died in Indiana in 1816 and 1857, respectively, and Jesse—who during his eventful life was both a preacher and a physician—moved to the Mormon town of Nauvoo in Illinois and then resided in Missouri and Iowa before he died in Nevada in the early 1860s.[33]

The large and unlikely gathering of characters from the Spurgin family drama in early nineteenth-century Indiana raises many questions. Was their shared destination merely coincidental? Were these various interrelated family groups pleased to have familiar people nearby to help them clear and cultivate new farms, just as their ancestors had worked together decades earlier in Virginia and North Carolina? Did the presumptive reunion of different branches of the Spurgin and Ruddick families mean that the revolutionary conflict and its attendant breakup of marriages and families left no hard feelings, even among men who, as children, had been abandoned as a result of William and Ann's elopement? Or did it signify that the ending of both the Spurgin and Ruddick marriages had been—despite Jane's and Solomon's strongly worded petitions—consensual, or maybe even amicable?

After Jane received her land grant in 1792, she had no further dealings with state or county authorities and thus disappeared from the historical record. Although years later her daughter Agnes recalled that "the rites of matrimony" that united her and Peter Bodenhamer, who had battled the Tories as a Whig militiaman during the war, were performed "at the house of her mother" in Abbotts Creek in 1793, Agnes's brother Joseph became at least the nominal head of Jane's household not long thereafter.[34]

Whatever the state's intent, the transferal of property from Jane to her (and William's) male heirs happened quickly. Although the first federal census listed Jane as a household head in 1790—before she officially secured title to the lost land—the census-takers gave her son Joseph that title in 1800. By then, all but one of Jane's surviving daughters had married local men, mostly from Baptist families in the Abbotts Creek neighborhood, and lived in Rowan County. In 1800, some of Jane's sons were also still nearby, but all save Joseph either died or left the state before the government conducted its next federal census in 1810. By then, Jane was also absent from the census, having died in August 1803 at the age of sixty-seven.[35]

In the coming years, Joseph Spurgin acquired more property in Abbotts Creek and elsewhere and embarked on a public career that surpassed his father's. When his younger brothers left for Indiana, Joseph bought their Abbotts Creek land, which they had acquired previously from Charles Bruce and others, thereby reassembling and slightly expanding the acreage his parents once owned there. Joseph became a justice of the peace and served one term as Rowan County's state senator. He later served two terms in the state assembly, where he represented Davidson County, which was formed from the eastern part of Rowan County in 1822. When Joseph died in 1859, the obituary for this "highly respectable citizen" appeared in newspapers across the state. He owned 733 acres in Abbotts Creek, in addition to a gristmill and an interest

FIGURE 8 | Jane Spurgin's gravestone. This stone marks the grave of Jane Welborn Spurgin, who was interred in the graveyard at Abbotts Creek Baptist Church, where she and her family were longtime members. The pierced stone design is the distinctive work of local stonecutters. The badly eroded inscription reads "Jane Spurgin / Was born June 20 1736 / Died August 3 1803." (Photograph by the author)

in a local gold mine. Although the 1850 census listed his occupation as "farmer," Joseph's landholdings were the most valuable in his neighborhood, and he also claimed ownership of fourteen enslaved people. In a county in which only twenty-one residents held twenty or more people in bondage, he ranked among Davidson County's largest slaveholders. Joseph Spurgin was buried in the cemetery of the Abbotts Creek Baptist Church, not far from the grave of his mother.[36]

When Jane died on 3 August 1803, her surviving children bought a substantial monument to mark her grave, one of the very first in the distinctive pierced stonework style that is unique to the Abbotts Creek area.[37] Along with her petitions, that carved headstone is one of few tangible artifacts of Jane's noteworthy life. Jane's petitions document her experiences during the Revolution and help to chart her changing personal relationships and political consciousness as a result of those experiences. The headstone effaces her distinctive political voice while attesting to her long-standing role as a respectable inhabitant of communities of family and faith, the more conventional worlds to which women mostly retreated in the postrevolutionary era.

Remembering the Revolution

IN 1775, NOT LONG AFTER the Battle of Bunker Hill, eighteen-year-old Joshua Campbell of Currituck County volunteered to march to Virginia with North Carolina's Whig militia. With his comrades, he fought alongside Virginia Whigs near Norfolk at the Battle of Great Bridge; he would go on to serve a total of three years as a soldier in the American war. Joshua Campbell's revolutionary fervor angered his Tory father, who disinherited him, he later claimed, "for no other Cause but that [he] wished to take an Active part with his Countrymen in the War." As a result of this rupture, after the war the younger Campbell sought to eradicate his connection to his by-then-deceased father. He submitted a memorial to the state assembly requesting to change his surname from Campbell to Pharaoh, the latter "Being the Maiden Name of his Mother, before her intermarriage with his said Father." The legislators looked favorably on his memorial and enacted a law that formally recognized his new identity. Joshua Pharaoh applied for, and received, a federal pension for his military service in 1833.[1]

By contrast, despite their mother's support for the Revolution and her public repudiation of her husband's political choices, there is no evidence that the next generation of Spurgins sought to distance themselves in any way from their loyalist father. When he composed his brief reminiscences in 1854, Joseph Spurgin ignored the collapse of his parents' marriage, privileged the public over the private, and crafted an image of William as a man of prodigious influence and honor. "In becoming a Justice he had taken the oath of allegiance to the king," he observed, "and although his wife and all her folks in Chatham and Orange counties were whigs, he said he felt himself bound to the British Crown, and held to the royal cause." Just as he overstated the revolutionary credentials of Jane's Welborn kin, Joseph exaggerated his father's prominence in both North Carolina and Upper Canada. At the time of the Revolution, he declared, "Col. Spurgin was offered two important offices by the Whig party if he would join them, and was finally offered the office of Governor." Later, when he moved to Canada, according to Joseph, William "was placed in some important office under the British government." Though clearly untrue, such assertions likely helped Joseph and his siblings to justify and accept the emotional and material losses they suffered as a result of William's Toryism and ultimate abandonment. Significantly, of the eleven of Jane and William's children who had male offspring, eight named a son in his honor. All but one of William's grandson-namesakes were born after the war, and all but three were born after he left his North Carolina family for good in 1790.[2]

For her part, Jane had the satisfaction of seeing three granddaughters bear her name—three additional Janes were born after she died in 1803—but if Joseph's recollections were at all representative, her children did not remember their mother as a patriot, and they did not they envision her as politically principled and engaged. In Joseph's short memoir of the revolutionary years, he mentioned Jane only briefly, recounting neither her wartime struggles to care for her family in William's absence nor her encounter with General Nathanael Greene, though the nine-year-old Joseph was certainly at home in Abbotts Creek when the American commander lodged there in 1781. Nor did Joseph even hint at Jane's dogged efforts to protect and then reclaim the family's property—most of which he himself inherited—or the assertive rhetoric she used when she petitioned the state assembly. In blandly noting that Jane had asked William to "join the Liberty party [or] have nothing to do further with the royal cause," Joseph implied that his mother was motivated more by fear than patriotism. In his telling, Jane became a well-meaning but largely apolitical deterrent to William's efforts to preserve his honor and integrity—an obstacle that the noble William circumvented by prioritizing his sworn allegiance to the king over his wife's desire for safety and security.[3]

As an old man in the 1850s, Joseph preferred to remember his mother as a woman whose vision and pursuits were wholly defined by home and family, or what by then many Americans commonly referred to as "woman's sphere." The postrevolutionary decades saw a backlash against politically minded women, justified in part by concerns that the fate of an increasingly partisan and contentious nation depended on women's virtue, piety, and devotion to their wifely and maternal duties within the home, which, in turn, would serve as a wholesome counterweight to and refuge from a rancorously amoral outside world. During this same period, remembering and commemorating the Revolution predictably assumed a central place in the construction of American national identity and civic consciousness. Political speeches, published histories, Independence Day rituals, and monuments all celebrated the Revolution—and hence the creation of the republic—as the achievement of famed Founders and, equally important, of brave white men who served as soldiers. If nothing else, Jane's story shows that women, and civilians generally, both contributed to the struggle for independence and endured hardships as a result of it. Yet those stories were largely elided from historical memory in the postrevolutionary era.[4]

But historical memory and civic rituals are inherently politicized and always contested, and not everyone accepted the prevailing narrative that celebrated a nation created by respectable white men united, as soldiers and statesman, in pursuit of a worthy common goal. African Americans and other antislavery activists promoted Black soldiers and especially Crispus Attucks—one of the Bostonians slain at the "massacre" of 1770—as patriot heroes, challenging the hypocrisy of white revolutionaries who fought for liberty while perpetuating slavery and rejecting the racialized view of citizenship that increasingly predominated in the postwar era. Others sought to reclaim women's place in the revolutionary story. Female patriots reprised their foremothers' efforts as boycotters of British goods and makers of homespun cloth in the years leading to the War of 1812; others wrote of women's revolutionary-era exploits. Elizabeth Fries Ellet led this literary effort to reconstruct the record of (white) women's contributions to the war effort especially, depending heavily on personal interviews to compensate for the "apparent dearth of information" in the form of surviving archival sources written by or about her subjects. Between 1845 and 1850, Ellet published three weighty volumes of biographical sketches of notable women of the revolutionary era, some famous and others less widely known, in addition to another book titled *Domestic History of the American Revolution.*[5]

Although she was a contemporary of Elizabeth Cady Stanton and others who demanded true equality for women, Ellet was no feminist. She saw the sexes as fundamentally different but nonetheless argued both that women could be committed patriots and that the support of patriotic women had been essential to the success of the American Revolution. "It is impossible now to appreciate the vast influence of woman's patriotism upon the destinies of the infant republic," she wrote, bemoaning the fact that their service and sacrifices had been nearly totally forgotten by subsequent generations. In her books, Ellet emphasized the power of women's domestic influence, as wives and mothers, in instilling patriotic virtues in their husbands and especially their sons. At the same time, however, she also chronicled the many other less conventionally domestic endeavors that women undertook to further the patriot cause. During the imperial crisis, she reminded her readers, women "formed themselves into associations renouncing the use of teas, and other imported luxuries, and engaging to card, spin, and weave their own clothing." Once the war began, they tended to the sick and wounded, collected funds to support the army, and ran the farms that produced the grain and bread that fed its soldiers. "The alarms of war—the roar of the strife itself, could not silence the voice of woman, lifted in encouragement or in prayer," she declared, adding, "The horrors of battle or massacre could not drive her from the post of duty."[6]

Jane Spurgin was not the subject of one of Ellet's brief biographies, but another antebellum historian, the North Carolinian E. W. Caruthers, did write about her. Born in Rowan County in 1793, Caruthers was an antislavery clergyman and local historian who produced two volumes in the 1850s in which he recounted "revolutionary incidents" that occurred in North Carolina, mostly in the backcountry. The second of these volumes, published in 1856, included the earliest published account of Jane's interaction with General Greene, as well as brief biographies of other

North Carolina women from the revolutionary era, most of whom either resolutely withstood enemy threats and insults as their homes were plundered or, using their "superior intelligence and shrewdness with a womanly dignity and manner and proper use of the tongue," outsmarted would-be plunderers. North Carolina's Whig women, Caruthers insisted, were "from principle, as patriotic as the men," and they "suffered so much from both the British and Tories" during the long and brutal war. Like Ellet, Caruthers regretted that the patriotism of such women had been forgotten, and like her he also drew on personal interviews to tell their stories. Even if Jane's own descendants were unwilling or unable to envision her as an avid supporter of the Revolution, someone in Rowan County remembered—and told Caruthers—that she had been "as true a Whig as her husband was a Tory" and that she had actively aided and abetted the revolutionary cause.[7]

In the spirit of Caruthers and Ellet, recent historians have shown how recovering the stories of previously little-known individuals can complicate and enrich our understanding of the Revolution and its significance, going beyond macrolevel generalizations about a glorious military victory that secured political independence and established republican government. For George Robert Twelves Hewes, an illiterate Boston shoemaker, the Revolution meant that he no longer had to enter the through the back door when he visited the palatial homes of John Hancock or other local grandees, with whom he shared a sense of rough equality as fellow-patriots in the postwar era. For Phillis Wheatley, an enslaved woman–turned–celebrity poet, revolutionary ideals of liberty and equality seemed both promising and painfully ironic, even as they empowered her to deploy her words deftly against slavery and racism, making the case for emancipation to General George Washington (who, perhaps not coincidentally, freed his enslaved workforce on his death in 1799). For impoverished and restless young people, such as Joseph Plumb Martin and Deborah Sampson (also known as Robert Shurtleff), the Revolution and its war presented an opportunity to leave home and have some adventures while earning modest wages by serving in the Continental Army, even if their actual experiences involved less glory than suffering and deprivation.[8]

What did the Revolution mean to Jane Spurgin? Before the imperial crisis and the war that followed, she had been the wife of one of the leading men in Rowan County, a justice of the peace who owned some 700 acres of improved land and who was one of relatively few men in the area who also claimed ownership of one or more enslaved people. William's loyalism and his eventual absence, coupled with the state's anti-Tory statutes, caused years of hardship and uncertainty for Jane and her family, while the war exposed them to dangers common to inhabitants of the backcountry, regardless of their political views. When the war was over, the Spurgins continued to pay the material costs of William's Toryism, despite the ultimate success of Jane's efforts to reclaim part of his former property. The stress of years of always impending homelessness must have been enormous. The loss of 300 acres, which substantially diminished the land that could be passed to the next generation, likely led her sons to join the stream of land-seeking migrants—offspring of Whigs and Tories alike—out of North Carolina and other more densely populated eastern states into Indian territory, which white settlers rapidly occupied and cultivated in the postrevolutionary decades.

In other ways, however, Jane may have seen her revolutionary experience in a more positive light. The war and its divisions, which either caused or facilitated the dissolution of the Spurgins' marriage, may have been fortuitous from her perspective, and her emergence from her postwar wrangling with the courts and the legislature as a property owner in her own right surely was a benefit. Jane's encounter with General Greene at her home in Abbotts Creek likely enhanced her self-image as a good citizen and a patriot, and it also gave her a terrific story to share in her declining years. It would be nice to think that she was among the attendees at the festive reception of President George Washington when he visited Salisbury during his celebrated tour of the southern states, or, better yet, that she was one of the twenty "ladies" who had tea with the great hero of the Revolution on that late spring day in 1791.[9] The ideals of the Revolution led Jane, like many other Americans, to confront authority and to reimagine her relationship to the polity and the men who ran it. Her experiences, though often difficult and costly, gave her the language to assert her rights and to ponder the meaning of republican citizenship.

Documents

This section brings together eight documents that were central to the process of reconstructing the Spurgins' family story, all of which have been amply quoted and cited in this book. The complete texts of these essential primary sources are provided here so that readers can get a feel for late eighteenth-century language and the standard forms used for petitions and other public documents and also so that they can read and interpret these documents for themselves.

I

Resolutions by inhabitants of Rowan County concerning resistance to Parliamentary taxation and the Provincial Congress of North Carolina (Rowan County Resolves)

Proceedings of the Freeholders in Rowan County[1]

August 8th 1774.
At a meeting August 8th 1774, the following resolves were unanimously agreed to.

Resolved, That we will at all times, when ever we are called upon for that purpose, maintain and defend at the Expense of our Lives and Fortunes, his Majesty's Right and Title to the Crown of Great Britain, and his Dominions in America to whose royal Person and Government we profess all due Obedience & Fidelity.

Resolved, That the Right to impose Taxes or Duties to be paid by the Inhabitants within this Province for any purpose whatsoever is peculiar and essential to the General Assembly in whom the legislative Authority of the Colony is vested.

Resolved, That any attempt to impose such Taxes or Duties by any other Authority is an Arbitrary Exertion of Power, and an Infringement of the Constitutional Rights and Liberties of the Colonies.

Resolved, That to impose a Tax or Duty upon Tea by the British Parliament in which the North American Colonies can have no Representation to be paid upon Importation by the inhabitants of the said Colonies, is an Act of Power without Right, it is subversive to the Liberties of the said Colonies, deprives them of their Property without their own Consent, and thereby reduces them to a State of Slavery.

Resolved, That the late cruel and Sanguinary Acts of Parliament to be executed by military force and Ships of War upon our Sister Colony of the Massachusetts Bay and Town of Boston, is a strong Evidence of the corrupt Enfluence obtained by the British Ministry in Parliament and a convincing Proof of their fixed Intention to deprive the Colonies of their Constitutional Rights and Liberties.

Resolved, That the Cause of the Town of Boston is the common Cause of the American Colonies.

Resolved, That it is the Duty and Interest of all the American Colonies, firmly to unite in an indissoluble Union and Association to oppose by every Just and proper means the Infringement of their common Rights and Privileges.

Resolved, That a general Association between all the American Colonies, not to import from Great Britain any Commodity whatsoever (except such things as shall be hereafter excepted by the general Congress of this Province) ought to be entered into and not dissolved till the just Rights of the said Colonies are restored to them, and the cruel Acts of the British Parliament against the Massachusetts Bay and Town of Boston are repealed.

Resolved, That no friend to the Rights and Liberties of America ought to purchase any Commodity whatsoever, except such as shall be excepted, which shall be imported from Great Britain after the general Association shall be agreed upon.

Resolved, That every kind of Luxury, Dissipation and Extravagance, ought to be banished from among us.

Resolved, That manufactures ought to be encouraged by opening Subscriptions for that purpose, or by any other proper means.

Resolved, That the African Trade is injurious to this Colony, obstructs the Population of it by freemen, prevents manufacturers, and other Useful Emigrants from Europe from settling among us, and occasions an annual increase of the Balance of Trade against the Colonies.

Resolved, That the raising of Sheep, Hemp and flax ought to be encouraged.

Resolved, That to be cloathed in manufactures fabricated in the Colonies ought to be considered as a Badge and Distinction of Respect and true Patriotism.

Resolved, That Messrs Samuel Young and Moses Winslow for the County of Rowan, and for the Town of Salisbury William Kennon Esqr be and they are hereby nominated and appointed Deputies, upon the Part of the Inhabitants and Freeholders of this County and Town of Salisbury, to meet such Deputies as shall be appointed by the other Counties and Corporations within this Colony at Johnston Court-House the 20th of this Instant.

Resolved, That at this important and alarming Crisis it be earnestly recommended to the said Deputies at their general Convention that they nominate and appoint one proper Person out of each District of this Province, to meet such Deputies in a general Congress, as shall be appointed upon the Part of the other Continental Colonies in America, to consult and agree upon a firm and indissoluble Union and Association for preserving by the best and most proper means their Common Rights and Liberties.

Resolved, That this Colony ought not to trade with any Colony which shall refuse to join in any Union and Association that shall be agreed upon by the greater Part of the other Colonies on this Continent, for preserving their common Rights and Liberties.

II

Petition of Jane Spurgin, 3 December 1785

The Petition of Jane Spurgin Humbly Sheweth[2] that She being the Wife of William Spurgin a late unhappy Man, is entirely deprived of Any thing to Subsist upon, as follows there were Different Suits commenced against the estate of Said Spurgin by Way of Original Attachment, And Judgments Were Obtained for considerable Sums & executions issued & Were levied upon the Whole of the Property of the Said Spurgin & Sold, notwithstanding the commissioner of confiscated property had directed that her thirds of the land Should not be sold & Very justly too, for Agreeable to the Act of Assembly, the Legislature does not even when a Man's estate is confiscated require that the Whole Shall be sold, but that the county court Shall Previous to any Sales Set apart so Much of the personal property as Will be Sufficient for the reasonable Support of the Wives, Widows & Children of any person Whose estate is, or may be confiscated & one third of the lands if Sufficient for their Support, but at their discretion to Assign the Whole of the land, therefore it cannot be expected that any Government Would place any individual or Set of individuals in a better

Situation than the whole community. Nor Would they She hopes after Giving her a right to a Sufficiency clear from the Publick do it for the purpose of Satisfying Some individuals Who had a Claim against her Husbands estate Generally, On Account of his Trespasses during the late Warr Which Occasioned the forfeiture of his estate. Therefore she hopes that as her husband is politically dead, & has no expectation of his return to assist in the Maintenance of herself & eight Small children, the Assembly after due consideration of her circumstances, will restore & give to her an indefeasible right to Seven hundred & four acres of land her husbands that is to say her thirds of the two tracts one tract containing three hundred & four acres & the Other four hundred. She hopes to get it out of both Tracts. All She requests of the personal property is a negro fellow Named Simon, relying on the humane & upright disposition of the General Assembly Your Petitioner waits with Great expectation.

III

Petition of Jane Spurgin, 11 November 1788

The Petition of Jean Spurgin of Rowan County humbly Sheweth[3]

That where as her husband William Spurgin by mistake and bad Conduct did in the last war draw on him the resentment of the Law, in so much as his Estate real and personal was Seized for the State and made Sale off, and he banished and not permitted to live at home and assist her, Your Petitioner has Sufferd great Callamities and hardships; for during the late War She was almost Continually harassed from the military who took from her grain, Meat, and many other Articles without the least recompense, that eaven for Several Years She and her family of Small Children enjoyed hardly any of the produce of her plantation; and Since the War, perticularly by this rigour and Severity that eaven that part of the plantation which was by Law allotted to her and had been laid off according to Law for the Subsistance of her and her Small Children, is now Seized and lays under ejectment, and She is now threatened every day to be turned out, She and her Children without Mercy. Other Women under the Same Circumstances are not treated in so hard a manner, nor can Your Petitioner believe it to be the meaning of the Law to punish without lenity, to give, only to be taken away again, and to make the Wife and Small Children entirely miserable on account of the Husbands and fathers transgressions Your Petitioner and her Children are thus worse Situated than a Widow and Orphants, and cannot forbare herewith to look up to the Honorable the Representatives of the State for redress, imploring your Mercy and justice to look into the premises, to take your Petitioners and her Childrens Circumstances into Consideration, and to give her and them Such releif as by Law originally intended. And your Petitioner as in Duty bound shall ever pray &c.

IV

Petition of Jane Spurgin, 28 November 1791

The memorial of Jennet Spurgen Humbly Sheweth[4]

That during the late war She furnished the regular Troops and Militia of this State with Provisions and Forriage some part of which, the officers that took it gave her certificates for. But the greater part that was taken from her She never got any vouchers for, owing to her husbands being disaffected to the government and owing to the same reason, the vouchers She did obtain would not be received and audited by the auditors of Salisbury District to whom they were presented for that Purpose. And tho it was your memorialists misfortune to be married to a man who was Enemical to the revolution it was an evil that was not in her power to remidy—and as She has always behaved herself as a good Citizen and well attached to the government She thinks it extreamly hard to be deprived of the Common rights of other Citizens. Your memorialist is advanced in life, and very much failed and had six Children to provide for, and no one to assist or help her, and is also in very low Circumstances her husband not having lived with her Since the war. She has therefore Stated her account for Such articles As She obtained vouchers for and humbly hopes your honorable body will grant her Such relief in the Premisses as you in your great wisdom's may think her entitled to. And your Memorialist as in duty bound will ever pray &c.

V

Petition of William Spurgin, 10 September 1792

I have been Wating three days to have Spake to your Exolencey[5] and as it is gods will to Continue you to be So unwell that I Cant be purmited to See you I Send you Sum Receipts Which I Obtained in ye Last War In ye province of North Carolina from ye Several Officers of Lord Cornwalles Armey When they Marched through that Place for horses and Provision Produced to them for his majesties Servis And has Never Received Any Satisfaction for ye Same And As I Lost All My Property on that Account taken and Solad from me by ye Reabils my Land my Negroes my Stock And household goods And All I most humbly Beg that your Exolencey Would be pleased to take those Receipts Which I Send to your hand And Assist me to ye Recovere of them If it is thought they Are Recoverable My Surcomstance is so Extreamly Lowe that I have nothing to Subsist Upon here Any Longer Nor I Cant Get my famuley Any further till I get Sum Releaf Which I was In hopes I could have got on ye Credit of these Receipts I have my famuley as far on as Pennsylvania State And there Lyes on [*illegible*] till I Can Return to them Agane I further Wanted to know of your Excelencey Wheather A number of famuleys might be Purmited to Settle to Geather In that part of ye Goverment Called ye Long point Or near About there If it would Please you to Resolve me I S[h]all Most humbly thank your Exelencey.

I further Wanted to know Wheater there Could be Any Assistance Alowed to poor People at ye furst Settling heare As I And Amaney Others Are Reduced So Lowe I Cant tell how we Could Rase Sum [Small] Crop Pray Sir be pleas to Return me A Answer if it Is not to much disturbing of you And I Shall for Ever Joine in prayer to ye Amighty god for your helth and Remaines your most Obeadient And humble Sarvant.

VI

Petition of Solomon Reddick (or Ruddick), 12 November 1796

To the Honorable the General Assembly of Virginia.[6]
The Petition of Solomon Reddick of Grayson Cty Humbly Sheweth

That about Seventeen years ago Your Petitioner Enter'd into Matrimony with a Certain Ann Bedsaul and with her continued uninterrupted for Twelve Years—that in the year One thousand Seven Hundred & Ninety She then abandoned by Virtue & Divested of all Conjugal affection and Matrimonial Tenderness Eloped with a Certaine William Spurgeon and left your petitioner With five Small & helpless Children in a Deplorable and Distrest Situation & your petitioner a friend to Virtue and Enemy to Vice being Desierous to frustrate all Future Connection with Such a woman and to Dissolve the bonds which [*illegible*] him & her, has Recourse to the Justice Magnanimity of your Honorable Body and praying that an act may pass Granting a devorce & your petitioner as in duty bound Shall Ever prey.

VII

Will of William Spurgin, 2 August 1806

In the Name of God Amen.[7]

I William Spurgin of the District of London and County of Norfolk, in the Province of upper Canada and township of Charlotteville Being weak in Body But of Perfect Mind and Memory thanks Be given unto god. Caulliing unto Mind the mortality of my Body and knowing that it is appointed for all men once to Die Doe make and ordain this my Last will and Testament that is to Say Principally and first of all I Give and Recommend my Soul into the hands of almighty God that Gave it and my Body. I Recommend to the Earth to be Buryed in a Decent Christian Like manner at the Discression of my Executors, Nothing Doubting But at the General Resurrection I shall Receive the Same again By the mighty Power of God and as touching Such Worldly Estate wherewith it hath pleased god to Bless me with in this Life I Give Devise and Dispence of the Same in the following manner and form—that is to Say first it is my Desire that all my Just Debts Should Be Lawfully paid and Discharged.

Item—I will and Bequeath unto my oldest Son John Spurgin the Sum of five Shillings Starling money of Great Britan.

Item—I will and Bequeath unto my Daughter Margret the Sum of five Shillings Starling money of great Britan.

Item—I will and Bequeath unto my Daughter Mary the Sum of five Shilling Starling money of great Britan.

Item—I will and Bequeath unto my Son William Spurgin the Sum of five Shillings Starling money of Great Britan.

Item—I will and Bequeath unto my Daughter Agness the Sum of five Shillings Starling money of Great Britan.

Item—I will and Bequeath unto my Daughter Jennete the Sum of five Shillings Starling money of Great Britan.

Item—I will and Bequeath to my Son Joseph Spurgin the Sum of five Shillings Starling money of Great Britan.

Item—I will and Bequeath to my Daughter Elisabeth the Sum of five Shillings Starling money of Great Britan.

Item—I will and Bequeath to my son Isaiah Spurgin the Sum of five Shillings Starling money of Great Britan.

Item—I will and Bequeath to my Son Josiah Spurgin the Sum of five Shillings Starling money of Great Britan.

Item—I will and Bequeath to my son Jessee Spurgin the Sum of five Shillings Starling money of Great Britan.

Also I will and Bequeath all and Singular my property Real and personal Lying and Being within the State or province of North Carolina in Roan County Recovered or to Be Recovered Hereafter to Be Divided as the Laws of that Province Directs amongst the above named famaly.

As to Touching and Concerning My Estate in the Province of Upper Canada

I will and Bequeath unto my son Aaron Spurgin one Lot of Land Containing two Hundred akers more Lying and Being in the township of Charlotteville Being Lot No. 11 in the Concession together with a Sorel Horse with a Blase face Name of fidler and a Bay Horse Named Smoker a year old Horse Colt Named Bird.

I will and Bequeath to my Son Samuel Spurgin one Lot of Land Containing two Hundred akers more or Less Being Number 1 in the Eleventh Concession of the township of Wallpool one Sorel mare Cauled Snip and a Bay mare Colt Sucking of Her.

I will and Bequeath to my Daugter Anne Spurgin one Lot of Land of two Hundred akers More or Less Being Lot No. 1 in the tenth Concession of the township of wallpool and one Large Brown Mare Cauled Plesh.

I will and Bequeath to my yongest Daughter Sarah Spurgin one Lot of Land No. two in the tenth Concession of the township of wallpool Containing two Hundred akers more or Less and one Bay mare Cauled Boney and a Colt Sucking of Her.

I will and Bequeath unto My Beloved Wife ann Spurgin one Horse, Her Bed and Bed Cloathes, one Chest, one Cloath Lume to Be Her own property. Furthermore it is my will and Desire that one yoke of working Cattle Together with all the Remainding part of my Cattle, Sheep, and Swine, one Wagon, together with all my Household goods and farming utencils to Be and Remain on my Homestead Place together with all my movable Property that I Shall Die Legally possessed of after Discharging the several Legacies Herein mentioned and to be mentioned and the payment of all my Just Debts and Funeral Charges for the use and Bringing up of my famaly of Children to be Left in the Care of my Said Beloved wife Ann Spurgin as Long as She my Said Loving wife Shall Continue to Be my widow, and on the Day of Her marrying to another then and in that Case I Devise that my Executors Shall take an Enventory of all and Singular the goods and Chattles that or may Be found Remainding and Continue in the Hands of Her my Said Loving wife at the descression of my Said Executors and after the marrage or Death of Her my Loving wife the place whereon I now Live in purssession of Being Lot No. Eleven Begin the front Concession of the township of Charlotteville in the County of Norfolk and District of London and the Province of Upper Canada to Be Equally Divided Between my two Sons and my two Daughters Aaron Spurgin, Samuel Spurgin, Anne Spurgin and Sarah Spurgin.

Hereby Revoking all former Wills By me made and I Do hereby nominate Constitute and Appoint Silas Secord, John Curn, farmers, together with my Son Aaron Spurgin, To Be Executors of this my Last will and testament. In Witness whereof I Have Hereunto Set my Hand and Seal the Second Day of August in the year of Our Lord one thousand Eight Hundred and Six and in the forty Sixth year of His Majestys Reign.

VIII

Historian E. W. Caruthers on Jane Spurgin and General Nathanael Greene in 1781

When [Greene] came to Abbott's Creek Meeting-House, [8] he halted two or three days to rest his troops. Or perhaps to wait for further developments. He made his headquarters at the house of Col. Spurgeon, who was in good circumstances, and lived about a mile from the church. He was a Tory Colonel, one of those commissioned by Gov. Martin, about the beginning of 1776, and had taken quite an active part in favor of the royal cause. Of course, he was not at home to receive his guest, and "treat him to the best he had;" but his wife, Mary [*sic*] Spurgen, was as true a Whig as her husband was a Tory, and, like Mrs. Steel in Salisbury, she showed him all the kindness, and gave him all the encouragement in her power. On arriving there, the first thing he did, was to select his ground for a battle, should it become necessary. It was a very eligible position, elevated, covered with a dense growth of large hickories, most of which are yet standing, and ample enough for all the evolutions that might be necessary, while he would have the buildings to protect him in case of emergency. As this locality was near the house, he told Mrs. Spurgen, that, if Cornwallis should overtake him, and compel him to fight, she must go into the cellar with her children, and remain there until the conflict was over; but fortunately for her and all concerned, the foe was still prevented from advancing by a higher power. Not having heard a word, however, of Cornwallis, or of his movements, since he left the Trading Ford, he felt very anxious to know whether he would cross there, as soon as the river became fordable, and pursue him, or remain on that side for the purpose of bringing the country into subjection, or cross up higher, with the view of getting between him and Virginia.

In such circumstances, a man of his patriotism and indomitable energy of character, could not rest. There was too much at stake, and he was of too noble a spirit to remain long inactive or in a state of suspense, while danger of the most alarming kind was so near. Having no other means of information, and knowing Mrs. Spurgen's patriotic spirit, he asked her if she knew of any one in whom he could put confidence, as he wished to send such a one back to the river, for the purpose of procuring some information respecting the movements of Cornwallis. She told him yes, he could put confidence in her son John. Feeling encouraged by this answer, and, at the same time, like a prudent man, fully awake to the perils that beset him, he repeated the question, and with a great deal of earnestness:

"Are you sure, Madam, that I can put confidence in John?"

"Yes, sir," was her prompt and womanly reply. "Yes, sir, you can put confidence in John, if he will consent to go, and I think he will."

That was enough; and John was called. General Greene then told him what he wanted,—that he wished him to take his own horse and go back to Trading Ford to see if he could find out anything about the movements of the British, and if he saw nothing of them there, to go up the river for a number of miles. He promptly consented, and set off at once. He rode a fine horse, and with proper vigilance, had not much to dread. On going to the river, he could neither see nor hear anything of them; but, in obedience to orders, he went up a number of miles without any better success. He then returned and told Gen. Greene how far he had gone, but without obtaining the least information. Greene told him he must go again, for he must have the information, and he must have it soon; and, if he saw nothing of them, to continue up the river to Shallow Ford. Young Spurgen set out again, and on reaching Shallow Ford, some thirty miles, more or less, from home, he found they were crossing. Then returning as fast as his horse could carry him, he reported that they were crossing at that ford. Instantly, Gen. Greene ordered his horse, and was off for Martinville, where he arrived on the evening of the 7th, and found Gen, Huger there, who had just arrived with the main body of the army. By this time, the designs of Cornwallis were manifest and Greene's situation admitted of no delay; but perhaps we ought to observe how much service the wife and son of a Tory Colonel, though a mere lad at the time, rendered at this critical juncture of affairs.

NOTES

Abbreviations

CSRNC   *The Colonial and State Records of North Carolina.* Edited by William L. Saunders et al. 30 vols. Raleigh, Winston, Goldsboro, and Charlotte: various publishers, 1886–1914.

GASR   General Assembly Sessions Papers

LAC   Library and Archives of Canada, Ottawa

LVA   Library of Virginia, Richmond

SANC   State Archives of North Carolina, Raleigh

Introduction

1. Petition of Jennet Spurgin, 28 Dec. 1791, GASR, Dec. 1791–Jan. 1792, box 1, SANC. See also Kierner, *Southern Women in Revolution,* esp. xix–xxii, 150–57, 163–66; and Bradburn, *Citizenship Revolution,* 1–3, 17–18.
2. See the classic Trouillot, *Silencing the Past,* esp. 48–53; and the more recent Fuentes, *Dispossessed Lives,* and Miles, *All That She Carried.* Some of the most revealing work on slavery, resistance, and antislavery during this period includes Pybus, *Epic Journeys of Freedom;* Bell, *Running from Bondage;* Polgar, *Standard-Bearers of Equality;* Bonner, *Remaking the Republic;* and, more generally, Holton, *Liberty Is Sweet.* See Nash, *Race and Revolution,* 57, for the characterization of the Revolution as "the largest slave uprising in our history."
3. R. Brown, "Microhistory and the Post-Modern Challenge," 15.
4. The widely accepted 40 percent estimate is from Paul H. Smith, "American Loyalists," 268–69. Scholars who emphasize pervasive violence and shifting loyalties include W. E. Lee, *Crowds and Soldiers;* Van Buskirk, *Generous Enemies;* Gigantino, *William Livingston's American Revolution;* Piecuch, *Three Peoples, One King;* Hoock, *Scars of Independence;* and Sullivan, *Disaffected.*

5. The best accounts of the Revolution in the North Carolina backcountry are A. Roger Ekirch, "Whig Authority and Public Order in Backcountry North Carolina, 1776–1783," in *Uncivil War,* ed. Hoffman et al., 99–124; and Jeffrey J. Crow, "Liberty Men and Loyalists: Disorder and Disaffection in the North Carolina Backcountry," ibid., 125–78. Both agree that "disaffection" was widespread at the beginning of the war. Ekirch argues that many backcountry residents moved to the Whig side after the Carolinas became the site of sustained armed conflict; Crow contends that the state government's brutality during that same period cemented opposition to the Whig regime. Oddly, both arguments are persuasive.

6. Page Smith, "David Ramsay and the Causes of the American Revolution," 55–61. Ramsay wrote two histories of the Revolution, in addition to another in which he also chronicled the colonial history of his home state: *History of the Revolution of South-Carolina, from a British Province to an Independent State; History of the American Revolution;* and *Ramsay's History of South Carolina.* For Caruthers, see *Revolutionary Incidents* and *Interesting Revolutionary Incidents.*

7. Commission to appoint Allan MacDonald et al. as officers of loyalist militias, 10 Jan. 1776, in *CSRNC,* 10:396–97; An Act directing the sale of Confiscated Property, 1782, ibid., 24:424–29; Josiah Martin to Welbore Ellis, Baron Mendip, 7 Mar. 1782, ibid., 22:617–18.

8. Jasanoff, *Liberty's Exiles;* Seeley, *Race, Removal, and the Right to Remain,* esp. chap. 4; Taparata, "Refugees as You Call Them."

9. Abigail Adams to John Adams, 31 Mar. 1776, *Founders Online,* https://founders .archives.gov/documents/Adams/04-01-02-0241; Charlene Boyer Lewis, "'The Tender Heart of the Chief Could Not Support the Scene': General Washington, Margaret Arnold, and the Treason at West Point," in *Women of George Washington's World,* ed. Lewis and Boudreau, 88–112.

10. Bloch, "The American Revolution, Wife Beating, and the Emergent Value of Privacy," 223–51.

1. Settling the Backcountry

1. Gabriel Johnston to Earl of Granville, 13 Mar. 1750, quoted in Ekirch, *"Poor Carolina,"* 9; Ramsey, *Carolina Cradle,* 23; Merrens, *Colonial North Carolina,* 53–55; List of taxables in North Carolina, in *CSRNC,* 7:145–46.

2. Arthur Dobbs to Board of Trade, 9 Nov. 1754, in *CSRNC,* 5:149.

3. Land, *Colonial Maryland,* 98–88, 104–5. On the Welborn family, see Welborn, *Welborns and Related Families,* 5–6, with significant corrections and additional documentation at "William Welborn Sr (1712–1773)," https://www.wikitree.com /wiki/Welborn-467.

4. Will of Edward Welbourne, 23 Jan. 1730, Will Books, Maryland Archives, transcribed at https://www.wikitree.com/wiki/Welborn-467; Land, *Colonial Maryland,* 119–20.

5. Welborn, *Welborns and Related Families,* 6; "William Welborn Sr (1712–1773)," https://www.wikitree.com/wiki/Welborn-467; Tracey, *Pioneers of Old Monocacy,* 345n; Williams, *History of Frederick County,* 10–11.

6. Sollers, "Transported Convict Laborers in Maryland," 20–27; A. Smith, *Colonists in Bondage,* 232; Williams, *History of Frederick County,* 1–11; Land, *Colonial Maryland,* 199–202; Tracey, *Pioneers of Old Monocacy,* 368.

7. Ekirch, *Bound for America*, 1, 17–19, 26–27, 48–55; *Proceedings of the Old Bailey, 1674–1913*, 25 Feb. 1719, https://www.oldbaileyonline.org/browse.jsp?id=t17190225 -2-defend32&div=t17190225-2#highlight and https://www.oldbaileyonline.org /browse.jsp?id=t17190225-3-defend36&div=t17190225-3#highlight. On Mary Stiles, see ibid., https://www.oldbaileyonline.org/browse.jsp?div=s17280605-1.

8. Ekirch, *Bound for America*, 103–8, 112–20, 129, 142, 176–80; *Proceedings of the Old Bailey, 1674–1913*, 25 Feb. 1719; *Archives of Maryland: Provincial Court Land Records, 1719–1723*, 8 Sept. 1719, http://aomol.msa.maryland.gov/000001/000721/html /am721-7.html.

9. Coldham, *Complete Book of Emigrants in Bondage*, 754; Singewald, *Report on the Iron Ores of Maryland*, 128–32; "Iron Production: Maryland's Industrial Past," https://www.hmdb.org/m.asp?m=104641; Kamoie, *Irons in the Fire*, 71, 83–84; McCleskey, *Road to Black Ned's Forge*, esp. 93–94. For the 1705 agreement, see *Archives of Maryland: Provincial Court Land Records, 1749–1756*, https://msa.mary land.gov/megafile/msa/speccol/sc2900/sc2908/000001/000701/html/am701-2 .html.

10. For the elder William's landholdings in Frederick County, Maryland, and Orange (later Frederick) County, Virginia, see *Spurgin Quarterly*, no. 20 (Dec. 1989): 491.

11. Ramsey, *Carolina Cradle*, 21–22.

12. Hofstra, *Planting of New Virginia*, 53–56, 146, 176–77; Lemon, *Best Poor Man's Country*, 43, 68, 72, 76, 85; Vickers, "Competency and Competition," 3–29; Williams, *History of Frederick County*, 30–40. For the Welborns, see Bynum, *Free State of Jones*, 20–22, 223, 226; "William Welborn Sr (1712–1773)," https://www.wikitree.com /wiki/Welborn-467, and "Isaac Welborn," https://www.findagrave.com/memorial /68312432/isaac-welborn.

13. Meehan, "Not Made out of Levity," 443–46; Instructions to Colonial Governors, 19 Nov. 1773, in *CSRNC*, 11:242–43.

14. Spruill, *Women's Life and Work in the Southern Colonies*, 178–84, 340–44; Lebsock, *Free Women of Petersburg*, 68–69; Sword, *Wives Not Slaves*, esp. chaps. 5–6.

15. Gilreath, *Frederick County (Va.) Deed Books*, 164; Linn, *Abstracts of the Deeds*, 4:30, 31; *Spurgin Quarterly*, no. 4 (Aug. 1985): 90–91.

16. Linn, *Abstracts of the Deeds*, 4:30, 31; Petition of William Spurgin, 30 Aug. 1793, Land Petitions of Upper Canada, LAC. On land prices, see also Merrens, *Colonial North Carolina*, 63–64. For references to "Spurgeon's Creek," see Enochs, *Rowan County, NC, Vacant Land Entries*, 109; and Powell and Hill, *North Carolina Gazetteer*, 500.

17. Ramsey, *Carolina Cradle*, 21–24, 50, 73–76, 92–93; Hofstra, *Planting of New Virginia*, 168; O'Dell, *Pioneers of Old Frederick County*, 73–77; Arthur Dobbs to Board of Trade, 24 Aug. 1755, in *CSRNC*, 5:355.

18. Spangenberg diary, 1752, in Fries, *Records of the Moravians*, 1:59.

19. Ibid., 1:41, 48; Ekirch, "'New Government of Liberty,'" 632, 638; Ekirch, *"Poor Carolina,"* 127–28.

20. Spangenberg diary, 1:48, 51–52.

21. Fries, *Records of the Moravians*, 1:13–15; Thorp, *Moravian Community in Colonial North Carolina*, chap. 5; Thorp, "Taverns and Tavern Culture," 661–88; Johanna Miller Lewis, *Artisans in the North Carolina Backcountry*, esp. chap. 3; Ramsay, *Carolina Cradle*, 169–70; Merrens, *Colonial North Carolina*, 162–66.

22. Cantrell, *History, Heritage & Memories*, 19–25. The church's earliest (and seemingly partial) membership list from 1783 includes five Teagues, three Swaims, two

Spurgins, and two Welborns. On the Teague family, see O'Dell, *Pioneers of Old Frederick County*, 123–26; and "Isabella Mary (Teague) Welborn, (1742–1812)," https://www.wikitree.com/wiki/Teague-255.

23. Paschal, *History of North Carolina Baptists*, 1:290–91; Morgan, "Great Awakening in North Carolina," 269–70, 273–74; Bynum, *Free State of Jones*, 21; Fries, *Records of the Moravians*, 1:352.

24. "Autobiography of Col. William Few," 343–44; Osterud, "Gender and the Transition to Capitalism," 19–20; Jensen, *Loosening the Bonds*, 46–48.

25. Ulrich, *Midwife's Tale*, 75–79; Osterud, "Gender and the Transition to Capitalism," 19–20, 23; Kierner, *Beyond the Household*, 13.

26. Vickers, "Competency and Competition," 3–8, 25; Thorp, "Doing Business in the Backcountry," 391–92, 399; Merrens, *Colonial North Carolina*, 113. On women as producers of alcoholic beverages, see Meacham, *Every Home a Distillery*.

27. Merrens, *Colonial North Carolina*, 112–19, 136–37, 145, 158–60; Thorp, "Taverns and Tavern Culture," 664–65; Lewis, *Artisans in the North Carolina Backcountry*, 58–61; Kars, *Breaking Loose Together*, 20.

28. Jensen, *Loosening the Bonds*, 37–38; Lewis, *Artisans in the North Carolina Backcountry*, 66.

29. Jensen, *Loosening the Bonds*, 38; Ulrich, *Good Wives*, 20–29; Kierner, *Beyond the Household*, 13–17.

30. Jensen, *Loosening the Bonds*, 38; Laurel Thatcher Ulrich, "Martha Ballard and Her Girls: Women's Work in Eighteenth-Century Maine," in *Work and Labor in Early America*, ed. Innes, esp. 70–73; Norton, *Liberty's Daughters*, 66–67, 75–83, 93–96.

31. Linn, *Rowan County, North Carolina, Tax Lists*, 33, 100; Merrens, *Colonial North Carolina*, 74–81; Morgan, *Slave Counterpoint*, 209–11, 252–53.

32. Caruthers, *Interesting Revolutionary Incidents*, 280; Linn, *Abstracts of the Deeds*, 4:375.

33. Minutes of the governor's council, 11 Aug. 1764, in *CSRNC*, 6:1077; Linn, *Abstracts of the Minutes of the Court of Pleas and Quarter Sessions*, 2:32; William Tryon to Earl of Shelburne, 29 June 1767, in Tryon, *Correspondence of William Tryon*, 1:522; Kars, *Breaking Loose Together*, 69; Ekirch, *"Poor Carolina,"* 173; Ramsey, *Carolina Cradle*, 177.

34. William Tryon to Earl of Shelburne, 29 June 1767, in Tryon, *Correspondence of William Tryon*, 1:522.

35. Kars, *Breaking Loose Together*, 68–69; Ekirch, *"Poor Carolina,"* 52; Roeber, *Faithful Magistrates and Republican Lawyers*, 42–43, 73–77; Bellesiles, "Establishment of Legal Structures on the Frontier," 906–7.

36. See Ramsey, *Carolina Cradle*, 26–28, 35, 37–38, 40, 50–56, for biographical information on most of Rowan's earliest justices. For a list of Rowan County's original fourteen appointees, see ibid., 50n.

37. Ramsey, *Carolina Cradle*, 26–28, 40, 56. For lists of members of the colonial legislature, see https://www.carolana.com/NC/Royal_Colony/House_of_Burgesses/home.html.

38. Isaac, *Transformation of Virginia*, 90–94; Roeber, *Faithful Magistrates and Republican Lawyers*, 79–80; William Tryon to Earl of Shelburne, 29 June 1767, in Tryon, *Correspondence of William Tryon*, 1:522. On the first Rowan County courthouse in Salisbury, which was completed in 1756, see Rumple, *History of Rowan County*, 72–76.

2. An Enemy to His Country

1. Spindel, "Law and Disorder," 7–13; Fries, *Records of the Moravians*, 1:305, 306; William Tryon to Lords of the Treasury, 5 Apr. 1766, in *CSRNC*, 7:195–96. For the text of the Declaratory Act, see https://avalon.law.yale.edu/18th_century/declaratory_act _1766.asp.
2. Becker, "Revolution and Reform," 419–21. The literature on the Regulators is extensive. Useful overviews of their grievances can be found in Ekirch, *"Poor Carolina,"* chap. 6; Kars, *Breaking Loose Together*, chaps. 2–3; and Troxler, *Farming Dissenters*, esp. xi, 21. See also Chandler, "Unawed by the Laws of Their Country," 120–45.
3. Kars, *Breaking Loose Together*, 111–12; Chandler, "Unawed by the Laws of their Country," 126; Regulators' Advertisement No. 1, Aug. 1766, in *CSRNC*, 7:249–50.
4. Ekirch, *"Poor Carolina,"* 170, 171; Kars, *Breaking Loose Together*, 72–73; Hudson, "Songs of the North Carolina Regulators," 477; *American National Biography Online*, s.v. "Fanning, Edmund," by Ann Gorman Condon, www.anb.org.
5. Ekirch, *"Poor Carolina,"* 136, 139, 169; Kars, *Breaking Loose Together*, 32–33.
6. Minutes of the Rowan County Court, 14–18 Oct. 1768, 15–18 Nov. 1769, 14–18 Aug. 1770, in *CSRNC*, 7:856–57; 8:156–57, 227.
7. For an excellent concise summary of the Regulators' petitioning efforts, see Chandler, "Unawed by the Laws of Their Country," 129–35. For the petitions, neither of which is reprinted in *CSRNC*, see Petition of Inhabitants of the County of Roan [*sic*] and Orange, 4 Oct. 1768, GASR, SANC, and Petition of Inhabitants of Orange County Bordering on Cumberland, 11 Nov. 1768, ibid. The October petition is printed in Butler and Watson, *North Carolina Experience*, 113–14.
8. Chandler, "Unawed by the Laws of Their Country," 132–36; Petition from inhabitants of Orange and Rowan Counties, Oct. 1769, in *CSRNC*, 8:81–84; Stewart, *Redemption from Tyranny*, 61–65.
9. For a brief summary of the events leading to the Battle of Alamance, see Ekirch, *"Poor Carolina,"* 164–65. The best extended treatment of these events and their significance is Kars, *Breaking Loose Together*, chaps. 1–3.
10. Petition from inhabitants of Guilford and Orange Counties concerning the pardon of Thomas Welborn, 25 Aug. 1771, in *CSRNC*, 9:25–27; Quinn, "Flower Swift Militia Company."
11. Kars, *Breaking Loose Together*, 1, 143–44.
12. Linn, *Abstracts of the Deeds*, 4:99; Klutz, *Abstract of Deed Books 15–19*, 65; *Spurgin Quarterly*, no. 4 (Aug. 1985): 81–82; Linn, *Rowan County, North Carolina, Tax Lists*, 100.
13. William Tryon to Earl of Shelburne, 29 June 1767, in Tryon, *Correspondence of William Tryon*, 1:522; Michael G. Kammen, "The American Revolution as a *Crise de Conscience*: The Case of New York," in *Society, Freedom, and Conscience*, ed. Jellison, 135–37; Kars, *Breaking Loose Together*, 171–72; Ekirch, *"Poor Carolina,"* 168–74.
14. Here and elsewhere, I have tracked William's court attendance using the appropriate volumes of Linn, *Abstracts of the Minutes of the Court of Pleas and Quarter Sessions*. See also Troxler, *Farming Dissenters*, 61–62; and Kars, *Breaking Loose Together*, 68–69, 169–70.
15. Bynum, *Free State of Jones*, 20–22; Paschal, *History of North Carolina Baptists*, 2:185; Fries, *Records of the Moravians*, 2:796; Regulators' Advertisement No. 6, 4 Apr. 1768, in *CSRNC*, 7:702–3; Agreement between Rowan County public officials and the Regulators, 7 Mar. 1771, ibid., 8:521–22; Kars, *Breaking Loose Together*, 158.

16. Nelson, *William Tryon and the Course of Empire*, 27–31; Kars, *Breaking Loose Together*, 84–86, 107–10, 125–29, 155–56, 180–81; Paschal, *History of North Carolina Baptists*, 1:335–60.

17. Isaac, *Transformation of Virginia*, 163–72; Kars, *Breaking Loose Together*, 95–106, 127, 129; Paschal, *History of North Carolina Baptists*, 1:333–34, 2:183; Morgan, "Great Awakening in North Carolina," 280.

18. Linn, *Abstracts of the Deeds*, 111, 121; Caruthers, *Revolutionary Incidents*, 40; Josiah Martin to William Legge, Early of Dartmouth, 28 Nov. 1772, in *CSRNC*, 9:357–60.

19. For recent scholarly assessments of the connections between Regulators and revolutionaries, or lack thereof, see Kars, *Breaking Loose Together*, chap. 12; Troxler, *Farming Dissenters*, 121–24; and Ekirch, *"Poor Carolina,"* 209–11. On Husband, see Stewart, *Redemption from Tyranny*, esp. chap. 4.

20. A List of Magistrates for Rowan County, 1771, GASR, SANC. Subsequent activities of nineteen of the men on this list have been tracked by consulting *CSRNC*, and these other sources: *The American Revolution in North Carolina*, https://www.carolana .com/NC/Revolution/home.html, for militia officers and legislators; and Rockwell, *Rowan County*, for county committees. One of the twenty-three JPs died before 1776, and three others could not be identified. For Matthew Locke, see *NCpedia*, s.v. "Locke, Matthew," by James S. Brawley, https://www.ncpedia.org/biography/locke -matthew.

21. Ekirch, *"Poor Carolina,"* 203–9; James Hunter to William Butler, 6 Nov. 1772, in *Regulators in North Carolina*, ed. Powell et al., 537.

22. Breen, *Marketplace of Revolution*, chap. 7 (quotation on 261); Merritt, *Trouble with Tea*, 63–77.

23. Carp, *Defiance of the Patriots*, esp. chaps. 6 and 9; Merritt, *Trouble with Tea*, chap. 4.

24. Maier, *From Resistance to Revolution*, chaps. 6 and 8; Watson, "Committee of Safety and the Coming of the American Revolution," 133–34; Resolutions by inhabitants of Rowan County concerning resistance to Parliamentary taxation and the Provincial Congress of North Carolina, 8 Aug.1774, in *CSRNC*, 9:1024–26.

25. Minutes of the Rowan County Committee of Safety, 23 Sept. 1774, in *CSRNC*, 9:1072– 75. Lists of committee members for 1774 through 1776 are in Rockwell, *Rowan County*, 120. For attendance of JPs in court during this period, see Linn, *Abstracts of the Minutes of the Court of Pleas and Quarter Sessions*, vol. 3, passim.

26. A cumulative list of men who signed the various Regulator petitions (not all of whom were from Rowan County) is in Troxler, *Farming Dissenters*, 159–66.

27. Resolutions by inhabitants of Rowan County concerning resistance to Parliamentary taxation and the Provincial Congress of North Carolina, 8 Aug.1774, in *CSRNC*, 9:1024–26. On comparably self-serving anti–slave-trade rhetoric in Virginia, see Holton, *Forced Founders*, 104–5.

28. Josiah Martin to North Carolina Council, 12 Aug. 1774, in *CSRNC*, 9:1028; Martin to Earl of Dartmouth, 4 Nov. 1774, ibid., 9:1083. See also Jasanoff, *Liberty's Exiles*, 25–27. On conflicting contemporary understandings of Parliamentary sovereignty and the place of the monarchy in the British constitution, see Wood, *Creation of the American Republic*, esp. 10–36, 127–32.

29. Rowan County Committee Minutes, 23 Sept. 1774, in *CSRNC*, 9:1072–75. For useful accounts of the Dunn and Boote story, see DeMond, *Loyalists in North Carolina*, 108–9; and *NCpedia*, s.v. "Dunn, John Ross," by Carole Watterson Troxler, https:// www.ncpedia.org/biography/dunn-john-ross.

30. Rowan County Committee Minutes, Nov. 1774, in *CSRNC*, 9:1079–80; Troxler, "Dunn, John Ross."
31. Rowan County Committee Minutes, Nov. 1774, in *CSRNC*, 9:1079–80; Larson, *Trials of Allegiance*, 51–55; Anderson, *Martyr and the Traitor*, 90. The text of the second resolution did not include the words "Abbotts Creek" but rather stipulated that the meeting would occur "at Spraikers." The Spraiker (or Spraker or Sprecher) family resided in Abbotts Creek near the Spurgins (see Linn, *Rowan County, North Carolina, Tax Lists*, 100–103).
32. On Virginia, see Isaac, *Transformation of Virginia*, chaps. 11–12.
33. Address of Sundry Inhabitants of the Counties of Rowan and Surry to Governor Martin, spring 1775, in *CSRNC*, 9:1160; Fries, *Records of the Moravians*, 2:702, 847, 913. The list of signers of the loyal address to Martin is not printed in *CSRNC*, nor has it survived with the original document, which is in the Thomas Gage Papers, William Clements Library, University of Michigan.
34. Rowan County address to the militia, June 1775, in *CSRNC*, 10:10–11; Minutes of Rowan County Committee of Safety, 1 Aug. 1775, in *CSRNC*, 10:135. See, generally, Parkinson, *Common Cause*, esp. chap. 2.
35. Minutes of Rowan County Committee of Safety, 1 Aug. 1775, in *CSRNC*, 10:134.
36. Minutes of Rowan County Committee of Safety, 10–11 Nov. 1775, in *CSRNC*, 10:316–17; Kammen, "American Revolution as a *Crise de Conscience*," 145–46, 158–61; Sullivan, *Disaffected*, 30–31. On Jacob Beck, see "Devault Theobald Beck (abt. 1715—abt. 1789)," https://www.wikitree.com/wiki/Beck-901.
37. Proclamation by Governor Josiah Martin, 15 Aug. 1775, in *CSRNC*, 10:150; Manifesto by Donald MacDonald concerning recruitment of loyalist troops in North Carolina, 5 Feb. 1776, ibid., 10:443–44.
38. Kammen, "American Revolution as a *Crise de Conscience*," 157; Martin, "*Nemo Potest Exuere Patriam*," 205–18.
39. Fries, *Records of the Moravians*, 2:846, 850–51.

3. William's War

1. Commission to appoint Allan MacDonald et al. as officers of loyalist militias, 10 Jan. 1776, in *CSRNC*, 10:396–97; An Act directing the sale of Confiscated Property, 1782, ibid., 24:424–29; Josiah Martin to Welbore Ellis, Baron Mendip, 7 Mar. 1782, ibid., 22:617–18.
2. Katcher, "Provincial Corps of the British Army," 164–71; DeMond, *Loyalists in North Carolina*, 61; Rankin, *North Carolina Continentals;* Paul H. Smith, "American Loyalists," 263–66.
3. Paul H. Smith, "American Loyalists," 268–69; Adams quoted in Ekirch, *"Poor Carolina,"* 211; Ambuske, "Loss Sustain'd by the Immense Drain of Men," 322–37; Josiah Martin to George Sackville Germain, 21 Mar. 1776, in *CSRNC*, 10:492.
4. Manifesto by Donald McDonald concerning recruitment of loyalist troops in North Carolina, 10 Feb. 1776, in *CSRNC*, 10:443–44; Waightsill Avery to Richard Richardson, 3 Dec. 1775, Draper Mss. 1KK14, State Historical Society of Wisconsin; Statement of James Henderson, 29 Mar. 1776, ibid. 1KK16–17; Cann, "Prelude to War," 197–214.
5. For population, see Boyd, *Some Eighteenth-Century Tracts Concerning North Carolina*, 415–17; Minutes of Rowan County Committee of Safety, 10–11 Nov. 1775,

in *CSRNC*, 10:316–17; Commission to appoint Allan MacDonald et al. as officers of loyalist militias, 10 Jan. 1776, in *CSRNC*, 10:396–97. The proximity of the Spurgin and Sappenfield residences can be deduced from the county tax lists (see Linn, *Rowan County, North Carolina, Tax Lists*, 100).

6. W. Brown, *King's Friends*, 334. It is telling that, for various reasons, none of these three men submitted postwar claims to the Loyalist Claims Commission in London.

7. North Carolina Provincial Council Report, 10 Apr. 1776, in *CSRNC*, 10:599; Minutes of the Rowan County Committee of Safety, 1 Aug. 1775, ibid., 10:137; "Johann (Johannes) Matthias Sappenfield biography," https://www.wikitree.com/wiki/Sappenfield-23; Linn, *Abstracts of the Minutes of the Court of Pleas and Quarter Sessions*, 1:33, 42, 51; 2:22; Cross and McKeehan, "Names of North Carolina Regulators," http://www.sons ofdewittcolony.org/mckstmerrframe.htm.

8. Ramsey, *Carolina Cradle*, 28–37; DeMond, *Loyalists in North Carolina*, 55–56, 67; Address of inhabitants of Rowan and Surry Counties to Josiah Martin concerning loyalty to Great Britain, [spring 1775], in *CSRNC*, 9:1160; Rawdon to Cornwallis, 4 July 1780, in Cornwallis, *Cornwallis Papers*, 1:192.

9. Commission to appoint Allan MacDonald et al. as officers of loyalist militias, 10 Jan. 1776, in *CSRNC*, 10:396–97; Manifesto by Donald McDonald concerning recruitment of loyalist troops in North Carolina, 10 Feb. 1776, ibid., 10:443–44; Fries, *Records of the Moravians*, 2:702, 3:1025–26, 1047; Caruthers, *Revolutionary Incidents*, 50.

10. Caswell to the North Carolina Provincial Congress, 29 Feb. 1776, in *American Archives*, ed. Force, 5:62. The two best accounts are Rankin, "Moore's Creek Bridge," 23–60; and Wilson, *Southern Strategy*, chap. 3.

11. Caswell to the North Carolina Provincial Congress, 29 Feb. 1776, in *American Archives*, ed. Force, 5:62; Rankin, "Moore's Creek Bridge," 56–57; Jones, *Captives of Liberty*, 111–12; Farquhard Campbell to Richard Caswell, 3 Mar. 1777, in *CSRNC*, 11:403–5; Josiah Martin to George Sackville Germain, 23 Jan. 1778, ibid., 13:368; *NCpedia*, s.v. "Campbell, Farquhard," by William C. Fields, https://www.ncpedia.org /biography/campbell-farquhard; DeMond, *Loyalists in North Carolina*, 111, 232; Letter of administration for the estate of Matthias Sappenfield, 21 Sept. 1781, listed in Pelletreau et al., *Abstracts of Wills*, 9:323.

12. W. E. Lee, *Crowds and Soldiers*, 154–55. For MacDonald and McCrummin, see "British Legion Biographical Sketches, Infantry Officers," at *The On-Line Institute for Advanced Loyalist Studies*, http://www.royalprovincial.com/military/rhist /britlegn/blinf1.htm. For McLeod, see Egerton, *Royal Commission on the Losses and Service of American Loyalists*, 214–15.

13. Rankin, "Moore's Creek Bridge," 55–56; Memoir by Hugh McDonald [Extract], 1853, in *CSRNC*, 11:835–36; Fries, *Records of the Moravians*, 3:1054.

14. Fries, *Records of the Moravians*, 3:1139, 1143. On Bryan, see Carole W. Troxler, "Before and after Ramsour's Mill: Cornwallis's Complaints and Historical Memory of Southern Backcountry Loyalists," in *Consequences of Loyalism*, ed. Brannon and Moore, 87.

15. Wilson, *Southern Strategy*, chaps. 2–4. See also Carp, *Great New York Fire of 1776*.

16. W. E. Lee, *Crowds and Soldiers*, chap. 6; Minutes of the Provincial Congress, 13 May 1776, in *CSRNC*, 10:585; Ordinances of the Convention, 22 Nov. 1776, ibid., 23:985; Ganyard, "Threat from the West," 47–61.

17. Fries, *Records of the Moravians*, 3:1139, 1144.

18. Troxler, *Loyalist Experience*, 9; Sullivan, *Disaffected*, 22, 30–31; Michael G. Kammen, "The American Revolution as a *Crise de Conscience:* The Case of New York," in *Society, Freedom, and Conscience*, ed. Jellison, 144–45.

19. *CSRNC*, 24:9–12. The process of defining and punishing treason was similar in other states. See, for instance, Larson, *Trials of Allegiance*, 70–77.

20. *CSRNC*, 24:9–12; Troxler, *Loyalist Experience*, 9.

21. *North Carolina Gazette*, 25 July 1777, in *CSRNC*, 11:743; DeMond, *Loyalists in North Carolina*, 181–84; *American National Biography Online*, s.v. "Howard, Martin," by Noel Yancey, www.anb.org.

22. *CSRNC*, 24:88–89.

23. Ibid.; Sappington, "North Carolina and the Non-Resistant Sects," 29–47.

24. Linn, *Abstracts of the Minutes of the Court of Pleas and Quarter Sessions*, 3:41–43; Welborn, *Welborns and Related Families*, 11–12; Rowan County tax list, 1778, SANC.

25. Memorial from militia officers of Rowan County concerning service in the Continental Army, 1778, in *CSRNC*, 13:289–90; W. E. Lee, *Crowds and Soldiers*, 168–69. For a helpful explanation of the relationship between Continental recruitment, the states, and the county militia in one Maryland community, see J. B. Lee, *Price of Nationhood*, 134–48.

26. Coleman, *American Revolution in Georgia*, 116–23; Frey, *Water from the Rock*, 86–107; Allison and Ferreiro, *American Revolution as a World War*.

27. DeMond, *Loyalists in North Carolina*, 171–74; Harrell, "North Carolina Loyalists," 580–88; in *CSRNC*, 22:880–89, 24: 424–25, 263–64; Linn, *Abstracts of the Minutes of the Court of Pleas and Quarter Sessions*, 3:150; Troxler, "Before and after Ramsour's Mill," 83; Fries, *Records of the Moravians*, 3:1205–6.

28. Minutes of the North Carolina House of Commons, 10 Feb. 1779; in *CSRNC*, 13:717; Resolution of the North Carolina General Assembly, 12 Feb. 1779, ibid., 15:388; W. E. Lee, *Crowds and Soldiers*, 167; Troxler, *Loyalist Experience*, 21–25.

29. Davis, *Kettle Creek*, 30–32, 59–60; Davis, "Loyalist Trials at Ninety Six," 172–73; Campbell, *Journal of* [. . .] *Archibald Campbell Esquire*, 58; Garden, *Anecdotes of the American Revolution*, 86; Troxler, "Before and after Ramsour's Mill," 85–87; Chesney, *Journal of Alexander Chesney*, 79–81; Memorial of Zacharias Gibbs to the Loyalist Claims Commission, Loyalist Claims Commission Papers, AO 46/145–52; Memorial of Christopher Neeley to the Loyalist Claims Commission, ibid., AO 49/320–29; "Case of the Loyalists in North Carolina," 266. Robert Scott Davis, a leading authority on the battle at Kettle Creek, names John Spurgin, not William, as Boyd's third-in-command, but for a persuasive alternate interpretation, see the exhaustively researched Elliott, *Stirring Up a Hornet's Nest*, esp. 8–9.

30. Memorial of Christopher Neeley; Clyde R. Ferguson, "Carolina and Georgia Patriot and Loyalist Militia in Action, 1778–1783," in *Southern Experience in the American Revolution*, ed. Crow and Tise, 174–99.

31. Three comprehensive modern accounts are Ashmore and Olmstead, "Battles of Kettle Creek and Brier Creek," 85–100, and the more balanced and well-documented Davis, *Kettle Creek*, and McDaniel, "Georgia's Forgotten Battlefields," 88–96. An important early account is McCall, *History of Georgia*, 396–99. See also Joseph Cartwright deposition, 1779, Draper Mss. 3 VV, 250–53, State Historical Society of Wisconsin; Ramsay, *History of the Revolution of South-Carolina*, 2:15.

32. Garden, *Anecdotes of the American Revolution*, 87; Piecuch, *Three Peoples, One King*, 172. For instance, Kettle Creek is not mentioned in either edition of the massive classic Middlekauff, *Glorious Cause*, or in the more recent (and less elite-focused) Holton, *Liberty Is Sweet*.

33. McCall, *History of Georgia*, 396–97; Elliott, *Stirring Up a Hornet's Nest*, 8–9, 21–22, 60; Ashmore and Olmstead, "Battles of Kettle Creek and Brier Creek," 96, 98;

Bacon, *History of Georgia,* 2:191; Davis, *Georgians in the Revolution,* 23; *Gazette of South Carolina,* 7 April 1779; Davis, *Kettle Creek,* 64–65. On Hugh McCall, see John C. Inscoe, "Hugh McCall (1767–1824)," *New Georgia Encyclopedia.* Neither William nor his brother John appears in the exhaustive standard genealogical reference for southern loyalists (Clark, *Loyalists in the Southern Campaign*).

34. Davis, *Kettle Creek,* 59–64. See also Lambert, *South Carolina Loyalists,* 82; Parkinson, *Common Cause,* 448–49. On Pickens, see Andrew, *Life and Times of General Andrew Pickens.* Biographical sketches of all of these men, and many others, appear in Elliott, *Stirring Up a Hornet's Nest.*

35. Davis, "Loyalist Trials at Ninety Six," 172–75, 180; Piecuch, *Three Peoples, One King,* 140–42; "Case of the Loyalists in North Carolina," 266; Memorial of Zacharias Gibbs.

36. Jones, *Captives of Liberty,* esp. 4–6, 11, 185–86; W. E. Lee, *Crowds and Soldiers,* 185–88; Davis, "Loyalist Trials at Ninety Six," 176–80; *Gazette of the State of South-Carolina,* 14 Apr. 1779; Memorial of Zacharias Gibbs; Memorial of Christopher Neeley.

37. Ramsay, *History of the Revolution of South Carolina,* 2:15.

38. Fries, *Records of the Moravians,* 3:1282, 1302, 1304–8; 4:1516; W. E. Lee, *Crowds and Soldiers,* 171.

39. Pancake, *This Destructive War,* chaps. 4 and 6; W. E. Lee, *Crowds and Soldiers,* 171–75; Cornwallis to Clinton, 30 June 1780, in Cornwallis, *Cornwallis Papers,* 1:162.

40. *NCpedia,* s.v. "Ramsour's Mill, Battle of," by Daniel W. Barefoot, https://www.ncpedia .org/ramsours-mill-battle; *NCpedia,* s.v. "Bryan, Samuel," by John K. Bryan Jr., https://www.ncpedia.org/biography/bryan-samuel; Rawdon to Cornwallis, 4 July 1780, in Cornwallis, *Cornwallis Papers,* 1:192.

41. Fries, *Records of the Moravians,* 4: 1549.

42. Ramsay, *Ramsay's History of South Carolina,* 266.

4. Jane's World

1. Pancake, *This Destructive War,* 164–66; Stumpf, *Josiah Martin,* 192–94; Petition of William Spurgin, 10 Sept. 1792, Land Petitions of Upper Canada, LAC; Caruthers, *Interesting Revolutionary Incidents,* 39–40; Joseph Spurgin's Statement of Revolutionary Events, 1854, *Spurgin Quarterly* 18 (May 1989): 435; Casper Hinkle pension application, 29 Nov. 1833, *Southern Campaign American Revolution Pension Statements & Rosters,* http://revwarapps.org/s16875.pdf. Greene's stay at Abbotts Creek can be tracked through his correspondence, which does not mention any member of the Spurgin family explicitly (see Greene, *Papers of General Nathanael Greene,* 253–57).

2. Petition of Jennet (Jane) Spurgin, 28 Nov. 1791, GASR, SANC.

3. Skemp, *Benjamin and William Franklin;* Van Buskirk, *Generous Enemies,* 50; Petition of Joshua Campbell, [1791], GASR, SANC.

4. Daniels, *Randolphs of Virginia,* 85–94; Young, "George Robert Twelves Hewes (1742–1840)," 597; Anderson, *Martyr and the Traitor,* 168, 173–74, 180, 187; Van Buskirk, *Generous Enemies,* 48.

5. Zabin, *Boston Massacre,* 222–28; Stark, *Loyalists of Massachusetts,* 368; Kimberly Nath, "Left Behind: Loyalist Women in Philadelphia during the American Revolu-

tion," in *Women in the American Revolution,* ed. Oberg, 212, 221; Martha J. King, "'A Lady of New Jersey': Annis Boudinot Stockton, Patriot and Poet in an Age of Revolution," ibid., 103–4, 108–12.

6. Gundersen, "Independence, Citizenship, and the American Revolution," 68. See also the discussion in Tillman, "What Is a Female Loyalist?"

7. Norton, *Liberty's Daughters,* chap. 6; Kierner, *Beyond the Household,* 78–81, 88; Cynthia A. Kierner, "The Edenton Ladies: Women, Tea, and Politics in Revolutionary North Carolina," in *North Carolina Women,* ed. Gillespie and McMillen, 12–33; Mayer, *Belonging to the Army,* esp. chap. 4; Young, *Masquerade;* Holton, *Liberty Is Sweet,* 300, 402.

8. *South Carolina Gazette and American General Gazette,* 21 Sept. 1776; *Virginia Gazette* (Purdie and Dixon), 2 June 1774; *Virginia Gazette* (Purdie), 4 July 1777; Proceedings of the Committee of Safety of Rowan County, 8 May 1776, in *CSRNC,* 10:594.

9. Martha Ryan's cipher book, 1781, Southern Historical Collection, University of North Carolina at Chapel Hill, https://finding-aids.lib.unc.edu/01940/#folder_1#1; Application of William Gipson, in *Revolution Remembered,* ed. Dann, 187–89; Kerber, *Women of the Republic,* esp. 199–204, 283–87.

10. Norton, *Liberty's Daughters,* chap. 7; Fries, *Records of the Moravians,* 3:1143, 4:1516. The Rowan County tax list for 1775 reported William Spurgin as owning an enslaved man named Neel, whereas Jane sought to recover another enslaved man named Simon in 1785 (see Rowan County tax list, 1775, SANC; Petition of Jane Spurgin, 3 Dec. 1785, GASR, SANC; Petition of Charles Bruce, Nov. 1790, GASR, SANC).

11. Kierner, *Beyond the Household,* 75–76, 89; *Virginia Gazette* (Dixon and Hunter), 21 Sept. 1776; *North Carolina Gazette,* 14 Nov. 1777.

12. Ashe, *History of North Carolina,* 600, 626–27, 715; Rowan County tax list, 1778, SANC; Linn, *Rowan County, North Carolina, Tax Lists,* 135, 249.

13. Minutes of the Provincial Congress, 13 May 1776, in *CSRNC,* 10:585.

14. *CSRNC,* 24:9–12; Kerber, *No Constitutional Right to Be Ladies,* 16–17.

15. *CSRNC,* 24:10, 85, 429; Kerber, *No Constitutional Right to Be Ladies,* 17–18.

16. Enochs, *Rowan County, NC, Vacant Land Entries,* i–vi.

17. Ibid., 109; Casper Hinkle pension application.

18. Klutz, *Abstract of Deed Books 15–19,* 63; Troxler, *Loyalist Experience,* 30; Will of William Spurgin, 13 Aug. 1806, London District, Upper Canada, Surrogate Court Register A, 1800–1817, 67–71. On gender and inheritance generally, see Salmon, *Women and the Law of Property in Early America,* 18–22, 142, 158.

19. Norton, *Liberty's Daughters,* 213–16, 226–27; Holton, *Abigail Adams,* esp. chap. 13; Petition of Jane Spurgin, 11 Nov. 1788, GASR, SANC.

20. Fraser, *United Empire Loyalists,* 1:280–81; Carole W. Troxler, "Before and after Ramsour's Mill: Cornwallis's Complaints and Historical Memory of Southern Backcountry Loyalists," in *Consequences of Loyalism,* ed. Brannon and Moore, 78; Family Central Family History Services, http://www.familycentral.net/index/family.cfm?ref1=6074:382&ref2=6074:383.

21. See generally A. Roger Ekirch, "Whig Authority and Public Order in Backcountry North Carolina, 1776–1783," in *Uncivil War,* ed. Hoffman et al., 99–124; Jeffrey J. Crow, "Liberty Men and Loyalists: Disorder and Disaffection in the North Carolina Backcountry," ibid., 125–78; Lee, *Crowds and Soldiers,* chap. 7.

22. Fries, *Records of the Moravians,* 4:1549, 1556, 1565, 1621–22, 1642, 1649, 1655; Cornwallis to Clinton, 2 June 1780, 6 Aug. 1780, in Cornwallis, *Cornwallis Papers,* 1:55, 177; Petition of William Spurgin, 14 July 1794, Land Petitions of Upper Canada, LAC.

23. Fries, *Records of the Moravians*, 4: 1562, 1625, 1629, 1630–31, 1644; Ekirch, "Whig Authority and Public Order," 107–8, 111–15; Crow, "Liberty Men and Loyalists," 141, 145.

24. Caruthers, *Revolutionary Incidents*, 420–22.

25. Count based on Lewis, "The Known Battles & Skirmishes in North Carolina," https://www.carolana.com/NC/Revolution/NC_Revolutionary_War_Known _Battles_Skirmishes.htm/.

26. Fries, *Records of the Moravians*, esp. 4:1657, 1659, 1682–83, 1691, 1709, 1718, 1723, 1749–55, 1770–71, 1774–75, 1777–78; Fenn, *Pox Americana*, 116–26; D. F. Johnson, *Occupied America*, 15. 113, 117–25; Godbeer, *World of Trouble*, 157–67; Sylvia Whitlock to William Davidson, 20 Jan. 1781, in Cornwallis, *Cornwallis Papers*, 4:93; Petition of Jane Spurgin, 11 Nov. 1788, GASR, SANC.

27. Speech of Waightsill Avery to the Grand Jury, March 1777, Draper Mss., 1 VV (unpaginated), State Historical Society of Wisconsin; Wilkinson, *Letters of Eliza Wilkinson*, 29–31, 46; Fries, *Records of the Moravians*, 4:1576, 1652, 1781; Troxler, *Loyalist Experience*, 27.

28. Block, *Rape and Sexual Power in Early America*, 80–81, 230–37; Hoock, "*Jus in Bello*," 83–87; D. F. Johnson, *Occupied America*, 94–96.

29. Elizabeth Steele to Ephraim Steele, 19 Apr. 1781, in Steele, *Papers of John Steele*, 10–11. On Steele, see Cory Joe Stewart, "Elizabeth Maxwell Steele: 'A Great Politician' and the Revolution in the Southern Backcountry," in *North Carolina Women*, ed. Gillespie and McMillen, 54–72.

30. Caruthers, *Interesting Revolutionary Incidents*, 40.

31. Casper Hinkle pension application; Caruthers, *Interesting Revolutionary Incidents*, 40–42; Fries, *Records of the Moravians*, 4:1674. Caruthers identified Greene's scout as John Spurgin, a "mere lad," but it was clearly a different son because John, the eldest, was born in 1753.

32. Babits and Howard, *Long, Obstinate, and Bloody*, chap. 9.

33. Cornwallis to Germain, 8 Apr. 1781, in Cornwallis, *Cornwallis Papers*, 4:106; Troxler, "Before and after Ramsour's Mill," 265–67; Returns of Charles Cornwallis' Brigade of the British Army (2), in *CSRNC*, 1781, 17:1009, 1027.

34. Petition of William Spurgin, 14 July 1794, Land Petitions of Upper Canada, LAC.

35. Ibid.; J. A. Houlding, *Oxford Dictionary of National Biography*, s.v. "Simcoe, John Graves," www.oxforddnb.

36. Cornwallis to Rawdon, 17 Mar. 1781, in Cornwallis, *Cornwallis Papers*, 4:46; Cornwallis to Clinton, 10 Apr. 1781, ibid., 4:111; Pancake, *The Destructive War*, chap. 11 (quotation on p. 186).

37. John Quillin deposition, 24 Aug. 1833, *Southern Campaign American Revolution Pension Statements & Rosters*, http://revwarapps.org/s9461.pdf; Fries, *Records of the Moravians*, 4:1695, 1698, 1704, 1781.

38. Nathanael Greene to Thomas Burke, 12 Aug. 1781, in *CSRNC*, 15:605; Watterson, "Ordeal of Governor Burke," 104–10.

39. Thomas Robeson to Alexander Martin, 24 Jan. 1782, in *CSRNC*, 22:608; Diary of a North Carolina soldier [Extract], Apr. 1782, ibid., 16:607; Fries, *Records of the Moravians*, 4:1782.

40. Josiah Martin to Welbore Ellis, Baron Mendip, 7 Mar. 1782, in *CSRNC*, 22:617–18; An Act directing the sale of Confiscated Property, 1782, ibid., 24:424–29. Martin praised the efforts of "John Spurgin," but he must have meant William because John had died in 1779 and William, not John, was a resident of North Carolina.

5. The Tory's Wife

1. Fries, *Records of the Moravians*, 4:1834–35, 1668–69, 1885; Travers, *Celebrating the Fourth*, 17–41.
2. Address of Alexander Martin to the General Assembly, 19 Apr. 1783, in *CSRNC*, 16:773–74.
3. Ibid.; Act of Pardon and Oblivion, 1783, ibid., 24:489–90.
4. Proclamation of Alexander Martin, 28 July 1783, ibid., 16:850–81; Brannon, *From Revolution to Reunion*, esp. chap. 4; DeMond, *Loyalists in North Carolina*, 251–55; Harrell, "North Carolina Loyalists," 579–80; Jasanoff, *Liberty's Exiles*, 6, 130–31, 386n.
5. Siebert, *Loyalists in East Florida*, 1:101–59; Raynor, *Patriots and Loyalists in Piedmont Carolina*, 10–21; Will of Samuel Bryan, 15 Aug. 1798, Rowan County Will Book D, 121–23, SANC.
6. Treaty of Paris, 3 Sept. 1783, *Primary Documents in American History*, https://www.loc.gov/law/help/us-treaties/bevans/b-gb-ust000012-0008.pdf.
7. DeMond, *Loyalists in North Carolina*, 58, 170–74, 240–50; Harrell, "North Carolina Loyalists," 586–89; Morrill, *Practice and Politics of Fiat Finance*, 35–38.
8. DeMond, *Loyalists in North Carolina*, 240–50; Pruitt, *Abstract of Land Entries*, 85; Hammersmith and Stein, *Old Guilford, North Carolina Court Minutes*, D, entry 21.
9. William Spurgin to John Graves Simcoe, 10 Sept. 1792, Land Petitions of Upper Canada, LAC; Jasanoff, *Liberty's Exiles*, 120–23, 130–31.
10. For a helpful explanation of these common forms of credit, see Hartigan-O'Connor, *Ties That Buy*, esp. 74–78.
11. Joseph Spurgin's Statement of Revolutionary Events, 1854, *Spurgin Quarterly* 18 (May 1989): 436; Petition of Jane Spurgin, 28 Nov. 1791, GASR, SANC; Sink and Matthews, *Pathfinders Past and Present*, 32; Linn, *Abstracts of the Minutes of the Court of Pleas and Quarter Sessions*, 3:90–91.
12. Petition of Jane Spurgin, 3 Dec. 1785, GASR, SANC; Rowan County Census, 1790, in *CSRNC*, 26:1027, 1028; Jacob Idol pension application, 1833, *Southern Campaigns American Revolution Pension Statements & Rosters*, http://revwarapps.org/w7859.pdf; *Tarboro Free Press*, 20 Mar. 1832. In her petition, Jane stated that William owned two tracts totaling 704 acres; court records give a slightly different count of 706 acres.
13. Linn, *Abstracts of the Deeds*, 204.
14. Salisbury District Superior Court Minutes, 1783, *Rowan Register* 9 (1994): 2086–87.
15. Linn, *Rowan County, North Carolina, Tax Lists*, 219–20, 245–46, 249.
16. Linn, *Abstracts of the Deeds*, 204; A True Bill by David Reese, Sept. 1785, Salisbury District Court, Criminal Action Papers, SANC; Salisbury District Superior Court minutes, Sept. 1785, *Rowan County Register* 16 (2001): 3726–27.
17. A True Bill by David Reese, Sept. 1785, Salisbury District Court, Criminal Action Papers, SANC.
18. Ibid.; Salisbury District Superior Court minutes, Sept. 1785, *Rowan County Register* 16 (2001): 3726–27; An Act to Prevent Horse-Stealing, 1784, in *CSRNC*, 24:688; Coates, "Punishment for Crime in North Carolina," 205–6.
19. An Act to Alter the Mode of Punishing Horse Stealing [. . .], 1787, in *CSRNC*, 24:795; Kotch, *Lethal State*, 9–11; Maestro, "Pioneer for the Abolition of Capital Punishment," 463–68.
20. An Act to Alter the Mode of Punishing Horse Stealing [. . .], 1787, in *CSRNC*, 24:795.

21. Petition of Jane Spurgin, 3 Dec. 1785, GASR, SANC.
22. Bailey, *Popular Influence upon Public Policy,* 9–16; Higginson, "Short History of the Right to Petition"; *Petitions, memorials, and other documents,* 1–9.
23. Although the courts typically handled emancipation petitions in North Carolina, see the petition of Ned Griffin, 4 Apr. 1784, and that of Grace and Richard Davis, 14 Dec. 1791, both in GASR, SANC.
24. Wood, *Creation of the American Republic,* chap. 5; Peterson, "Messages, Petitions, Communications, and Memorials to Congress"; Schamel, "Untapped Resources."
25. Based on Minutes of the North Carolina House of Commons, 19 Nov.–29 Dec. 1785, in *CSRNC,* 17:264–425. For statistics on petitioning in North Carolina between 1750 and 1775, and on women's petitioning between 1776 and 1800, see Kierner, *Southern Women in Revolution,* xxi, 231.
26. For references to these petitions in the legislative minutes, see *CSRNC,* 17:283, 284, 292–93, 294, 308, 315, 320, 322, 347–48, 370, 371, 379, 388, 391, 401, 419. See also Petition of Martha Dixon, 20 Oct. 1785, GASR, SANC.
27. Petition of Margaret Cotton, 15 Aug. 1778, GASR, SANC; Petition of Elizabeth Torrence, 24 Oct. 1783, GASR, SANC; *NCpeida,* s.v. "Cotton, James," by Robert M. McBride, https://www.ncpedia.org/biography/cotton-james. See also Kierner, *Southern Women in Revolution,* chap. 3.
28. Petition of Jane Spurgin, 3 Dec. 1785, GASR, SANC.
29. Petition of Jane Spurgin, 10 Nov. 1788, GASR, SANC.
30. Petition of Jane Spurgin, 3 Dec. 1785, GASR, SANC.
31. Ibid.
32. Linn, *Abstracts of the Minutes of the Court of Pleas and Quarter Sessions,* 3: 150; DeMond, *Loyalists in North Carolina,* 250.
33. Klutz, *Abstract of Deed Books 11–14,* 1:8; Quinn, "The Flower Swift Militia Company;" Petition of Jean Spurgin, 11 Nov. 1788, GASR, SANC. Solomon and Ann's surname is rendered variously as Reddick, Riddick, or Ruddick. In choosing "Ruddick," I am deferring to the usage in the main published family history, which also gives a later birthdate for Aaron Spurgin (Hanneman, *Ruddick Family in America,* 15). Nevertheless, Aaron's gravestone in Iowa and his entry in the 1860 US census verify his true birthdate and birthplace, respectively. See https://www.findagrave.com/memorial /32271591/aaron-spurgin and https://www.familysearch.org/ark:/61903/3:1:33S7 -9B9N-3D6L?i=13&cc=1473181&personaUrl=%2Fark%3A%2F61903%2F1%3A1%3AM 8L3-G2P.
34. Petition of Jane Spurgin, 10 Nov. 1788, GASR, SANC.
35. Ibid.
36. Ibid.
37. Connections to Abbotts Creek Baptist Church have been established primarily by membership lists in the manuscript records of the Abbotts Creek Primitive Baptist Church (Davidson County, NC), ca. 1783, Special Collections & Archives, Z. Smith Reynolds Library, Wake Forest University Library; Cantrell, *History, Heritage & Memories,* 32; and by burials in the extant church graveyard, where the first body (that of Johan Christian Bodenhamer, whose two sons would wed Jane's daughters, Agnes and Elizabeth) was interred in 1788. See https://www.findagrave.com /cemetery/2386134/memorial-search?orderby=d&page=1#sr-15165166.
38. Family connections have been established via the *Spurgin Quarterly* and various online genealogy sites. On the Klinert (or Kleinert or Clinard family), see "Kleinert to Clinard, 1700s in Pennsylvania."

39. William Ledford pension application, 13 Feb. 1844, *Southern Campaigns American Revolution Pension Statements & Rosters,* http://revwarapps.org/r6238.pdf; Daniel Malsinger [*sic*] pension application, 6 June 1843, ibid.; *Southern Campaigns American Revolution Pension Statements & Rosters,* http://revwarapps.org/r7145 .pdf. On Hinkle, see "Nathaniel Hinkle (1759–1848)," https://www.wikitree.com /wiki/Hinkle-224.

40. Petition of Jane Spurgin, 10 Nov. 1788, and supporting documents, GASR, SANC.

41. Rowan County census, 1790, in *CSRNC,* 26: 1028. Ann Bedsaul Ruddick's husband, Solomon, claimed that his wife "Eloped with a Certain William Spurgeon" in 1790 (Petition of Solomon Ruddick, 12 Nov. 1796, Legislative Petitions, LVA). On the ill-fated state of Franklin, see Barksdale, *Lost State of Franklin;* and for John Spurgin's involvement, see Petition of the inhabitants of the western county, Dec. 1787, in *CSRNC,* 22:705–14. On William Spurgin, one of the less well-documented of Jane's children, see https://www.findagrave.com/memorial/113233079/william-spurgin.

6. The Common Rights of Other Citizens

1. An Act to Restrain all Married Persons from Marrying Again Whilst Their Former Wives or Former Husbands are Living, 1790, in *CSRNC,* 25:74.

2. Crow, "Slave Rebelliousness and Social Conflict in North Carolina"; Bradburn, *Citizenship Revolution,* 12–13, 46–54, 236–63; Gundersen, "Independence, Citizenship, and the American Revolution." For an overview of changing attitudes toward and practices concerning divorce during this period, see Kerber, *Women of the Republic,* chap. 6. A classic cultural history of the overall challenge to patriarchy, in a trans-Atlantic context, is Fliegelman, *Prodigals and Pilgrims.*

3. Kerber, *Women of the Republic,* 159; Dewey, "Thomas Jefferson's Notes on Divorce," 219; Sword, *Wives Not Slaves,* 256; Basch, *Framing American Divorce,* 3–4, 38–41; Petition of James Garret and Mary Hofler Garret, 21 Nov. 1787, GASR, SANC; Petition of John Christian Smith, 19 Jan. 1791, Legislative Papers, South Carolina State Archives, Columbia. On the growing importance of affection and companionship in marriage and family relations during this period, see also Jan Lewis, *Pursuit of Happiness.*

4. Meehan, "Not Made out of Levity," 441–43; Kerber, *Women of the Republic,* 159, 180–81; Sword, *Wives Not Slaves,* 259–60.

5. Kierner, *Southern Women in Revolution,* 195, 196n; Ferrell, "Early Statutory and Common Law Divorce in North Carolina," 607–11; G. G. Johnson, *Ante-Bellum North Carolina,* 217–22.

6. Petition of Susannah Wersley, 20 Nov. 1786, Legislative Petitions, Hanover County, LVA. Wersley's petition was the fourth divorce petition that Virginia's assembly considered, the first of which was filed by Francis Hill in 1782.

7. Petition of Solomon Riddick, 12 Nov. 1796, Legislative Petitions, Grayson County, LVA; Petition of Ezra Bostick, 8 Dec. 1791, GASR, SANC; Petition of James Martin, 1779, quoted in Meehan, "Not Made out of Levity," 449. Solomon Ruddick's unsigned petition, likely penned by a clerk, gives his surname as "Reddick," but the document is listed as the petition of Solomon "Riddick" in the Library of Virginia.

8. Petition of Solomon Riddick; Godbeer, *World of Trouble,* 7; Worrall, *Friendly Virginians,* 202–3, 217–19; Quinn, "Flower Swift Militia Company." The Virginia legislature did not grant a divorce petition until 1802 (see Buckley, *Great Catastrophe of My Life,*

22–23). The Ruddick family genealogy erroneously asserts that Solomon received his divorce and later remarried (see Hanneman, *Ruddick Family in America*, 13–14).

9. D. F. Johnson, *Occupied America*, 89, 153, 158, 161, 167, 170; McBurney, *Spies in Revolutionary Rhode Island*, 258–59.

10. Cohen, "What Man Hath Put Asunder," 121, 131–39. Citations for complete petitions (all of which at in the New Hampshire State Archives in Concord) are as follows: Elizabeth Rogers, 26 Jan. 1778; Martha Stevens, 4 June 1779; Rebekah Davis, 13 Apr. 1780; Charity Welch, 13 June 1781.

11. Kierner, *Southern Women in Revolution*, 200, 223–29; Lebsock, *Free Women of Petersburg*, 68–69.

12. Petition of Jennet Spurgin, 28 Dec. 1791, GASR, SANC; Affidavit of Jennet Spurgin, 25 Nov. 1791, ibid.

13. Petition of Jennet Spurgin, 28 Dec. 1791, GASR, SANC.

14. Bradburn, *Citizenship Revolution*, 1–3, 17–18; Royster, *Revolutionary People at War*, esp. chaps. 1 and 7.

15. All revolutionary-era state constitutions are available and fully searchable at *Avalon Project*.

16. On education and intellect as arguments for women's inclusion in the polity, see Bilder, *Female Genius;* and Kerber, *Women of the Republic*, esp. chaps. 7–8.

17. Zagarri, "Rights of Man and Woman in Post-Revolutionary America," 203, 216–21; Jan Lewis, "Of Every Age, Sex & Condition," 363–71.

18. Holton, "Equality as Unintended Consequences."

19. Kierner, *Southern Women in Revolution*, esp. xix–xxii, 150–57, 163–66. See also Ami Pflugrad-Jackisch, "'What Am I but an American?': Mary Willing Byrd and Westover Plantation during the American Revolution," in *Women in the American Revolution*, ed. Oberg, 171–91; Abigail Adams to John Adams, 31 Mar. 1776, *Founders Online*, https://founders.archives.gov/documents/Adams/04-01-02-0241.

20. Committee report on Petition of Jane Spurgin, 3 Jan. 1792 (files with petition), GASR, SANC.

21. Minutes of the Rowan Court of Pleas and Quarter Sessions, 10 May 1792, *Rowan Register* 11 (1996): 2600.

22. Klutz, *Abstracts of Deed Books 11–14 of Rowan County*, 79.

23. Demond, *Loyalists in North Carolina*, 173–74, 178–80; Lucas, "Cooling by Degrees," esp. 56–60.

24. Jasanoff, *Liberty's Exiles*, esp. 120–21, 130–45.

25. Petition of William Spurgin, 10 Sept. 1792, Land Petitions of Upper Canada, LAC; *Dictionary of Canadian Biography*, s.v. "Simcoe, John Graves," by S. R. Mealing, vol. 5, http://www.biographi.ca/en/bio/simcoe_john_graves_5E.html. Birth and death dates for the children of William and Ann can be found via findagrave.com.

26. Will of William Spurgin, [1806], Norfolk County Copybooks of Instruments and Deeds, RG 61-37, microfilm GS 2856, 188–90, Ontario Archives, Toronto.

27. Taylor, "Late Loyalists."

28. Petitions of William Spurgin, 10 Sept. 1792, 30 Aug. 1793, 14 July 1794, 3 May 1796, Land Petitions of Upper Canada, LAC. Notations on the verso side of the last petition indicate that William's grants were finalized and recorded only in 1798.

29. Petition of William Spurgin, 3 May 1796, Land Petitions of Upper Canada, LAC.

30. Will of William Spurgin, [1806]. As late as 1820, Aaron Spurgin, who fought for Canada in the War of 1812, appeared in Canadian records as a "yeoman" (https://

www.bac-lac.gc.ca/eng/discover/military-heritage/war-of-1812/Pages/item.aspx
?IdNumber=11060&DotsIdNumber=).

31. Seeley, *Race, Removal, and the Right to Remain*, 167–68, 281; Rose, "Upland South-
    erners," 242, 244, 253; Swierenga, "Settlement of the Old Northwest," 80, 85, 89;
    Gibson and Jung, *Historical Census Statistics*, 57.

32. Hanneman, *Ruddick Family*, 13–15; Hening, *Statutes at Large*, 12: 691; Rose, "Upland
    Southerners," 244–48.

33. Hanneman, *Ruddick Family*, 13–15; *Spurgin Quarterly* (Dec. 1989): 495–96; "Jesse
    Spurgin," https://ancestors.familysearch.org/en/LZSS-RLR/jesse-spurgin-1780
    -1865; "Jesse Spurgin," *Nauvoo Community Project*, http://nauvoo.byu.edu/Search
    Results.aspx?GivenName=Jesse&Surname=Spurgin&Gender=M.

34. Peter Bodenhamer pension application [filed by Agnes Spurgin Bodenhamer], Apr.
    1846, *Southern Campaign American Revolution Pension Statements and Rosters*,
    https://revwarapps.org/r982.pdf.

35. *Second Federal Census, 1800: Rowan County, N.C.; Third Federal Census, 1810, Rowan
    County, N.C.*

36. Klutz, *Abstracts of Deed Books 15–19 of Rowan County*, 68, 79, 81, 144; 3: 52, 75, 76, 141;
    Seventh Federal Census and Slave Schedule, Davidson, County, N.C.; Will of Joseph
    Spurgin, 20 Dec. 1848, Davidson County will book, SANC; Sandrock, "Slaveholders
    before and after the Civil War," 7, 11–12, 95–96; *Fayetteville Observer*, 6 June 1859;
    [Raleigh] *Spirit of the Age*, 8 June 1859; Joseph Spurgin, https://www.findagrave.com
    /memorial/17740968/joseph-spurgin. A useful compilation of members of both
    houses of the North Carolina legislature is at "North Carolina in the 1800s," https://
    www.carolana.com/NC/1800s/nc_1800s_general_assembly.html.

37. Little, *Sticks and Stones;* Individual Property Form for Abbotts Creek Primitive
    Baptist Church Cemetery, https://files.nc.gov/ncdcr/nr/DV0076.pdf.

Postscript

1. Petition of Joshua Campbell, [1791], GASR, SANC; A bill to alter the names of certain
   persons therein mentioned, Jan. 1792, ibid.; Joshua Pharaoh pension application,
   15, June 1833, *Southern Campaign American Revolution Pension Statements &
   Rosters*, http://revwarapps.org/s16509.pdf.

2. Joseph Spurgin's Statement of Revolutionary Events, 1854, *Spurgin Quarterly*
   18 (May 1989): 435–36. For family names and dates, see the various pages for the
   Spurgin children via links at "William Spurgin (1734–1806)," https://ancestors
   .familysearch.org/en/L5B5-YT1/william-spurgin-1734-1806.

3. "Joseph Spurgin's Statement," 435–36.

4. See, generally, Zagarri, *Revolutionary Backlash;* Purcell, *Sealed with Blood;* O'Keefe,
   "Monuments to the American Revolution;" and Kierner, "Genteel Balls and Republican Parades."

5. Ellet, *Women of the American Revolution*, 1:x; Casper, "Uneasy Marriage of Sentiment and Scholarship;" Kantrowitz, *More Than Freedom*, 28–33; Bonner, *Remaking
   the Republic*, esp. 137–40, 151–54; McDonnell et al., *Remembering the Revolution*, esp.
   1–5.

6. Ellet, *Women of the American Revolution*, 1:13–16- 21.

7. Caruthers, *Interesting Revolutionary Incidents*, esp. 39–40, 266–67, 270–71, 276–82;

NCpedia, s.v. "Caruthers, Eli Washington," by W. Conrad Gass, https://www.ncpedia .org/biography/caruthers-eli-washington.

8. Young, *Shoemaker and the Tea Party;* Young, *Masquerade;* James Basker, "George Washington and Phillis Wheatley: The Indispensable Man and the Poet Laureate of the American Revolution," in *Women of George Washington's World,* ed. Lewis and Boudreau, 113–36; David Waldstreicher, "Women's Politics, Antislavery Politics, and Phillis Wheatley's American Revolution," in *Women in the American Revolution,* ed. Oberg, 147–68; William Hunting Howell, "'Starving Memory': Antinarrating the American Revolution," in *Remembering the Revolution,* ed. McDonnell et al., 93–109; Martin, *Ordinary Courage.*

9. Washington, *Diaries of George Washington,* vol. 6: *1 January 1790–13 December 1799,* 151–52.

Appendix

1. *CSRNC,* 9:1024–26.
2. Petition of Jane Spurgin, 3 Dec. 1785, GASR, Nov.–Dec. 1785, box 1, SANC.
3. Petition of Jean Spurgin, 11 Nov. 1788, GASR, Nov.–Dec. 1788, box 1, SANC.
4. Petition of Jennet Spurgin, 28 Dec. 1791, GASR, Dec. 1791–Jan. 1792, SANC.
5. Petition of William Spurgin, 10 Sept. 1792, Land Petitions of Upper Canada, 1763–1865, LAC.
6. Petition of Solomon Reddick, 12 Nov. 1796, Legislative Petitions of the General Assembly, 1776–1865, box 92, folder 3, LVA.
7. Will of William Spurgin, [1806], Norfolk County Copybooks of Instruments and Deeds, RG 61-37, microfilm GS 2856, 188–90, Ontario Archives, Toronto.
8. Caruthers, *Interesting Revolutionary Incidents,* 39–42.

BIBLIOGRAPHY

Primary Sources
Manuscripts

BRITISH ARCHIVES, LONDON
Loyalist Claims Commission Papers (microfilm)

LIBRARY AND ARCHIVES OF CANADA, OTTAWA
Land Petitions of Upper Canada

LIBRARY OF VIRGINIA, RICHMOND
Legislative Petitions

MARYLAND ARCHIVES, ANNAPOLIS
Will Books

NEW HAMPSHIRE STATE ARCHIVES, CONCORD
General Court Petitions

ONTARIO PROVINCIAL ARCHIVES, TORONTO
Surrogate Court Estate Files (microfilm)

SOUTHERN HISTORICAL COLLECTION,
UNIVERSITY OF NORTH CAROLINA, CHAPEL HILL
Martha Ryan's Cipher Book

STATE ARCHIVES OF NORTH CAROLINA

Davidson County Wills
General Assembly Sessions Papers
Rowan County Wills
Salisbury District Court, Criminal Action Papers

WILLIAM CLEMENTS LIBRARY, UNIVERSITY OF MICHIGAN, ANN ARBOR

Thomas Gage Papers

WISCONSIN HISTORICAL SOCIETY, MADISON

Draper Manuscripts (microfilm)

Z. SMITH REYNOLDS LIBRARY, WAKE FOREST UNIVERSITY, WINSTON-SALEM, NC

Abbotts Creek Primitive Baptist Church Records

Newspapers and Periodicals

Fayetteville Observer
Gazette of South Carolina
North Carolina Gazette
Rowan Register
South Carolina Gazette and American General Gazette
Spirit of the Age (Raleigh)
Spurgin Quarterly
Tarboro [NC] Free Press
Virginia Gazette

Published Primary Sources

Archives of Maryland: Provincial Court Land Records, 1719–1723. http://aomol.msa.mary land.gov/000001/000721/html/index.html.
Archives of Maryland: Provincial Court Land Records, 1749–1756. http://aomol.msa.mary land.gov/000001/000701/html/index.html.
The Avalon Project: Documents in Law, History and Diplomacy. https://avalon.law.yale .edu/.
"Autobiography of Col. William Few of Georgia." *Magazine of American History* 7 (1881): 343–58.
Bacon, William Stevens. *A History of Georgia: From Its First Discovery by Europeans to the Adoption of the Present Constitution in MDCCXCVIII.* 2 vols. New York: D. Appleton, 1847–59.
Boyd, William K. *Some Eighteenth-Century Tracts Concerning North Carolina.* Raleigh, NC: Edwards and Broughton, 1927.
Campbell, Colin, ed. *Journal of an Expedition against the Rebels of Georgia in North America under the Orders of Archibald Campbell Esquire* [. . .]. Darien, GA: Ashantilly, 1981.

Caruthers, E. W. *Revolutionary Incidents: And Sketches of Character, Chiefly in the "Old North State."* Philadelphia: Hayes and Zell, 1854.

———. *Interesting Revolutionary Incidents: And Sketches of Character, Chiefly in the "Old North State,"* 2nd series. Philadelphia: Hayes and Zell, 1856.

"Case of the Loyalists in North Carolina: The Exertions and Sufferings during the Rebellion." *Political Magazine & Parliamentary, Naval, Military & Literary Journal* 4 (April 1783): 265–67.

Chesney, Alexander. *The Journal of Alexander Chesney: A South-Carolina Loyalist in the Revolution and After.* Edited by E. Alfred Jones. Columbus: Ohio State University, 1921.

Cornwallis, Charles. *The Cornwallis Papers: The Campaigns of 1780 and 1781 in the Southern Theatre of the American Revolutionary War.* 4 vols. Edited by Ian Saberton. Uckfield, UK: Naval and Military Press, 2010.

Dann, John C., ed. *The Revolution Remembered: Eyewitness Accounts of the War for Independence.* Chicago: University of Chicago Press, 1980.

Egerton, Hugh Edward, ed. *The Royal Commission on the Losses and Services of American Loyalists, 1783 to 1785.* 1915. New York: Franklin Burt, 1971.

Ellet, Elizabeth F. *The Women of the American Revolution.* 3 vols. New York: Baker and Scribner, 1848–50.

Enochs, Richard A., ed. *Rowan County, NC, Vacant Land Entries, 1778–1789.* Indianapolis, IN: R. A. Enochs, 1988.

First Federal Census, 1790: Rowan County, N.C.

Force, Peter, ed. *American Archives: Fourth Series* [. . .] *from* [. . .] *March 7, 1774, to the Declaration of Independence by the United States.* 6 vols. Washington, DC: M. St. Clair Clarke and Peter Force, 1837–46.

Founders Online: Correspondence and Writings of Seven Major Shapers of the United States. At https://founders.archives.gov/.

Fries, Adelaide L., ed. *Records of the Moravians in North Carolina.* 7 vols. Raleigh, NC: Edwards and Broughton Print Co., 1922–47.

Garden, Alexander. *Anecdotes of the American Revolution.* 1822. Charleston, SC: A. E. Miller, 1828.

Gibson, Campbell, and Kay Jung. *Historical Census Statistics on Population Totals by Race, 1790 to 1990, and by Hispanic Origin, 1970 to 1990, for the United States, Regions, Divisions, and States.* Washington, DC: US Census Bureau, 2002.

Gilreath, Amelia C., comp. *Frederick County (Va.) Deed Books, 1743–1785.* Vol. 1: *Deed Books 1, 2, 3, 4: 1743–1758.* Nokesville, VA: A. C. Gilreath, 1989.

Greene, General Nathanael. *The Papers of General Nathanael Greene.* Edited by Richard K. Showman et al. 13 vols. Chapel Hill: University of North Carolina Press, 1976–2005.

Hammersmith, Mary Powell, and Nancy Hawlick Stein, eds. *Old Guilford, North Carolina Court Minutes, 1781–1788, & Genealogical Implications of the Laws in Effect.* Hartford, KY: McDowell, 1978.

Hening, William Waller, comp. *The Statutes at Large: Being a Collection of All the Laws of Virginia* [. . .]. 13 vols. Richmond: Printed for the Editor, 1819–23.

Klutz, James W., ed. *Abstract of Deed Books 15–19 of Rowan County, North Carolina, 1797–1807.* Landis, NC: J. W. Klutz, 1996.

Linn, Jo White, comp. *Abstracts of the Deeds of Rowan County, North Carolina, 1753–1785.* Vols. 1–10. Salisbury, NC: J. W. Linn, 1983.

———. *Abstracts of the Minutes of the Court of Pleas and Quarter Sessions, Rowan County, North Carolina.* 3 vols. Salisbury, NC: J. W. Linn, 1977.

————. *Rowan County, North Carolina, Tax Lists, 1757–1800: Annotated Transcriptions.* Salisbury, NC: J. W. Linn, 1995.

Martin, James Kirby, ed. *Ordinary Courage: The Revolutionary War Adventures of Joseph Plumb Martin.* Malden, MA: Blackwell, 2008.

McCall, Hugh. *The History of Georgia: Containing Brief Sketches of the Most Remarkable Events up to the Present Day (1784).* 1811–16. Atlanta: Caldwell, 1909.

Pelletreau, William Smith, et al., eds. *Abstract of Wills on File in the Surrogate's Office, City of New York, 1665–1801.* 17 vols. New York: New-York Historical Society, 1893–1913.

Powell, William S., et al., eds. *The Regulators in North Carolina: A Documentary History, 1759–1776.* Raleigh: North Carolina Division of Archives and History, 1971.

The Proceedings of the Old Bailey, 1674–1913. https://www.oldbaileyonline.org/.

Pruitt, A. B., ed. *Abstract of Land Entries: Rowan County, North Carolina, Feb. 1778–Dec. 1778.* N.p., 1987.

Ramsay, David. *History of the American Revolution.* Philadelphia: R. Aitken and Son, 1789.

————. *The History of the Revolution of South-Carolina, from a British Province to an Independent State.* 2 vols. Trenton, NJ: Isaac Collins, 1785.

————. *Ramsay's History of South Carolina, from Its First settlement in 1670 to the Year 1808.* 1809, Newberry, SC: W. J. Duffie, 1858.

Saunders, William L., et al., eds. *The Colonial and State Records of North Carolina.* 30 vols. Raleigh, Winston, Goldsboro, and Charlotte: various publishers, 1886–1914.

Second Federal Census, 1800: Rowan County, N.C.

Seventh Federal Census and Slave Schedule, Davidson, County, N.C

Siebert, Wilbur Henry, ed. *Loyalists in East Florida, 1774 to 1785; the Most Important Documents Pertaining Thereto.* 2 vols. Deland: Florida State Historical Society, 1929.

Southern Campaigns American Revolution Pension Statements & Rosters. http://revwarapps.org.

Steele, John. *The Papers of John Steele.* Edited by Henry McGilbert Wagstaff. 2 vols. Raleigh, NC: Edwards and Broughton Print Co., 1924.

Third Federal Census, 1810: Rowan County, N.C.

Tryon, William. *The Correspondence of William Tryon and Other Selected Papers.* Edited by William S. Powell. 2 vols. Raleigh: North Carolina Division of Archives and History, 1980–81.

Washington, George. *The Diaries of George Washington.* Edited by Donald Jackson and Dorothy Twohig. Vol. 6: *1 January 1790–13 December 1799.* Charlottesville: University Press of Virginia, 1979.

Wilkinson, Eliza. *Letters of Eliza Wilkinson: During the Invasion and Possession of Charlestown, S.C., by the British in the Revolutionary War.* Edited by Caroline Gilman. 1839. New York: New York Times; Arno Press, 1969.

Secondary Sources

Allison, David, and Larrie D. Ferreiro, eds. *The American Revolution as a World War.* Washington, DC: Smithsonian Books, 2018.

Ambuske, James A. "'The Loss it Sustain'd by the Immense Drain of Men': The Imperial Politics of Scottish Emigration to Revolutionary America, 1756–1803." PhD diss., University of Virginia, 2016.

American National Biography Online. www.anb.org.

Anderson, Virginia DeJohn. *The Martyr and the Traitor: Nathan Hale, Moses Dunbar, and the American Revolution.* New York: Oxford University Press, 2017.

Andrew, Rod, Jr. *The Life and Times of General Andrew Pickens: Revolutionary War Hero, American Founder.* Chapel Hill: University of North Carolina Press, 2017.

Ashe, Samuel A. *History of North Carolina,* 2 vols. Raleigh: Edwards and Broughton Print Co., 1925.

Ashmore, Otis, and Charles H. Olmstead. "The Battles of Kettle Creek and Brier Creek." *Georgia Historical Quarterly* 10 (1926): 85–100.

Babits, Lawrence Edward, and Joshua B. Howard. *Long, Obstinate, and Bloody: The Battle of Guilford Courthouse.* Chapel Hill: University of North Carolina Press, 2009.

Bailey, Raymond C. *Popular Influence upon Public Policy: Petitioning in Eighteenth-Century Virginia.* Westport, CT.: Greenwood, 1979.

Barksdale, Kevin T. *The Lost State of Franklin: America's First Secession.* Lexington: University Press of Kentucky, 2009.

Basch, Norma. *Framing American Divorce: From the Revolutionary Generation to the Victorians.* Berkeley: University of California Press, 1999.

Becker, Robert A. "Revolution and Reform: An Interpretation of Southern Taxation, 1763 to 1783." *William and Mary Quarterly,* 3rd ser., 32 (1975): 417–42.

Bell, Karen Cook. *Running from Bondage: Enslaved Women and Their Remarkable Fight for Freedom in Revolutionary America.* New York: Cambridge University Press, 2021.

Bellesiles, Michael A. "The Establishment of Legal Structures on the Frontier: The Case of Revolutionary Vermont." *Journal of American History* 73 (1987): 895–915.

Bilder, Mary Sarah. *Female Genius: Eliza Harriot and George Washington at the Dawn of the Constitution.* Charlottesville: University of Virginia Press, 2022.

Bloch, Ruth H. "The American Revolution, Wife Beating, and the Emergent Value of Privacy." *Journal of Early American Studies* 5 (2007): 223–51.

Block, Sharon. *Rape and Sexual Power in Early America.* Chapel Hill: University of North Carolina Press, 2006.

Bonner, Christopher James. *Remaking the Republic: Black Politics and the Creation of American Citizenship.* Philadelphia: University of Pennsylvania Press, 2020.

Bradburn, Douglas. *The Citizenship Revolution: Politics and the Creation of the American Union, 1774–1804.* Charlottesville: University of Virginia Press, 2009.

Brannon, Rebecca. *From Revolution to Reunion: The Reintegration of the South Carolina Loyalists.* Columbia: University of South Carolina Press, 2016.

Brannon, Rebecca, and Joseph S. Moore, eds. *The Consequences of Loyalism: Essays in Honor of Robert M. Calhoon.* Columbia: University of South Carolina Press, 2019.

Breen, T. H. *Marketplace of Revolution: How Consumer Politics Shaped American Independence.* New York: Oxford University Press, 2004.

"British Legion Biographical Sketches, Infantry Officers." *The On-Line Institute for Advanced Loyalist Studies.* http://www.royalprovincial.com/military/rhist/britlegn/blinf1.htm.

Brown, Richard D. "Microhistory and the Post-Modern Challenge." *Journal of the Early Republic* 23 (2003): 1–20.

Brown, Wallace. *The King's Friends: The Composition and Motives of the American Loyalist Claimants.* Providence, RI: Brown University Press, 1965.

Buckley, Thomas E. *The Great Catastrophe of My Life: Divorce in the Old Dominion.* Chapel Hill: University of North Carolina Press, 2002.

Butler, Lindsay S., and Alan D. Watson, eds. *The North Carolina Experience: An Interpretive and Documentary History.* Chapel Hill: University of North Carolina Press, 2010.

Bynum, Victoria E. *The Free State of Jones: Mississippi's Longest Civil War.* Chapel Hill: University of North Carolina Press, 2016.

Cann, Marvin L. "Prelude to War: The First Battle of Ninety Six: November 19–21, 1775." *South Carolina Historical Magazine* 76 (1975): 197–214.

Cantrell, Rufus Roy. *History, Heritage & Memories Abbotts Creek Missionary Baptist Church High Point, North Carolina, 1756–2006.* Nashville, TN: Fields, 2008.

Carp, Benjamin L. *Defiance of the Patriots: The Boston Tea Party and the Making of America.* New Haven, CT: Yale University Press, 2010.

——. *The Great New York Fire of 1776: A Lost Story of the American Revolution.* New Haven, CT: Yale University Press, 2023.

Casper, Scott E. "An Uneasy Marriage of Sentiment and Scholarship: Elizabeth F. Ellet and the Domestic Origins of American Women's History." *Journal of Women's History* 4 (1992): 10–35.

Chandler, Abby. "'Unawed by the Laws of their Country': Local and Imperial Legitimacy in North Carolina's Regulator Rebellion." *North Carolina Historical Review* 93 (2016): 120–45.

Clark, Murtie June. *Loyalists in the Southern Campaign of the Revolution.* 3 vols. Baltimore, MD: Genealogical Publishing, 1981.

Coates, Albert. "Punishment for Crime in North Carolina." *North Carolina Law Review* 17 (1938–39): 205–32.

Cohen, Sheldon S. "What Man Hath Put Asunder: Divorce in New Hampshire, 1681–1784." *Historical New Hampshire* 41 (1986): 118–41.

Coldham, Peter Wilson. *The Complete Book of Emigrants in Bondage, 1614–1775.* Baltimore, MD: Genealogical Publishing, 1988.

Coleman, Kenneth. *The American Revolution in Georgia.* Athens: University of Georgia Press, 1958.

Corbitt, David Leroy. *The Formation of the North Carolina Counties, 1663–1943.* Raleigh, NC: State Department of Archives and History, 1950.

Cross, Jerry, and Wallace L. McKeehan, "Names of North Carolina Regulators." http://www.sonsofdewittcolony.org/mckstmerrframe.htm.

Crow, Jeffrey J. "Slave Rebelliousness and Social Conflict in North Carolina, 1775 to 1802." *William and Mary Quarterly,* 3rd ser., 37 (1980): 79–102.

Crow, Jeffrey J., and Larry E. Tise, eds. *The Southern Experience in the American Revolution.* Chapel Hill: University of North Carolina Press, 1978.

Daniels, Jonathan. *The Randolphs of Virginia.* Garden City, NY: Doubleday, 1972.

Davis, Robert Scott. *Georgians in the Revolution: At Kettle Creek (Wilkes Co.) and Burke County.* Easley, SC: Southern Historical Press, 1986.

——. *Kettle Creek: The Battle of the Cane Brakes, Wilkes County, Georgia.* Atlanta: Georgia Dept. of Natural Resources, Office of Planning and Research, Historic Preservation Section, 1975.

——. "The Loyalist Trials at Ninety Six in 1779." *South Carolina Historical Magazine* 80 (1979): 172–81.

Demond, Robert O. *The Loyalists in North Carolina during the Revolution.* 1940; Hamden, CT: Archon, 1964.

Dewey, Frank L. "Thomas Jefferson's Notes on Divorce." *William and Mary Quarterly,* 3rd ser., 39 (1982): 221–23.

Dictionary of Canadian Biography. http://www.biographi.ca/en/.

Ekirch, A. Roger. *Bound for America: The Transportation of British Convicts to the Colonies, 1718–1775.* New York: Oxford University Press, 1987.

———. "'A New Government of Liberty': Hermon Husband's Vision of Backcountry North Carolina, 1755." *William and Mary Quarterly*, 3rd ser., 34 (1977): 632–50.

———. *"Poor Carolina": Politics and Society in Colonial North Carolina, 1729–1776*. Chapel Hill: University of North Carolina Press, 1981.

Elliott, Daniel T. *Stirring Up a Hornet's Nest: The Kettle Creek Battlefield Survey*. Lamar Institute Publication Series, Report Number 131. http://www.npshistory.com /publications/kecr/rpt-131.pdf.

Family Central Family History Services. http://www.familycentral.net.

Fenn, Elizabeth A. *Pox Americana: The Great Smallpox Epidemic of 1775–1782*. New York: Hill and Wang, 2001.

Ferguson, E. James. *The Power of the Purse: A History of American Public Finance, 1776–1790*. Chapel Hill: University of North Carolina Press, 1961.

Ferrell, J. S. "Early Statutory and Common Law Divorce in North Carolina." *North Carolina Law Review* 41 (1963): 608–20.

Find a Grave. https://www.findagrave.com/.

Fliegelman, Jay. *Prodigals and Pilgrims: The American Revolution against Patriarchal Authority, 1750–1800*. Cambridge: Cambridge University Press, 1982.

Fraser, Alexander, ed. *United Empire Loyalists; Enquiry into the Losses and Services in Consequence of Their Loyalty* [. . .]. 2 vols. Toronto: Ontario Department of Public Records and Archives, 1904–5.

Frey, Sylvia R. *Water from the Rock: Black Resistance in a Revolutionary Age*. Princeton, NJ: Princeton University Press, 1991.

Fuentes, Marisa J. *Dispossessed Lives: Enslaved Women, Violence, and the Archive*. Philadelphia: University of Pennsylvania Press, 2016.

Ganyard, Robert L. "Threat from the West: North Carolina and the Cherokee, 1776–1778." *North Carolina Historical Review* 45 (1968): 47–66.

Gigantino, James J., II. *William Livingston's American Revolution*. Philadelphia: University of Pennsylvania Press, 2018.

Gillespie, Michele K., and Sally G. McMillen, eds. *North Carolina Women: Their Lives and Times*. Vol. 1. Athens: University of Georgia Press, 2014.

Godbeer, Richard. *World of Trouble: A Philadelphia Quaker Family's Journey through the American Revolution*. New Haven, CT: Yale University Press, 2019.

Gundersen, Joan R. "Independence, Citizenship, and the American Revolution." *Signs* 13 (1987): 59–77.

Hanneman, John W. *The Ruddick Family in America*. Oakland, CA: J. W. Hanneman, 1993.

Harrell, Isaac S. "North Carolina Loyalists." *North Carolina Historical Review* 3 (1926): 575–90.

Hartigan-O'Connor, Ellen. *The Ties That Buy: Women and Commerce in Revolutionary America*. Philadelphia: University of Pennsylvania Press, 2009.

Higginson, Stephen A. "A Short History of the Right to Petition Government for the Redress of Grievances." *Yale Law Journal* 96 (1986): 142–66.

Hoffman, Ronald, et al., eds. *An Uncivil War: The Southern Backcountry during the American Revolution*. Charlottesville: University Press of Virginia, 1985.

Hofstra, Warren R. *The Planting of New Virginia: Settlement and Landscape in the Shenandoah Valley*. Baltimore, MD: Johns Hopkins University Press, 2004.

Holton, Woody. *Abigail Adams: A Life*. New York: Free Press, 2009.

———. "Equality as Unintended Consequences: The Contracts Clause and the Married Women's Property Acts." *Journal of Southern History* 81 (2015): 313–40.

———. *Forced Founders: Indians, Debtors, Slaves, and the Making of the American Revolution in Virginia.* Chapel Hill: University of North Carolina Press, 1999.

———. *Liberty Is Sweet: The Hidden History of the American Revolution.* New York: Simon and Schuster, 2021.

Hoock, Holger. "*Jus in Bello:* Rape and the British Army in the American Revolutionary War." *Journal of Military Ethics* 14 (2015): 74–97.

———. *Scars of Independence: America's Violent Birth.* New York: Crown, 2017.

Hudson, Arthur Palmer. "Songs of the North Carolina Regulators." *North Carolina Historical Review* 4 (1947): 470–85.

Innes, Stephen, ed. *Work and Labor in Early America.* Chapel Hill: University of North Carolina Press, 1988.

"Iron Production: Maryland's Industrial Past." *HMdb.org: The Historical Marker Database.* https://www.hmdb.org/m.asp?m=104641.

Isaac, Rhys. *The Transformation of Virginia, 1740–1790.* Chapel Hill: University of North Carolina Press, 1983.

"Isaac Welborn." https://www.findagrave.com/memorial/68312432/isaac-welborn.

"Isabella Mary (Teague) Welborn, (1742–1812)." https://www.wikitree.com/wiki/Teague-255.

Jasanoff, Maya. *Liberty's Exiles: American Loyalists in a Revolutionary World.* New York: Knopf, 2011.

Jellison, Richard M., ed. *Society, Freedom, and Conscience: The Coming of the Revolution in Virginia, Massachusetts, and New York.* New York: Norton, 1976.

Jensen, Joan M. *Loosening the Bonds: Mid-Atlantic Farm Women, 1750–1850.* New Haven, CT: Yale University Press, 1986.

"Johann (Johannes) Matthias Sappenfield biography." https://www.wikitree.com/wiki/Sappenfield-23.

Johnson, Donald F. *Occupied America: British Military Rule and the Experience of Revolution.* Philadelphia: University of Pennsylvania Press, 2020.

Johnson, Guion Griffis. *Ante-Bellum North Carolina: A Social History.* Chapel Hill: University of North Carolina Press, 1937.

Jones, T. Cole. *Captives of Liberty: Prisoners of War and the Politics of Vengeance in the American Revolution.* Philadelphia: University of Pennsylvania Press, 2020.

Kamoie, Laura Croghan. *Irons in the Fire: The Business History of the Tayloe Family and Virginia's Gentry, 1700–1860.* Charlotteville: University of Virginia Press, 2007.

Kantrowitz, Stephen. *More Than Freedom: Fighting for Black Citizenship in a White Republic, 1829–1889.* New York: Penguin, 2012.

Kars, Marjoleine. *Breaking Loose Together: The Regulator Rebellion in Pre-Revolutionary North Carolina.* Chapel Hill: University of North Carolina Press, 2002.

Katcher, Philip. "The Provincial Corps of the British Army, 1775–1783." *Journal of the Society for Army Historical Research* 54 (1976): 164–71.

Kerber, Linda K. *No Constitutional Right to Be Ladies: Women and the Obligations of Citizenship.* New York: Hill and Wang, 1998.

———. *Women of the Republic: Ideology and Intellect in Revolutionary America.* Chapel Hill: University of North Carolina Press, 1980.

Kierner, Cynthia A. *Beyond the Household: Women's Place in the Early South, 1700–1835.* Ithaca, NY: Cornell University Press, 1998.

———. "Genteel Balls and Republican Parades: Gender and Early Southern Civic Rituals." *Virginia Magazine of History and Biography* 104 (1996): 185–210.

———. *Southern Women in Revolution: Personal and Political Narratives, 1750–1800.* Columbia: University of South Carolina Press, 1998.

"Kleinert to Clinard, 1700s in Pennsylvania." https://busybeetraveler.wordpress.com /2012/08/02/chapter-4-kleinerts-to-clinard-1700s-in-pennsylvania/.

Klinghoffer, Judith Apter, and Lois Elkis. "The Petticoat Electors: Women's Suffrage in New Jersey, 1776–1807." *Journal of the Early Republic* 12 (1992): 159–93.

Kotch, Seth. *Lethal State: A History of the Death Penalty in North Carolina.* Chapel Hill: University of North Carolina Press, 2019.

Kukla, Jon. *Patrick Henry: Champion of Liberty.* New York: Simon and Schuster, 2017.

Lambert, Robert Stansbury. *South Carolina Loyalists in the American Revolution.* Columbia: University of South Carolina Press, 1987.

Land, Aubrey C. *Colonial Maryland: A History.* Millwood, NY: KTO, 1981.

Larson, Carlton F. W. *The Trials of Allegiance: Treason, Juries, and the American Revolution.* New York: Oxford University Press, 2019.

Lebsock, Suzanne D. *The Free Women of Petersburg: Status and Culture in a Southern Town, 1784–1860.* New York: Norton, 1984.

Lee, Jean B. *The Price of Nationhood: The American Revolution in Charles County.* New York: Norton, 1994.

Lee, Wayne E. *Crowds and Soldiers in Revolutionary North Carolina.* Gainesville: University Press of Florida, 2001.

Lemon, James T. *The Best Poor Man's Country: A Geographical Study of Early Southeastern Pennsylvania.* Baltimore, MD: Johns Hopkins University Press, 1972.

Lewis, Charlene Boyer, and George W. Boudreau, eds. *The Women of George Washington's World.* Charlottesville: University of Virginia Press, 2022.

Lewis, J. D. "The Known Battles & Skirmishes in North Carolina." https://www.carolana .com/NC/Revolution/NC_Revolutionary_War_Known_Battles_Skirmishes.htm/.

Lewis, Jan. "'Of Every Age, Sex & Condition': The Representation of Women in the Constitution." *Journal of the Early Republic* 15 (1995): 359–87.

———. *The Pursuit of Happiness: Family and Values in Jefferson's Virginia.* Cambridge: Cambridge University Press, 1983.

Lewis, Johanna Miller. *Artisans in the North Carolina Backcountry.* Lexington: University of Kentucky Press, 1995.

Little, M. Ruth. *Sticks and Stones: Three Centuries of North Carolina Gravemarkers.* Chapel Hill: University of North Carolina Press, 1998.

Lucas, Jeffrey P. "Cooling by Degrees: Reintegration of Loyalists in North Carolina, 1776–1790." Master's thesis, North Carolina State University, 2007.

Maestro, Marcello. "A Pioneer for the Abolition of Capital Punishment: Cesare Beccaria." *Journal of the History of Ideas* 34 (1973): 463–68.

Maier, Pauline. *From Resistance to Revolution: Colonial Radicals and the Development of American Opposition to Britain, 1765–1776.* New York: Knopf, 1972.

Martin, Thomas S. "*Nemo Potest Exuere Patriam:* Indelibility of Allegiance and the American Revolution." *American Journal of Legal History* 35 (1991): 205–18.

Mayer, Holly A. *Belonging to the Army: Camp Followers and Community during the American Revolution.* Columbia: University of South Carolina Press, 1996.

McBurney, Christian M. *Spies in Revolutionary Rhode Island.* Charleston, SC: History Press, 2012.

McCleskey, Turk. *The Road to Black Ned's Forge: A Story of Race, Sex, and Trade on the Colonial American Frontier.* Charlottesville: University of Virginia Press, 2014.

McDaniel, Matthew F. K. "Georgia's Forgotten Battlefields: A Survey of and Recommendations for Selected Revolutionary War Battlefields and Sites in the State." Master's thesis, University of Georgia, 2002.

McDonnell, Michael A., et al., eds. *Remembering the Revolution: Memory, History, and Nation Making from Independence to Civil War*. Amherst: University of Massachusetts Press, 2013.

Meacham, Sarah Hand. *Every Home a Distillery: Alcohol, Gender, and Technology in the Colonial Chesapeake*. Baltimore, MD: Johns Hopkins University Press, 2009.

Meehan, Thomas R. "'Not Made out of Levity': Evolution of Divorce in Early Pennsylvania." *Pennsylvania Magazine of History and Biography* 92 (1968): 441–64.

Merrens, Harry Roy. *Colonial North Carolina in the Eighteenth Century: A Study in Historical Geography*. Chapel Hill: University of North Carolina Press, 1964.

Merritt, Jane T. *The Trouble with Tea: The Politics of Consumption in the Eighteenth-Century Global Economy*. Baltimore: Johns Hopkins University Press, 2017.

Middlekauff, Robert. *The Glorious Cause: The American Revolution, 1763–1789*. 1982. New York: Oxford University Press, 2005.

Miles, Tiya. *All That She Carried: The Journey of Ashley's Sack, a Black Family Keepsake*. New York: Random House, 2021.

Morgan, David T., Jr. "The Great Awakening in North Carolina, 1740–1775: The Baptist Phase." *North Carolina Historical Review* 45 (1968): 264–83.

Morgan, Philip D. *Slave Counterpoint: Black Culture in the Eighteenth-Century Chesapeake and Low Country*. Chapel Hill: University of North Carolina Press, 1998.

Nash, Gary B. *Race and Revolution*. Madison: University of Wisconsin Press, 1990.

Nauvoo Community Project. http://nauvoo.byu.edu/.

NCPedia. https://www.ncpedia.org.

Nelson, Paul David. *William Tryon and The Course of Empire: A Life in British Imperial Service*. Chapel Hill: University of North Carolina Press, 1990.

New Georgia Encyclopedia. https://www.georgiaencyclopedia.org.

Norton, Mary Beth. *Liberty's Daughters: The Revolutionary Experience of American Women, 1750–1800*. Boston: Little Brown, 1980.

Oberg, Barbara B., ed. *Women in the American Revolution: Gender, Politics, and the Domestic World*. Charlottesville: University of Virginia Press, 2019.

O'Dell, Cecil. *Pioneers of Old Frederick County, Virginia*. Marceline, MO: Walsworth, 1995.

O'Keefe, Kieran J. "Monuments to the American Revolution." *Journal of the American Revolution*, 17 September 2019. https://allthingsliberty.com/2019/09/monuments-to-the-american-revolution/

Osterud, Nancy Grey. "Gender and the Transition to Capitalism in Rural America." *Agricultural History* 67 (1993): 14–29.

Oxford Dictionary of National Biography. www.oxforddnb.com.

Pancake, John S. *This Destructive War: The British Campaign in the Carolinas, 1780–1782*. Tuscaloosa: University of Alabama Press, 1985.

Parkinson, Robert G. *The Common Cause: Race and Nation in the American Revolution*. Chapel Hill: University of North Carolina Press, 2016.

Paschal, George Washington. *History of North Carolina Baptists*. 2 vols. Raleigh: North Carolina Baptist State Convention, 1930–55.

Peterson, R. Eric. "Messages, Petitions, Communications, and Memorials to Congress." *CRS Report for Congress*. Washington, DC, 2007. https://www.everycrsreport.com/files/20070816_98-839_24a0874b321c7d0059f567a0b29f2eb59a2a0285.pdf.

Petitions, Memorials, and Other Documents Submitted for the Consideration of Congress,

March 4, 1789 to December 14, 1795: A Staff Study [. . .]. Washington, DC: US Government Printing Office, 1986.

Piecuch, Jim. *Three Peoples, One King: Loyalists, Indians, and Slaves in the Revolutionary South*. Columbia: University of South Carolina Press, 2008.

Polgar, Paul W. *Standard-Bearers of Equality: America's First Abolition Movement*. Chapel Hill: University of North Carolina Press, 2019.

Powell, William S., and Michael Hill, eds. *The North Carolina Gazetteer: A Dictionary of Tar Heel Places and Their History*. 2nd ed. Chapel Hill: University of North Carolina Press, 2010.

Purcell, Sarah. *Sealed with Blood: War, Sacrifice, and Memory in Revolutionary America*. Philadelphia: University of Pennsylvania Press, 2002.

Pybus, Cassandra. *Epic Journeys of Freedom: Runaway Slaves of the American Revolution and Their Global Quest for Liberty*. Boston: Beacon, 2006.

Quinn, James A. "The Flower Swift Militia Company of Montgomery Co., Virginia, 1779–1783: Reconstruction of a Vanished Community in Today's Carroll and Grayson Counties." https://www.newrivernotes.com/carroll_history_1779-1783_flower_swift _company.htm.

Ramsey, Robert W. *Carolina Cradle: Settlement of the Northwest Carolina Frontier, 1747– 1762*. Chapel Hill: University of North Carolina Press, 1964.

Rankin, Hugh F. "The Moore's Creek Bridge Campaign, 1776." *North Carolina Historical Review* 30 (1953): 23–60.

———. *The North Carolina Continentals*. Chapel Hill: University of North Carolina Press, 1971.

Raynor, George. *Patriots and Tories in the Carolina Piedmont*. Salisbury, NC: Salisbury Post, 1990.

Rockwell, E. *Rowan County, North Carolina, in 1774*. Boston: C. Benjamin Richardson, 1869.

Roeber, A. G. *Faithful Magistrates and Republican Lawyers: Creators of Virginia's Legal Culture, 1680–1810*. Chapel Hill: University of North Carolina Press, 1981.

Rose, Gregory S. "Upland Southerners: The County Origins of Southern Migrants to Indiana by 1850." *Indiana Magazine of History* 82 (1986): 242–63.

Royster, Charles. *A Revolutionary People at War: The Continental Army and American Character, 1775–1783*. Chapel Hill: University of North Carolina Press, 1979.

Rumple, Jethro. *A History of Rowan County, North Carolina*. Salisbury, NC: J. J. Bruner, 1881.

Sabine, Lorenzo. *Biographical Sketches of Loyalists of the American Revolution, with an Historical Essay*. 2 vols. Boston: Little, Brown, 1864.

Salmon, Marylynn. *Women and the Law of Property in Early America*. Chapel Hill: University of North Carolina Press, 1989.

Sandrock, Marguerite. "Slaveholders before and after the Civil War: Davidson County, North Carolina, 1820–1880." Master's thesis, University of North Carolina, Greensboro, 1979.

Sappington, Roger E. "North Carolina and the Non-Resistant Sects during the American War of Independence." *Quaker History* 60 (1971): 29–47.

Schamel, Charles E. "Untapped Resources: Private Claims and Private Legislation in the Records of the U.S. Congress." *Prologue Magazine* 27 (Spring 1995). https://www .archives.gov/publications/prologue/1995/spring/private-claims-1.html.

Seeley, Samantha. *Race, Removal, and the Right to Remain: Migration and the Making of the United States*. Chapel Hill: University of North Carolina Press, 2021.

Bibliography

Singewald, Joseph T., Jr. *Report on the Iron Ores of Maryland, with an Account of the Iron Industry.* Baltimore, MD: Johns Hopkins University Press, 1911.

Sink, Margaret, and Mary Green Matthews. *Pathfinders Past and Present: A History of Davidson County, North Carolina.* High Point, NC: Hall Printing, 1972.

Skemp, Sheila L. *Benjamin and William Franklin: Father and Son, Patriot and Loyalist.* Boston: Bedford, 1994.

Smith, Abbot Emerson. *Colonists in Bondage: White Servitude and Convict Labor in America, 1607–1776.* Chapel Hill: University of North Carolina Press, 1947.

Smith, Page. "David Ramsay and the Causes of the American Revolution." *William and Mary Quarterly,* 3rd ser., 17 (1960): 51–77.

Smith, Paul H. "The American Loyalists: Notes on Their Organization and Numerical Strength." *William and Mary Quarterly,* 3rd ser., 25 (1968): 259–77.

Sollers, Basil. "Transported Convict Laborers in Maryland during the Colonial Period." *Maryland Historical Magazine* 2 (1907): 17–47.

Spindel, Donna J. "Law and Disorder: The North Carolina Stamp Act Crisis." *North Carolina Historical Review* 67 (1980): 1–16.

Spruill, Julia Cherry. *Women's Life and Work in the Southern Colonies.* Chapel Hill: University of North Carolina Press, 1938.

Stark, James H. *The Loyalists of Massachusetts and the Other Side of the American Revolution.* Boston: W. B. Clarke, 1907.

Stewart, Bruce E. *Redemption from Tyranny: Herman Husband's American Revolution.* Charlottesville: University of Virginia Press, 2020.

Stumpf, Vernon O. *Josiah Martin: The Last Royal Governor of North Carolina.* Durham, NC: Carolina Academic Press, 1986.

Sullivan, Aaron. *The Disaffected: Britain's Occupation of Philadelphia during the American Revolution.* Philadelphia: University of Pennsylvania Press, 2019.

Swierenga, Robert P. "The Settlement of the Old Northwest: Ethnic Pluralism in a Featureless Plain." *Journal of the Early Republic* 9 (1989): 73–105.

Sword, Kirsten. *Wives Not Slaves: Patriarchy and Modernity in the Age of Revolution.* Chicago: University of Chicago Press, 2021.

Taparata, Evan. "'Refugees as You Call Them': The Politics of Refugee Recognition in the Nineteenth-Century United States." *Journal of American Ethnic History* 38 (2019): 9–35.

Taylor, Alan. "The Late Loyalists: Northern Reflections of the Early American Republic." *Journal of the Early Republic* 27 (2007): 1–34.

Thorp, Daniel B. "Doing Business in the Backcountry: Retail Trade in Colonial Rowan County, North Carolina." *William and Mary Quarterly,* 3rd. ser., 48 (1991): 387–408.

———. *The Moravian Community in Colonial North Carolina: Pluralism on the Southern Frontier.* Knoxville: University of Tennessee Press, 1989.

———. "Taverns and Tavern Culture on the Southern Colonial Frontier: Rowan County, North Carolina, 1753–1776." *Journal of Southern History* 62 (1996): 661–88.

Tillman, Kacy. "What Is a Female Loyalist?" *Commonplace: The Journal of Early American Life* (Summer 2013). http://commonplace.online/article/what-is-a-female-loyalist/.

Tracey, Grace L. *Pioneers of Old Monocacy: The Early Settlement of Frederick County, Maryland, 1721–1743.* Baltimore, MD: Genealogical Publishing, 1987.

Travers, Len. *Celebrating the Fourth: Independence Day and the Rites of Nationalism in the Early Republic.* Amherst: University of Massachusetts Press, 1997.

Trouillot, Michel-Rolph. *Silencing the Past: Power and the Production of History.* 1995. Boston: Beacon, 2015.

Troxler, Carole Watterson. *Farming Dissenters: The Regulator Movement in Piedmont North Carolina.* Chapel Hill: University of North Carolina Press, 2011.

———. *The Loyalist Experience in North Carolina.* Raleigh: North Carolina Division of Archives and History, 1976.

Ulrich, Laurel Thatcher. *Good Wives: Image and Reality in the Lives of Women in Northern New England, 1650–1750.* New York: Oxford University Press, 1980.

———. *A Midwife's Tale: The Life of Martha Ballard, Based on Her Diary, 1785–1812.* New York: Knopf, 1990.

Van Buskirk, Judith L. *Generous Enemies: Patriots and Loyalists in Revolutionary New York.* Philadelphia: University of Pennsylvania Press, 2002.

Vickers, Daniel. "Competency and Competition: Economic Culture in Early America." *William and Mary Quarterly,* 3rd ser., 47 (1990): 3–29.

Watson, Alan D. "The Committee of Safety and the Coming of the American Revolution in North Carolina." *North Carolina Historical Review* 73 (1996): 131–55.

Watterson, John S., III. "The Ordeal of Governor Burke." *North Carolina Historical Review* 48 (1971): 95–117.

Welborn, Gene. *Welborns and Related Families with Roots in North and South Carolina.* Greenwood, SC: Gene Welborn, 1994.

"William Welborn Sr (1712–1773)." https://www.wikitree.com/wiki/Welborn-467.

Williams, Thomas J. C. *History of Frederick County, Maryland, from the Earliest Settlements to the Beginning of the War between the States.* Frederick, MD: L. R. Titsworth, 1910.

Wilson, David K. *The Southern Strategy: Britain's Conquest of South Carolina and Georgia, 1775–1780.* Columbia: University of South Carolina Press, 2005.

Wood, Gordon S. *The Creation of the American Republic, 1776–1787.* Chapel Hill: University of North Carolina Press, 1969.

Worrall, Jay, Jr. *The Friendly Virginians: America's First Quakers.* Athens, GA: Iberian, 1994.

Young, Alfred F. "George Robert Twelves Hewes (1742–1840): A Boston Shoemaker and the Memory of the American Revolution." *William and Mary Quarterly,* 3rd ser., 38 (1981): 561–623.

———. *Masquerade: The Life and Times of Deborah Sampson, Continental Soldier.* New York: Knopf, 2005.

———. *The Shoemaker and the Tea Party.* Boston: Beacon, 1999.

Zabin, Serena. *The Boston Massacre: A Family History.* Boston: Houghton Mifflin Harcourt, 2020.

Zagarri, Rosemarie. *Revolutionary Backlash: Women and Politics in the Early American Republic.* Philadelphia: University of Pennsylvania Press, 2007.

———. "The Rights of Man and Woman in Post-Revolutionary America." *William and Mary Quarterly,* 3rd ser., 55 (1998): 203–30.

INDEX

Italicized page numbers refer to illustrations.

Creadlebaugh, Tilman, 123

crime, 13–14, 15, 29, 67, 112–15, 128; capital punishment and, 13, 68, 113, 114, 128; corporal punishment and, 14, 114

Cross Creek, N.C., 25, 59, 62, 64

Cumberland County, N.C., 62

currency: paper, 71, 88; scarcity of, 34, 37, 109

Currituck County, N.C., 151

Custer, Peter, 112

dairying, 24, 25, 26

Davidson County, N.C., 148, 149

Davis, Hannah, 118

Davis, Rebekah, 134

Davis, William, 110–11, 121

debt, 17, 30, 36, 88, 105, 115, 139; litigation for, 109, 110–12, 120, 141; state appropriation of Tory, 72, 108; Tories barred from collecting, 67, 72, 110

Declaration of Independence, 53, 67, 130

Declaratory Act (1766), 34

disease, 79, 98

divorce, 17, 128–29, 130–31, 142; petitions for, 130, 131–35, 163–64

Dixon, Martha, 116

Dobbs, Arthur, 12, 20, 28

Dobbs County, N.C., 118

Dooly, John, 74

dower, 90, 103, 118, 120–21, 122, 138, 139, 140, 142

Dunbar, Moses, 82–83

Dunn, John, 49–51

East India Company, 46

Edenton, N.C., 84, *85*, 116

education, 35, 84, 85–86, 116, 138

Ellet, Elizabeth Fries, 153–54

enslaved people, 4, 14, 15, 29, 155; American Revolution and, 4, 58, 71, 72, 73, 106, 115, 129; in Carolina backcountry, 27, 30, 86, 149. *See also* slavery

Eutaw Springs, Battle of, 77

Fairfax, Lord, 16

families: division of labor in, 11, 24–27; political differences in, 82–84, 129, 133–34, 151–52; Revolution's impact on, 129–30, 132, 140, 146–47, 148, 152, 156

Fanning, David, 101–2, 106

Fanning, Edmund, 35–36, 43

Fayetteville, N.C., 25

ferries, 29

Few, William, 24

Fields, Robert, 102

Fields, William, 102

Florida, 74, 107

Fourth of July, 104, 153

France, 71

Franklin (state), 126

Franklin, Benjamin, 82

Franklin, William, 82

Frederick, Md. (town), 64

Frederick County, Md., 13, 16, 23

Frederick County, Va., 16, 20, 23

French and Indian War, 17, 32, 107

Garret, James, 130

Garret, Mary Hofler, 130

George III (king of Great Britain), 6, 106; colonial allegiance to, 32, 47, 53

Georgia, 71, 73, 74, 76, 77, 78

Germans, 13, 20, 23, 60. *See also* Moravians

Gibbs, Zacharias, 73, 78

Gipson, William, 86

Goss, Frederick, 95–96

Goss, Jacob, 95–96

grain, 12, 17, 20. *See also* agriculture; gristmills; wheat

Granville, Earl of, 21, 36, 91

Granville District, N.C., 21–22, 72

Great Awakening, 23

Great Bridge, Battle of, 66, 151

Great Britain: Tory refugees in, 65, 69

Great Wagon Road, 11, *18*, 22, 77

Greene, Nathanael, 1, 81, 82, 94, 95, 98–99, 101, 152, 154, 156, 167–68

Greensboro, N.C., 99

gristmills, 20, 22, 29, 93, 144, 148

Groff, John, 91, 93

Guilford County, N.C., 45, 108, 110–11

Guilford Courthouse, Battle of, 99–101

Hadden family, 82

Halifax, N.C., 64

Hamm, Andrew, 93

Hamm, Barbara, 93

Hancock, John, 155

Pickens, Andrew, 74, 77
Potomac River, 16
pregnancy, 14, 26–27. *See also* childbirth
Presbyterians, 23, 42, 52
Prince George's County, Md., 13
prisoners of war, 64, 68, 77–78, 96, 105
Proclamation of 1763, 32, 53
property: confiscation of, 66–69, 72, 83, 89, 91, 93, 103, 108, 115; recovery of confiscated, 107, 118, 120, 126, 135, 142, 143
property rights, 19, 67, 108, 135, 138, 139; married women's, 139–40. *See also* coverture
provisions, military, 71, 86, 96–97, 115, 135–36, 141
Pryor, John, 37
Puritans, 17

Quakers, 35, 38, 42, 61, 70, 121, 133, 147
Quillin, John, 101
Quincy, Hannah, 83
Quincy, Samuel, 83

Ramsay, David, 6, 78, 80
Ramsour's Mill, Battle of, 79–80
Randolph, John, 82
Randolph, Peyton, 82
Randolph County, N.C., 102
rape, 97–98, 102, 106
Rawdon, Lord Francis, 61, 100, 101
Regulators, 5, 33, 39, 40, 42, 43, 45, 55; grievances of, 34–38, 41; and the Revolution, 42–43, *44*, 47, 52, 59, 60; suppression of, 38–39, 121
representation, legislative: of backcountry counties, 37, 45; and taxation, 32–33, 140
rights, 2, 115, 138, 139. *See also* citizenship; property rights
roads, 11, *18*, 22, 25, 29
Rowan County, N.C., 1, 25; agriculture in, 20, 24–26; confiscation of property in, 91, 103, 108; county courts in, 28, 29–31, 36, 43–44, 47, 110, 120, 123; partisan violence in, 65, 66, 86, 94, 95–96, 101–2; population of, 11, 27, 59–60; Regulators in, 33, 36, 38, 41–42; revolutionary committees in, 33, 47, 49–51, 53–55, 60, 62, 84–85, 157–60; Tories in, 44, 49–51,

52–53, 59–62, 65, 66, 70, 78, 93, 94, 123, 126
Ruddick, Ann Bedsaul. *See* Spurgin, Ann Bedsaul Ruddick
Ruddick, Solomon, 121, 129, 132–33, 146–47, 163–64
Rush, Benjamin, 114
Ryan, Ann, 85–86
Ryan, Elisabeth, 85–86
Ryan, Martha, 85–86, *87*

Salem, N.C., 22
Salisbury, N.C. (town), 30, 33, 40, 47, 49, 78, 97, 112, 156; British troops in, 81, 98, 100; as commercial hub, 22–23, 25
Salisbury District, N.C., 59, 73, 111, 136, 141
Sampson, Deborah, 84, 155
Sandy Creek Association, 35
Sappenfield, Catherine, 120–21, 122, 138
Sappenfield, Matthias, 54, 60–61, 64, 72, 108, 120–21
Savannah, Ga., 58, 71, 72, 99
Savannah River, 74
Scarborough, Edward, 121
Scots Highlanders, 59, 62, 64, 65
Scots-Irish, 13, 20, 23
Sharpe, William, 47
Simcoe, John Graves, 100, 108, 144, 145
Simon (enslaved man), 120
slavery, 4, 105, 129, 138, 149, 153, 155; growth of, 14, 22; and white fears of insurrection, 53. *See also* enslaved people
slave trade, 48, 105
smallpox, 79, 96
Smith, Flower, 133
Snowden, Richard, 15–16
soldiers, 79, 132, 135–36, 153, 155; British, 32, 46, 74, 97, 98, 132; recruitment of, 52, 55, 70–71, 73–74
Sons of Liberty, 35, 45
South Carolina, 38, 49, 78, 100; divorce in, 130, 131; Tories in, 59, 73–74, 78, 106
Southern Campaign, 58, 71–72, 76, 89, 99; backcountry battles in, 74–77, 79–80; violence of, 5–6, 82, 94–98, 101–2
Spain, 71, 107
Spangenberg, Gottlieb Augustus, 21–22, 23, 24

spies, 134
Spraiker family, 175n31
Spurgin, Aaron, 121, 129, 144, 146, 165, 166, 184n30
Spurgin, Agnes. *See* Bodenhamer, Agnes Spurgin
Spurgin, Ann Bedsaul Ruddick, 121, 128, 129, 132–33, 142, 144, 146, 164, 166
Spurgin, Anne, 165, 166
Spurgin, Elizabeth. *See* Bodenhamer, Elizabeth Spurgin
Spurgin, Israel Isaiah, 56, 147, 165
Spurgin, James, 13–16
Spurgin, Jane (daughter of Jane and William). *See* Jones, Jane Spurgin
Spurgin, Jane Welborn, xi, 1; childbirth and childrearing, 12, 26–27, 56, 65, 79, 80, 86, 103, 119; death and gravesite of, 3, *149*, 149–50; and domestic work, 26–28, 86–88; early life, 12–13, 17, 19; efforts to secure family property, 91–92, 93, 111–12, 115, 119–20, 121–23, *124–25*, 139–41; and enslaved labor, 86, 120; estranged from William, xi, 2, 92, 115, 121, 127, 128–29, 130, 143; as fictive widow, 103, 112, 115, 118, 122, 138, 140, 142; and Nathanael Greene, 1, 81, 82, 98–99, 152, 154, 156, 167–68; as landowner, 141–42, 144, 148, 152, 156; petitions of, xi, 1, 2, 3, 9, 92, 115, *117*, 119–20, 121–23, *124–25*, 127, 135–36, *137*, 140–41, 143, 145, 150, 160–62; and Regulators, 39, 42–43, 55; and Revolution, 6–8, 55–56, 81–82, 92–93, 94, 98, 150, 151–52, 153, 154–55, 156
Spurgin, Jesse, 79, 147, 165
Spurgin, John (brother of William Jr.), 16, 19, 77
Spurgin, John (son of Jane and William), 19, 26, 56, 70, 86, 92, 126, 144, 164
Spurgin, Joseph, 81, 148–49, 151–52, 165
Spurgin, Josiah, 65, 147, 165
Spurgin, Margaret, 27, 92, 164
Spurgin, Mary (daughter of Jane and William), 165
Spurgin, Mary (mother of William Jr.), 16, 19
Spurgin, Rebecca. *See* Hinkle, Rebecca Spurgin
Spurgin, Samuel (brother of William Jr.), 16, 19, 70, 123
Spurgin, Samuel (son of William and Ann), 144, 146, 165, 166
Spurgin, Sarah, 166
Spurgin, Sarah Ledford, 123
Spurgin, William (father of William Jr.), 13–16
Spurgin, William (son of Jane and William), 127, 144, 165
Spurgin, William, Jr. (husband of Jane), xi, 1, 16, 151; in Canada, 108, 133, 142, 143–46, 152, 163; and debt, 108–12, 120, 141; estranged from Jane, xi, 2, 92, 115, 121, 127, 128–29, 130, 143; evades capture and prosecution, 65, 67, 78, 88, 94; as justice of the peace, 28, 31, 32, 39–41, 47, 55, 156; as landowner, 16–17, 19–20, 28, 39, 65, 92, 93, 98, 108–9, 112–13, 142, 145, 146, 156; loss of property, 57, 72, 108–10; military career of, 2, 7, 43, 58, 59, 62, 73–74, 76–77, 81, 94, 98, 99–100, 101–2, 144; and Regulators, 33, 39, 40–41, 42–43; reputation of, 43, 61–62, 152; as slaveholder, 39, 86, 108, 112, 120, 179n10; Tory activities of, 1, 49–51, 52–53, 54–55, 73–74, 81, 106; will of, 92, 144, 146, 164–66
Stamp Act (1765), 32, 33, 34, 35, 37, 45, 84
Stanton, Elizabeth Cady, 154
Steele, Elizabeth, 98
Stiles, Mary, 14
Stockton, Annis Boudinot, 83
Stockton, Richard, 83
suffrage. *See* voting
Sugar Act (1764), 32, 33
Sullivan's Island, S.C., 66
Sumter, Thomas, 95
Surry County, N.C., 45, 52–53, 62, 101
Swaim, Charity Teague, 23
Swaim, John, 23

Tarleton, Banastre, 97
taverns, 22, 23, 25, 29, 30, 98, 123
taxes: colonial, 12, 15, 16, 29, 34, 42, 144; nonpayment of, 36–38, 43, 112; Parliamentary, 32, 33, 45–46, 47, 53; petitions for relief from, 2, 37, 38, 115; wartime, 70, 71, 88–89, 105, 109, 140

tea, 46, 84, 154, 156

Tea Act (1773), 46

Teague family, 23, 41, 70, 123

Tennessee, 127

Tories, 32, 55, 60, 62, 82, 83, 151; departure of, 65, 69, 93, 105, 106, 118; numbers of, 5, 59; postwar treatment of, 2, 102–3, 105–8, 110, 129, 143; prosecution of, 6, 49–51, 53–55, 57, 58, 67–70, 72; in Rowan County, 44, 49–51, 52–53, 59–62, 65, 66, 70, 78, 93, 94, 123, 126; in southern states, 58, 59, 60, 73–74, 78, 79–80, 107; wives of, 82, 83, 89, 93, 94, 98, 103, 112, 115, 118, 120, 122, 134, 135, 138, 140, 142

Torrence, Elizabeth, 118

Torrence, Thomas, 118

Townshend Duties Act (1767), 45–46

trade, 14–15, 23, 25, 33, 46, 48, 68, 105, 109

Transportation Act (1718), 13

treason, 67–68, 69, 78, 89, 105, 120

Treaty of Paris (1783), 57, 103, 104, 107, 108, 146

Tryon, William, 34, 37, 40, 45, 52; promotes Church of England, 41–42; suppresses the Regulators, 37, 38, 39, 42

Tryon County, N.C., 59

Upper Canada, 100, 143–44, 146, 152

Valley Forge, 8

Virginia, 12, 29, 52, 61, 82, 100, 114, 121, 151; divorce in, 17, 130, 132–33, 163–64; western settlements in, 7, 12, 16–17, 19, 20, 23, 123

voting, 138, 139

Wachovia, 21, 104

Wake County, N.C., 45

war: economic impact of, 71, 88–89, 96, 105, 109–10; partisan violence in, 58, 59, 64, 65, 66, 74, 78, 86, 94–96, 101–2; prisoners of, 64, 68, 77–78, 96, 105; and

social disruption, 129–30, 132, 134–35, 147, 148. *See also* Southern Campaign; *specific battles*

War of 1812, 153, 184n30

Washington, George, 8, 52, 155, 156

Washington, Martha, 8

Washington County, Ind., 147

weaving, 23, 26, 87–88, 153, 154. *See also* cloth; Moravians

Welborn, Ann Crabtree, 12, 13, 19

Welborn, Edward, 13

Welborn, Isaac, 19, 123

Welborn, Isabella Mary Teague, 23

Welborn, James, 23, 41, 42–43, 123

Welborn, Thomas, 39, 41

Welborn, William, 12, 13, 19, 41

Welborn family, 23, 24, 41, 70, 123, 152

Wersley. Susannah, 132

West Indies, 69, 71

wheat, 20, 25, 79

Wheatley, Phillis, 155

Whigs: local committees, 33, 46, 47, 49–51, 53–55, 60, 62, 84–85, 157–60; militia, 44, 52, 53, 62, 64–65, 71, 72–73, 74, 80, 94–95, 111. *See* also Continental Congress; war

Whitlock, Sylvia, 96

widows, 16, 19, 90, 116, 118, 120, 139, 140, 147; fictive, 103, 112, 115, 118, 122, 138, 140, 142

Wilkes County, Ga., 74

Wilkinson, Eliza, 97

Williamsburg, Va., *50*

Williamson, Andrew, 77

Wilmington, N.C., 25, 34, 62, 69, 76, 84, 99, 101, 102

Wire, Barny, 142

work, 24, 86–88; gender and, 11, 24–27

Yadkin River, 19, 20, 79, 80, 81, 96, 101

Yorktown, Battle of, 58, 93, 102, 103, 107

Younger, James, 23, 41

The Revolutionary Age